Mathematical Formulas for Economists

Springer
Berlin
Heidelberg
New York
Barcelona
Hong Kong
London
Milan
Paris
Tokyo

Bernd Luderer · Volker Nollau
Klaus Vetters

Mathematical Formulas for Economists

With 58 Figures and 6 Tables

Springer

Professor Dr. Bernd Luderer
Chemnitz University of Technology
Faculty of Mathematics
Straße der Nationen 62
09111 Chemnitz
Germany
bluderer@mathematik.tu-chemnitz.de

Professor Dr. Volker Nollau
Dr. Klaus Vetters
Dresden University of Technology
Faculty of Mathematics and Natural Science
Mommsenstraße 13
01062 Dresden
Germany
nollau@math.tu-dresden.de
vetters@math.tu-dresden.de

ISBN 3-540-42616-7 Springer-Verlag Berlin Heidelberg New York

Library of Congress Cataloging-in-Publication Data applied for
Die Deutsche Bibliothek – CIP-Einheitsaufnahme
Luderer, Bernd: Mathematical formulas for economists: with 6 tables / Bernd Luderer; Volker Nollau; Klaus Vetters. – Berlin; Heidelberg; New York; Barcelona; Hong Kong; London; Milan; Paris; Tokyo: Springer, 2002
ISBN 3-540-42616-7

Springer-Verlag Berlin Heidelberg New York
a member of BertelsmannSpringer Science+Business Media GmbH

http://www.springer.de

Softcover-Design: Erich Kirchner, Heidelberg

SPIN 10852378 43/2202-5 4 3 2 1 0 – Printed on acid-free paper

Preface

This collection of formulas constitutes a compendium of mathematics for economics and business. It contains the most important formulas, statements and algorithms in this significant subfield of modern mathematics and addresses primarily students of economics or business at universities, colleges and trade schools. But people dealing with practical or applied problems will also find this collection to be an efficient and easy-to-use work of reference.

First the book treats mathematical symbols and constants, sets and statements, number systems and their arithmetic as well as fundamentals of combinatorics. The chapter on sequences and series is followed by mathematics of finance, the representation of functions of one and several independent variables, their differential and integral calculus and by differential and difference equations. In each case special emphasis is placed on applications and models in economics.

The chapter on linear algebra deals with matrices, vectors, determinants and systems of linear equations. This is followed by the representation of structures and algorithms of linear programming. Finally, the reader finds formulas on descriptive statistics (data analysis, ratios, inventory and time series analysis), on probability theory (events, probabilities, random variables and distributions) and on inductive statistics (point and interval estimates, tests). Some important tables complete the work.

The present manual arised as a result of many years' teaching for students of economic faculties at the Institutes of Technology of Dresden and Chemnitz, Germany. Moreover, the authors could take advantage of experience and suggestions of numerous colleagues. For critical reading of the manuscript we feel obliged to thank Dipl.-Math. M. Richter and Dr K. Eppler. Our special thank is due to M. Schoenherr, Dr U. Wuerker and Dr J. Rudl, who contributed to technical preparation of the book.

After successful use by German readers it is a great pleasure for us to present this collection of formulas to the English auditorium. The translation is based on the third, revised German edition. We are greatly obliged to Springer-Verlag for giving us the opportunity to publish this book in English.

Finally we would like to emphasize that remarks and criticism are always welcome.

Chemnitz / Dresden,
July 2001

Bernd Luderer
Volker Nollau
Klaus Vetters

Contents

Mathematical Symbols and Constants

Notations and symbols

$\mathbb{N}$	– set of natural numbers
$\mathbb{N}_0$	– set of natural numbers inclusively zero
$\mathbb{Z}$	– set of integer numbers
$\mathbb{Q}$	– set of rational numbers
$\mathbb{R}$	– set of real numbers
$\mathbb{R}^+$	– set of nonnegative real numbers
$\mathbb{R}^n$	– set of n-tuples of real numbers (n-dimensional vectors)
$\mathbb{C}$	– set of complex numbers
$\sqrt{x}$	– nonnegative number y (square root) such that $y^2 = x$, $x \geq 0$
$\sqrt[n]{x}$	– nonnegative number y (n-th root) such $y^n = x$, $x \geq 0$
$\sum\limits_{i=1}^{n} x_i$	– sum of the numbers x_i: $x_1 + x_2 + \ldots + x_n$
$\prod\limits_{i=1}^{n} x_i$	– product of the numbers x_i: $x_1 \cdot x_2 \cdot \ldots \cdot x_n$
$n!$	– $1 \cdot 2 \cdot \ldots \cdot n$ (n factorial)
$\min\{a, b\}$	– minimum of the numbers a and b: a for $a \leq b$, b for $a \geq b$
$\max\{a, b\}$	– maximum of the numbers a and b: a for $a \geq b$, b for $a \leq b$
$\lceil x \rceil$	– smallest integer y such that $y \geq x$ (rounding up)
$\lfloor x \rfloor$	– greatest integer y such that $y \leq x$ (rounding down)
$\operatorname{sgn} x$	– signum: 1 for $x > 0$, 0 for $x = 0$, -1 for $x < 0$
$\lvert x \rvert$	– absolute value of the real number x: x for $x \geq 0$ and $-x$ for $x < 0$
(a, b)	– open interval, i. e. $a < x < b$
$[a, b]$	– closed interval, i. e. $a \leq x \leq b$
$(a, b]$	– half-open interval closed from the right, i. e. $a < x \leq b$
$[a, b)$	– half-open interval open at the right, i. e. $a \leq x < b$
$\leq$, $\geq$	– less or equal; greater or equal
$\pm$, $\mp$	– first plus, then minus; first minus, then plus
$\stackrel{\text{def}}{=}$	– equality by definition
$:=$	– the left-hand side is defined by the right-hand side

$\forall$	– for all; for any ...
$\exists$	– there exists ... ; there is (at least one) ...
$p \wedge q$	– conjunction; p and q
$p \vee q$	– disjunction; p or q
$p \Longrightarrow q$	– implication; from p it follows q
$p \Longleftrightarrow q$	– equivalence; p is equivalent to q
$\neg p$	– negation; not p
$a \in M$	– a is an element of the set M
$a \notin M$	– a is not an element of the set M
$n! = 1 \cdot 2 \cdot \ldots \cdot n$	– factorial
$\binom{n}{k}$	– binomial coefficient
$A \subset B$	– A subset of B
$\emptyset$	– empty set
$\lVert \cdot \rVert$	– norm (of a vector, matrix, ...)
rang $(\boldsymbol{A})$	– rank of the matrix $\boldsymbol{A}$
det $\boldsymbol{A}$, $\lvert\boldsymbol{A}\rvert$	– determinant of the matrix $\boldsymbol{A}$
δ_{ij}	– Kronecker's symbol: 1 for $i = j$ and 0 for $i \neq j$
$\lim\limits_{n\to\infty} a_n$	– limit of the sequence $\{a_n\}$ for n tending to infinity
$\lim\limits_{x\to x_0} f(x)$	– limit of the function f at the point x_0
$\lim\limits_{x\downarrow x_0} f(x)$	– limit from the right (right-hand limit) at the point x_0
$\lim\limits_{x\uparrow x_0} f(x)$	– limit from the left (left-hand limit) at the point x_0
$U_\varepsilon(x^*)$	– ε-neighbourhood of the point x^*
$f(x)\big\vert_a^b = \big[f(x)\big]_a^b$	$= f(b) - f(a)$

Mathematical constants

$\pi = 3.141\,592\,653\,589\,793\ldots$

$\mathrm{e} = 2.718\,281\,828\,459\,045\ldots$

$1^\circ = 0.017\,453\,292\,520\ldots = \dfrac{\pi}{180}$

$1' = 0.000\,290\,888\,209\ldots$

$1'' = 0.000\,004\,848\,137\ldots$

Sets and Propositions

Notion of a set

set M	– collection of well-defined, different objects
elements	– objects of a set $a \in M \iff a$ belongs to the set M $a \notin M \iff a$ does not belong to the set M
description	– 1. by enumeration of the elements: $M = \{a, b, c, \dots\}$ 2. by characterizing the properties of elements with the help of a sentence form: $M = \{x \in \Omega \mid A(x) \text{ true}\}$
empty set	– the set which does not contain any element; notation: $\emptyset$
disjoint sets	– sets without common elements: $M \cap N = \emptyset$

Relations between sets

Set inclusion (subset)

$M \subset N \iff (\forall x\colon x \in M \Longrightarrow x \in N)$	– M subset of N (inclusion)
$M \subset N \wedge (\exists x \in N : x \notin M)$	– M proper subset of N
$\mathcal{P}(M) = \{X \mid X \subset M\}$	– power set, set of all subsets of the set M
Properties:	
$M \subset M$	– reflexivity
$M \subset N \wedge N \subset P \Longrightarrow M \subset P$	– transitivity
$\emptyset \subset M \quad \forall M$	– $\emptyset$ is a subset of any set

- Other notation of a subset: $M \subseteq N$ (proper subset: $M \subset N$).

Equality of sets

$M = N \iff (\forall x\colon x \in M \iff x \in N)$	– equality
Properties:	
$M \subset N \wedge N \subset M \iff M = N$	– order property
$M = M$	– reflexivity
$M = N \Longrightarrow N = M$	– symmetry
$M = N \wedge N = P \Longrightarrow M = P$	– transitivity

Operations with sets

$M \cap N = \{x \mid x \in M \wedge x \in N\}$	–	intersection of the sets M and N; contains all elements belonging both to M and to N (1)
$M \cup N = \{x \mid x \in M \vee x \in N\}$	–	union of the sets M and N; contains all elements belonging either to M or to N (or to both of them) (2)
$M \setminus N = \{x \mid x \in M \wedge x \notin N\}$	–	difference of the sets M und N; contains all elements of M not belonging to N (3)
$\mathbf{C}_\Omega M = \overline{M} = \Omega \setminus M$	–	complement to M with respect to Ω; here Ω is some given basic set and $M \subset \Omega$ (4)

(1)

(2)

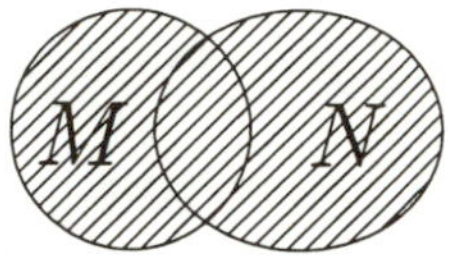

(3)

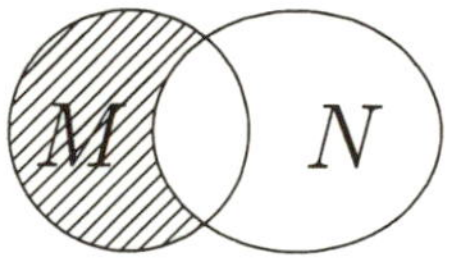

(4)

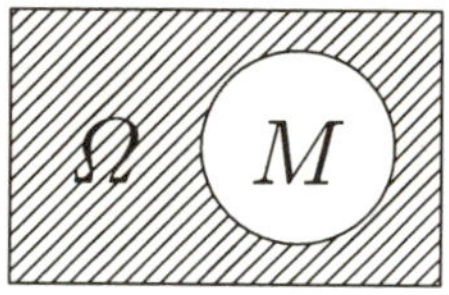

- Sets A, B for which $A \cap B = \emptyset$ (A, B having no elements in common) are called *disjoint*.
- Operations with sets are also called *connections* between sets.

Multiple connections

$$\bigcup_{i=1}^{n} M_i = M_1 \cup M_2 \cup \ldots \cup M_n = \{x \mid \exists i \in \{1,\ldots,n\} : x \in M_i\}$$

$$\bigcap_{i=1}^{n} M_i = M_1 \cap M_2 \cap \ldots \cap M_n = \{x \mid \forall i \in \{1,\ldots,n\} : x \in M_i\}$$

De Morgan's laws

$$\overline{(M \cup N)} = \overline{M} \cap \overline{N}, \qquad \overline{(M \cap N)} = \overline{M} \cup \overline{N} \qquad \text{(two sets)},$$

$$\overline{\bigcup_{i=1}^{n} M_i} = \bigcap_{i=1}^{n} \overline{M_i}, \qquad \overline{\bigcap_{i=1}^{n} M_i} = \bigcup_{i=1}^{n} \overline{M_i} \qquad (n \text{ sets})$$

Rules for operations with sets

Union and intersection

$A \cup (B \cap A) = A$	$A \cap (B \cup A) = A$
$A \cup (B \cup C) = (A \cup B) \cup C$	$A \cap (B \cap C) = (A \cap B) \cap C$
$A \cup (B \cap C) = (A \cup B) \cap (A \cup C)$	
$A \cap (B \cup C) = (A \cap B) \cup (A \cap C)$	

Union, intersection and difference

$$A \setminus (A \setminus B) = A \cap B$$
$$A \setminus (B \cup C) = (A \setminus B) \cap (A \setminus C)$$
$$A \setminus (B \cap C) = (A \setminus B) \cup (A \setminus C)$$
$$(A \cup B) \setminus C = (A \setminus C) \cup (B \setminus C)$$
$$(A \cap B) \setminus C = (A \setminus C) \cap (B \setminus C)$$
$$A \cap B = \emptyset \quad \Longleftrightarrow \quad A \setminus B = A$$

Union, intersection and difference in connection with inclusion

$$A \subset B \quad \Longleftrightarrow \quad A \cap B = A \quad \Longleftrightarrow \quad A \cup B = B$$
$$A \subset B \quad \Longrightarrow \quad A \cup C \subset B \cup C$$
$$A \subset B \quad \Longrightarrow \quad A \cap C \subset B \cap C$$
$$A \subset B \quad \Longleftrightarrow \quad A \setminus B = \emptyset$$

Union, intersection and complement

If both $A \subset \Omega$ and $B \subset \Omega$, then the following relations hold (all complements taken with respect to Ω):

$\overline{\emptyset} = \Omega$	$\overline{\Omega} = \emptyset$	
$A \cup \overline{A} = \Omega$	$A \cap \overline{A} = \emptyset$	
$\overline{A \cup B} = \overline{A} \cap \overline{B}$	$\overline{A \cap B} = \overline{A} \cup \overline{B}$	De Morgan's laws, s. p. 4
$\overline{(\overline{A})} = A$	$A \subset B \iff \overline{B} \subset \overline{A}$	

Product set and mappings

Product set

(x, y)	–	ordered pair; combination of the elements $x \in X$, $y \in Y$ in consideration of their order
$(x, y) = (z, w) \iff x = z \wedge y = w$	–	equality of two ordered pairs
$X \times Y = \{(x, y) \mid x \in X \wedge y \in Y\}$	–	product set, Cartesian product, cross or direct product

Cross product of n sets

$$\prod_{i=1}^{n} X_i = X_1 \times X_2 \times \ldots \times X_n = \{(x_1, \ldots, x_n) \mid \forall\, i \in \{1, \ldots, n\} : x_i \in X_i\}$$

$$\underbrace{X \times X \times \ldots \times X}_{n\ \text{times}} = X^n; \qquad \underbrace{\mathbb{R} \times \mathbb{R} \times \ldots \times \mathbb{R}}_{n\ \text{times}} = \mathbb{R}^n$$

• The elements of $X_1 \times \ldots \times X_n$, i. e. $(x_1, \ldots, x_n)$, are called *n-tuples*, for $n = 2$ *pairs*, for $n = 3$ *triples*; especially $\mathbb{R}^2$ denotes all pairs, $\mathbb{R}^n$ all n-tuples of real numbers (vectors with n components).

Mappings (relations)

$A \subset X \times Y$	–	mapping from X to Y; subset of the cross product of the sets X and Y
$D_A = \{x \in X \mid \exists\, y\colon (x, y) \in A\}$	–	domain of A
$W_A = \{y \in Y \mid \exists\, x\colon (x, y) \in A\}$	–	range of A
$A^{-1} = \{(y, x) \mid (x, y) \in A\}$	–	reciprocal mapping; mapping inverse to the mapping A

• Let $(x, y) \in A$. Then y is an element associated with the element x. A mapping A from X to Y is called *single-valued* if for any element $x \in X$ there is only one element $y \in Y$ associated with x. A single-valued mapping is called a *function* f. The mapping rule is denoted by $y = f(x)$. If both the mapping A and the inverse mapping A^{-1} (inverse function f^{-1}) are single-valued, then A (and f, resp.) are called *one-to-one mapping (function)*.

Linear mapping

$f(\lambda x + \mu y) = \lambda f(x) + \mu f(y)$	–	defining property of a linear mapping (function), $\lambda, \mu \in \mathbb{R}$

• The composition $h(x) = g(f(x))$ of two linear mappings (e. g. $f\colon \mathbb{R}^n \to \mathbb{R}^m$ and $g : \mathbb{R}^m \to \mathbb{R}^p$) is again a linear mapping ($h : \mathbb{R}^n \to \mathbb{R}^p$) denoted by $h = g \circ f$.

Propositional calculus

Sentences and sentence forms

sentence p	–	statement which expresses some proposition p having the truth value "true" (t) or "false" (f)
sentence form $p(x)$	–	sentence depending on a variable x; only after substitution of a concrete name of x a truth value results

• The determination of a truth value of a sentence form $p(x)$ can also take place by means of the *universal quantifier* $\forall$ ($\forall\, x : p(x)$; in words: "for all x the sentence $p(x)$ expresses a true proposition") or the *existential quantifier* $\exists$ ($\exists\, x\colon p(x)$; in words: "there is an x for which $p(x)$ is true").

Compound propositions

• The combination of propositions leads to new proposition defined with the help of truth tables. Compound propositions are unary relations (negation), dyadic relations (see the following table) or polyadic relations consisting of the operators $\neg$, $\wedge$, $\vee$, $\Longrightarrow$, $\Longleftrightarrow$.

• A *tautology* is always true, a *contradiction* is always false (independent of the truth value of the partial sentences).

Unary Relation (truth table)

negation $\neg p$ (not p)

p	$\neg p$
t	f
f	t

Dyadic relations (truth table)

Relation	read	p q	t t	t f	f t	f f
conjunction	p and q	$p \wedge q$	t	f	f	f
disjunction	p or q	$p \vee q$	t	t	t	f
implication	p implies q	$p \Longrightarrow q$	t	f	t	t
equivalence	p equivalent to q	$p \Longleftrightarrow q$	t	f	f	t

• The implication ("from p it follows q") is also denoted as proposition in "if ..., then ... " form, p is called the *premise* (assumption), q is the *conclusion* (assertion).

• The premise p is *sufficient* for the conclusion q, q is *necessary* for p. Other formulations for the equivalence are: "then and only then if ... " or "if and only if ... (iff)".

Tautologies of propositional calculus

$p \vee \neg p$	–	law of excluded middle (excluded third)
$\neg(p \wedge \neg p)$	–	law of contradiction
$\neg(\neg p) \Longleftrightarrow p$	–	negation of the negation
$\neg(p \Longrightarrow q) \Longleftrightarrow (p \wedge \neg q)$	–	negation of the implication
$\neg(p \wedge q) \Longleftrightarrow \neg p \vee \neg q$	–	De Morgan's law
$\neg(p \vee q) \Longleftrightarrow \neg p \wedge \neg q$	–	De Morgan's law
$(p \Longrightarrow q) \Longleftrightarrow (\neg q \Longrightarrow \neg p)$	–	law of contraposition
$[(p \Longrightarrow q) \wedge (q \Longrightarrow r)] \Longrightarrow (p \Longrightarrow r)$	–	law of transitivity
$p \wedge (p \Longrightarrow q) \Longrightarrow q$	–	rule of detachment
$q \wedge (\neg p \Longrightarrow \neg q) \Longrightarrow p$	–	principle of indirect proof
$[(p_1 \vee p_2) \wedge (p_1 \Longrightarrow q) \wedge (p_2 \Longrightarrow q)] \Longrightarrow q$	–	distinction of cases

Method of complete induction

Problem: A proposition $A(n)$ depending on a natural number n has to be proved for any n.

Basis of the induction: The validity of the proposition $A(n)$ is shown for some initial value (usually $n = 0$ or $n = 1$).

Induction hypothesis: It is assumed that $A(n)$ is true for $n = k$.

Induction step: Using the induction hypothesis, the validity of $A(n)$ is proved for $n = k + 1$.

Number Systems and their Arithmetic

Natural, integer, rational, and real numbers

Natural numbers: $\mathbb{N} = \{1, 2, 3, \dots\}$, $\mathbb{N}_0 = \{0, 1, 2, 3, \dots\}$

divisor	–	a natural number $m \in \mathbb{N}$ is called a divisor of $n \in \mathbb{N}$ if there exists a natural number $k \in \mathbb{N}$ such that $n = m \cdot k$
prime number	–	a number $n \in \mathbb{N}$ with $n > 1$ and the only divisors 1 and n
greatest common divisor	–	$\text{g.c.d.}(n,m) = \max\{k \in \mathbb{N}$ such that k divides n and $m\}$
least common multiple	–	$\text{l.c.m.}(n,m) = \min\{k \in \mathbb{N}$ such that n and m divide $k\}$

- Every number $n \in \mathbb{N}$, $n > 1$, can be written as a product of prime powers:

$$n = p_1^{r_1} \cdot p_2^{r_2} \cdot \ldots \cdot p_k^{r_k}$$ p_j prime numbers, r_j natural numbers

Integers: $\mathbb{Z} = \{\dots, -3, -2, -1, 0, 1, 2, 3, \dots\}$

Rational numbers: $\mathbb{Q} = \{\frac{m}{n} \mid m \in \mathbb{Z},\ n \in \mathbb{N}\}$

- The decimal representation of a rational number is finite or periodic. Every number with a finite or periodic decimal representation is a rational number.

Real numbers: $\mathbb{R}$

- The real numbers arise by "extending" $\mathbb{Q}$ by nonperiodic decimal numbers with infinitely many digits.

$$x = \sum_{j=-\infty}^{k} r_j g^j$$ – g-adic representation

$g = 2$: dual $g = 8$: octal $g = 10$: decimal representation

Conversion decimal $\longrightarrow$ g-adic

1. Decomposition of the positive decimal number x: $x = n + x_0$, $n \in \mathbb{N}$, $x_0 \in \mathbb{R}$
2. Conversion of the integer part n via *iterated division* by g:

$$q_0 = n, \qquad q_{j-1} = q_j \cdot g + r_j, \qquad 0 \le r_j < g, \qquad j = 1, 2, \dots$$

3. Conversion of the non-integer part x_0 via *iterated multiplication* by g:

$$g \cdot x_{j-1} = s_j + x_j, \qquad 0 < x_j < 1, \qquad j = 1, 2, \dots$$

4. Result: $x = (r_k \dots r_2 r_1 . s_1 s_2 \dots)_g$

Conversion g-adic $\longrightarrow$ decimal (by means of ▶ Horner's scheme)

$$x=(r_k \dots r_2 r_1 . s_1 s_2 \dots s_p)_g = (\dots((r_k g + r_{k-1})g + r_{k-2})g + \dots + r_2)g + r_1 + (\dots((s_p/g + s_{p-1})/g + s_{p-2})/g + \dots + s_1)/g$$

Calculation with real numbers

Elementary laws

$a+b=b+a$ $a \cdot b = b \cdot a$	– commutative laws
$(a+b)+c=a+(b+c)$ $(a \cdot b) \cdot c = a \cdot (b \cdot c)$	– associative laws
$(a+b) \cdot c = a \cdot c + b \cdot c$ $a \cdot (b+c) = a \cdot b + a \cdot c$	– distributive laws
$(a+b)(c+d) = ac+bc+ad+bd$	– multiplying out of brackets
$\frac{a}{b} = \frac{a \cdot c}{b \cdot c}$	– extension of a fraction $(b, c \neq 0)$
$\frac{a \cdot c}{b \cdot c} = \frac{a}{b}$	– reduction of a fraction $(b, c \neq 0)$
$\frac{a}{c} \pm \frac{b}{c} = \frac{a \pm b}{c}$	– addition/subtraction of fractions with equal denominator $(c \neq 0)$
$\frac{a}{c} \pm \frac{b}{d} = \frac{a \cdot d \pm b \cdot c}{c \cdot d}$	– addition/subtraction of arbitrary fractions $(c, d \neq 0)$
$\frac{a}{b} \cdot \frac{c}{d} = \frac{a \cdot c}{b \cdot d}$	– multiplication of fractions $(b, d \neq 0)$
$\frac{\frac{a}{b}}{\frac{c}{d}} = \frac{a}{b} : \frac{c}{d} = \frac{a \cdot d}{b \cdot c}$	– division of fractions $(b, c, d \neq 0)$

Definitions

$\sum_{i=1}^{n} a_i = a_1 + a_2 + \ldots + a_n$	– sum of elements of a sequence
$\prod_{i=1}^{n} a_i = a_1 \cdot a_2 \cdot \ldots \cdot a_n$	– product of elements of a sequence

Rules of operation

$\sum_{i=1}^{n}(a_i + b_i) = \sum_{i=1}^{n} a_i + \sum_{i=1}^{n} b_i$	$\sum_{i=1}^{n}(c \cdot a_i) = c \cdot \sum_{i=1}^{n} a_i$
$\sum_{i=1}^{n} a_i = n \cdot a \quad (\text{for } a_i = a)$	$\sum_{i=1}^{m}\sum_{j=1}^{n} a_{ij} = \sum_{j=1}^{n}\sum_{i=1}^{m} a_{ij}$
$\sum_{i=1}^{n} a_i = \sum_{i=0}^{n-1} a_{i+1}$	$\prod_{i=1}^{n} a_i = \prod_{i=0}^{n-1} a_{i+1}$
$\prod_{i=1}^{n}(c \cdot a_i) = c^n \cdot \prod_{i=1}^{n} a_i$	$\prod_{i=1}^{n} a_i = a^n \quad (\text{for } a_i = a)$

Independence of the index variable

$\sum_{i=1}^{n} a_i = \sum_{k=1}^{n} a_k$	$\prod_{i=1}^{n} a_i = \prod_{k=1}^{n} a_k$

Absolute values

Definition

$$|x| = \begin{cases} x & \text{for } x \geq 0 \\ -x & \text{for } x < 0 \end{cases}$$ – (absolute) value of the number x

Rules of operation and properties

$\|x\| = x \cdot \operatorname{sgn} x$	$\|-x\| = \|x\|$
$\|x\| = 0 \iff x = 0$	
$\|x \cdot y\| = \|x\| \cdot \|y\|$	$\left\|\frac{x}{y}\right\| = \frac{\|x\|}{\|y\|}$ for $y \neq 0$

Triangular inequalities:

$\|x + y\| \leq \|x\| + \|y\|$	(equality holds if and only if $\operatorname{sgn} x = \operatorname{sgn} y$)
$\big\|\|x\| - \|y\|\big\| \leq \|x + y\|$	(equality holds if and only if $\operatorname{sgn} x = -\operatorname{sgn} y$)

Factorial and binomial coefficients

Definitions

$n! = 1 \cdot 2 \cdot \ldots \cdot n$	– factorial ($n \in \mathbb{N}$)
$\binom{n}{k} = \dfrac{n \cdot (n-1) \cdot \ldots \cdot (n-k+1)}{1 \cdot 2 \cdot \ldots \cdot k}$	– binomial coefficient ($k, n \in \mathbb{N}$, $k \leq n$; read: "binomial n k" or "n choose k")
$\binom{n}{k} = \begin{cases} \dfrac{n!}{k!(n-k)!} & \text{for} \quad k \leq n \\ 0 & \text{for} \quad k > n \end{cases}$	– extended definition for $k, n \in \mathbb{N}_0$ with $0! = 1$

$$\binom{0}{0} = 1 \qquad \binom{n}{0} = 1 \qquad \binom{n}{1} = n \qquad \binom{n}{n} = 1$$

Pascals's triangle:

$$\begin{array}{lccccccccccc}
n=0: & & & & & & 1 & & & & & \\
n=1: & & & & & 1 & & 1 & & & & \\
n=2: & & & & 1 & & 2 & & 1 & & & \\
n=3: & & & 1 & & 3 & & 3 & & 1 & & \\
n=4: & & 1 & & 4 & & 6 & & 4 & & 1 & \\
n=5: & 1 & & 5 & & 10 & & 10 & & 5 & & 1
\end{array}$$

(diagonals labelled $k=1$, $k=2$, $k=3$)

....

Properties

$\binom{n}{k} = \binom{n}{n-k}$	– symmetry property
$\binom{n}{k} + \binom{n}{k-1} = \binom{n+1}{k}$	– addition property
$\binom{n}{0} + \binom{n+1}{1} + \ldots + \binom{n+m}{m} = \binom{n+m+1}{m}$	– addition theorems
$\binom{n}{0}\binom{m}{k} + \binom{n}{1}\binom{m}{k-1} + \ldots + \binom{n}{k}\binom{m}{0} = \binom{n+m}{k}$	
$\sum\limits_{k=0}^{n} \binom{n}{k} = 2^n$	

• The definition of the binomal coefficient is also used for $n \in \mathbb{R}$. In this case, the addition property and the addition theorems are valid either.

Equations

Transformation of expressions

$$(a \pm b)^2 = a^2 \pm 2ab + b^2 \qquad \text{(binomial formulas)}$$

$$(a+b)(a-b) = a^2 - b^2$$

$$(a \pm b)^3 = a^3 \pm 3a^2 b + 3ab^2 \pm b^3 \qquad (a \pm b)(a^2 \mp ab + b^2) = a^3 \pm b^3$$

$$\frac{a^n - b^n}{a-b} = a^{n-1} + a^{n-2}b + a^{n-3}b^2 + \ldots + ab^{n-2} + b^{n-1}, \quad a \neq b,\ n = 2, 3, \ldots$$

$$x^2 + bx + c = \left(x + \frac{b}{2}\right)^2 + c - \frac{b^2}{4} \qquad \text{(completion of the square)}$$

Binomial theorem

$$(a+b)^n = \sum_{k=0}^{n} \binom{n}{k} a^{n-k} b^k = a^n + \binom{n}{1} a^{n-1} b + \ldots + \binom{n}{n-1} ab^{n-1} + b^n, \qquad n \in \mathbb{N}$$

Transformation of equations

Two terms remain equal if the same rule of operation is applied to **both** of them.

$$a = b \implies a + c = b + c, \qquad c \in \mathbb{R}$$

$$a = b \implies a - c = b - c, \qquad c \in \mathbb{R}$$

$$a = b \implies c \cdot a = c \cdot b, \qquad c \in \mathbb{R}$$

$$a = b,\ a \neq 0 \implies \frac{c}{a} = \frac{c}{b}, \qquad c \in \mathbb{R}$$

$$a = b \implies a^n = b^n, \qquad n \in \mathbb{N}$$

$$a^2 = b^2 \implies \begin{cases} a = b & \text{for} \quad \operatorname{sgn} a = \operatorname{sgn} b \\ a = -b & \text{for} \quad \operatorname{sgn} a = -\operatorname{sgn} b \end{cases}$$

Solving of equations

If an equation contains variables, then for some values of these variables it can be true and for other values false. The determination of one or all values of the variables for which a given equation is **true** is denoted as *solving* of the equation.

$$ax+b=0 \quad\Longrightarrow\quad \begin{cases} x=-\frac{b}{a} & \text{for} \quad a\neq 0 \\ x \text{ arbitrary} & \text{for} \quad a=b=0 \\ \text{no solution} & \text{for} \quad a=0,\, b\neq 0 \end{cases}$$

$$(x-a)(x-b)=0 \quad\Longrightarrow\quad x=a \quad \text{or} \quad x=b$$

$$(x-a)(y-b)=0 \quad\Longrightarrow\quad (x=a \text{ and } y \text{ arbitrary}) \quad \textbf{or} \quad (x \text{ arbitrary and } y=b)$$

Quadratic equation for real x :

$$x^2+px+q=0 \quad\Longrightarrow$$

$$\begin{cases} x=-\dfrac{p}{2}\pm\sqrt{\dfrac{p^2}{4}-q} & \text{for} \quad p^2>4q \quad \text{(two different solutions)} \\ x=-\dfrac{p}{2} & \text{for} \quad p^2=4q \quad \text{(one real double solution)} \\ \text{no solution} & \text{for} \quad p^2<4q \end{cases}$$

Inequalities

Rules of operation

$x<y \ \wedge\ y<z$	$\Longrightarrow$	$x<z$	$(x,y,z,u,v\in\mathbb{R})$
$x<y$	$\Longrightarrow$	$x+z<y+z$	
$x<y \ \wedge\ z>0$	$\Longrightarrow$	$x\cdot z<y\cdot z$	
$x<y \ \wedge\ z<0$	$\Longrightarrow$	$x\cdot z>y\cdot z$	
$0<x<y \ \wedge\ 0<u<v$	$\Longrightarrow$	$x\cdot u<y\cdot v$	
$0<x<y$	$\Longrightarrow$	$\dfrac{1}{x}>\dfrac{1}{y}$	
$\dfrac{x}{y}<\dfrac{u}{v} \ \wedge\ y>0 \ \wedge\ v>0$	$\Longrightarrow$	$\dfrac{x}{y}<\dfrac{x+u}{y+v}<\dfrac{u}{v}$	

Bernoulli's inequality

$$(1+x)^n \geq 1+nx \qquad \text{for} \qquad x>-1,\ n\in\mathbb{N}$$

Cauchy-Schwarz inequality

$$\sum_{i=1}^{n} x_i y_i \leq \left(\sum_{i=1}^{n} x_i^2\right)^{\frac{1}{2}} \cdot \left(\sum_{i=1}^{n} y_i^2\right)^{\frac{1}{2}}$$

Finite sums

Arithmetic series:

$$a_{k+1} = a_k + d \qquad \Longrightarrow \qquad s_n = \sum_{k=1}^{n} a_k = \frac{n(a_1 + a_n)}{2}$$

Geometric series:

$$a_{k+1} = q \cdot a_k \qquad \Longrightarrow \qquad s_n = \sum_{k=1}^{n} a_k = a_1 \frac{q^n - 1}{q - 1} \qquad (q \neq 1)$$

Special finite sums

sum	value
$1 + 2 + 3 + \ldots + n$	$\frac{1}{2}n(n+1)$
$1 + 3 + 5 + \ldots + (2n-1)$	n^2
$2 + 4 + 6 + \ldots + 2n$	$n(n+1)$
$1^2 + 2^2 + 3^2 + \ldots + n^2$	$\frac{1}{6}n(n+1)(2n+1)$
$1^2 + 3^2 + 5^2 + \ldots + (2n-1)^2$	$\frac{1}{3}n(4n^2-1)$
$2^2 + 4^2 + 6^2 + \ldots + (2n)^2$	$\frac{2}{3}n(n+1)(2n+1)$
$1^3 + 2^3 + 3^3 + \ldots + n^3$	$\frac{1}{4}n^2(n+1)^2$
$1^3 + 3^3 + 5^3 + \ldots + (2n-1)^3$	$n^2(2n^2-1)$
$2^3 + 4^3 + 6^3 + \ldots + (2n)^3$	$2n^2(n+1)^2$
$1 + x + x^2 + \ldots + x^n$	$\frac{x^{n+1}-1}{x-1} \qquad (x \neq 1)$
$\sin x + \sin 2x + \ldots + \sin nx$	$\frac{\cos\frac{x}{2} - \cos(n+\frac{1}{2})x}{2\sin\frac{x}{2}}$
$\cos x + \cos 2x + \ldots + \cos nx$	$\frac{\sin(n+\frac{1}{2}x) - \sin\frac{x}{2}}{2\sin\frac{x}{2}}$

Powers and roots

Powers with integer exponents $(a \in \mathbb{R};\ n \in \mathbb{N};\ p, q \in \mathbb{Z})$

Powers with positive exponent: $a^n = \underbrace{a \cdot a \cdot \ldots \cdot a}_{n \text{ factors}}, \qquad a^0 = 1$

Powers with negative exponent: $a^{-n} = \dfrac{1}{a^n} \qquad (a \neq 0)$

Rules of operation

$a^p \cdot a^q = a^{p+q}$	$a^p \cdot b^p = (a \cdot b)^p$	$(a^p)^q = (a^q)^p = a^{p \cdot q}$
$\dfrac{a^p}{a^q} = a^{p-q}$	$\dfrac{a^p}{b^p} = \left(\dfrac{a}{b}\right)^p$	$(a, b \neq 0)$

Roots, powers with real exponents $(a, b \in \mathbb{R};\ a, b > 0;\ m, n \in \mathbb{N})$

n-th root: $u = \sqrt[n]{a} \iff u^n = a, \quad u \geq 0$

Rules of operation

$\sqrt[n]{a} \cdot \sqrt[n]{b} = \sqrt[n]{a \cdot b}$	$\dfrac{\sqrt[n]{a}}{\sqrt[n]{b}} = \sqrt[n]{\dfrac{a}{b}}$	$(b \neq 0) \quad (a, b > 0)$
$\sqrt[m]{\sqrt[n]{a}} = \sqrt[n]{\sqrt[m]{a}} = \sqrt[m \cdot n]{a}$	$\sqrt[n]{a^m} = (\sqrt[n]{a})^m$	$(a \geq 0)$

Powers with rational exponent: $a^{\frac{1}{n}} = \sqrt[n]{a}, \qquad a^{\frac{m}{n}} = \sqrt[n]{a^m}$

Powers with real exponent: $a^x = \lim\limits_{k \to \infty} a^{q_k}, \qquad q_k \in \mathbb{Q}, \ \lim\limits_{k \to \infty} q_k = x$

• For powers with real exponents the same rules of operation as for powers with integer exponents are true.

Logarithms

Logarithm to the base a: $x = \log_a u \iff a^x = u, \quad a > 1, \ u \geq 0$

Base $a = 10$: $\log_{10} u = \lg u$ – Briggsian logarithm

Base $a = \mathrm{e}$: $\log_{\mathrm{e}} u = \ln u$ – natural logarithm

Rules of operation

$\log_a (u \cdot v) = \log_a u + \log_a v$	$\log_a \left(\dfrac{u}{v}\right) = \log_a u - \log_a v$
$\log_a u^v = v \cdot \log_a u$	$\log_b u = \dfrac{\log_a u}{\log_a b} \quad (u, v > 0,\ b > 1)$

Complex numbers

i: $\mathrm{i}^2 = -1$	– imaginary unit
$z = a + b\,\mathrm{i}, \quad a, b \in \mathbb{R}$	– Cartesian form of the complex number $z \in \mathbb{C}$
$z = r(\cos\varphi + \mathrm{i}\sin\varphi) = r\mathrm{e}^{\mathrm{i}\varphi}$	– polar (trigonometric) form of the complex number $z \in \mathbb{C}$ (Euler's relation)
$\operatorname{Re} z = a = r\cos\varphi$	– real part of z
$\operatorname{Im} z = b = r\sin\varphi$	– imaginary part of z
$\|z\| = \sqrt{a^2 + b^2} = r$	– absolute value of z
$\arg z = \varphi$	– argument of z
$\overline{z} = a - b\,\mathrm{i}$	– complex number conjugate to $z = a + b\,\mathrm{i}$

Special complex numbers

$$\mathrm{e}^{\mathrm{i}0} = 1, \qquad \mathrm{e}^{\pm\mathrm{i}\frac{\pi}{3}} = \frac{1}{2}\left(1 \pm \sqrt{3}\,\mathrm{i}\right)$$

$$\mathrm{e}^{\pm\mathrm{i}\frac{\pi}{2}} = \pm\mathrm{i}, \qquad \mathrm{e}^{\pm\mathrm{i}\frac{\pi}{4}} = \frac{1}{2}\sqrt{2}(1 \pm \mathrm{i})$$

$$\mathrm{e}^{\pm\mathrm{i}\pi} = -1, \qquad \mathrm{e}^{\pm\mathrm{i}\frac{\pi}{6}} = \frac{1}{2}\left(\sqrt{3} \pm \mathrm{i}\right)$$

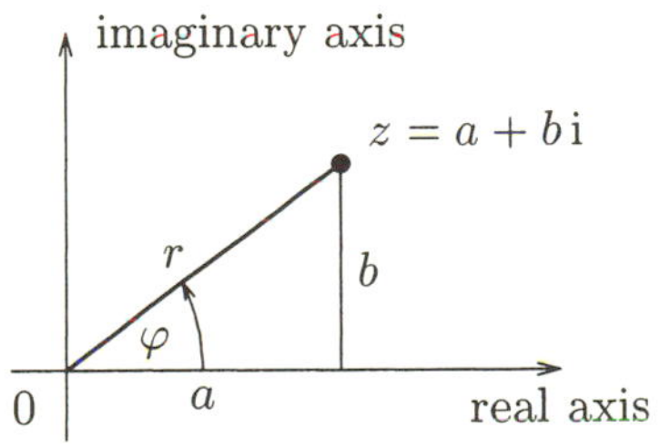

Transformation Cartesian ⟶ polar form

Given a, b $\Longrightarrow$ $r = \sqrt{a^2 + b^2}$,

φ is the solution of $\cos\varphi = \dfrac{a}{r}$, $\sin\varphi = \dfrac{b}{r}$

Transformation polar ⟶ Cartesian form

Given r, φ $\Longrightarrow$ $a = r \cdot \cos\varphi$, $\quad b = r \cdot \sin\varphi$

Rules of operation

Given $z_k = a_k + b_k\,\mathrm{i} = r_k(\cos\varphi_k + \mathrm{i}\sin\varphi_k) = r_k \mathrm{e}^{\mathrm{i}\varphi_k}$, $k = 1, 2$.

$$z_1 \pm z_2 = (a_1 \pm a_2) + (b_1 \pm b_2)\,\mathrm{i}$$

$$z_1 \cdot z_2 = (a_1 a_2 - b_1 b_2) + (a_1 b_2 + a_2 b_1)\,\mathrm{i}$$

$$z_1 \cdot z_2 = r_1 r_2 \left[\cos(\varphi_1 + \varphi_2) + \mathrm{i}\,\sin(\varphi_1 + \varphi_2)\right] = r_1 r_2\, \mathrm{e}^{\mathrm{i}(\varphi_1 + \varphi_2)}$$

$$\frac{z_1}{z_2} = \frac{r_1}{r_2}\left[\cos(\varphi_1 - \varphi_2) + \mathrm{i}\,\sin(\varphi_1 - \varphi_2)\right] = \frac{r_1}{r_2}\,\mathrm{e}^{\mathrm{i}(\varphi_1 - \varphi_2)}$$

$$\frac{z_1}{z_2} = \frac{z_1 \overline{z}_2}{|z_2|^2} = \frac{a_1 a_2 + b_1 b_2 + (a_2 b_1 - a_1 b_2)\,\mathrm{i}}{a_2^2 + b_2^2} \qquad (a_2^2 + b_2^2 > 0)$$

$$z \cdot \overline{z} = |z|^2 \qquad \frac{1}{z} = \frac{\overline{z}}{|z|^2}$$

Solution of $z^n = a$ (taking of the root)

Representing the number a in the polar form $a = r\mathrm{e}^{\mathrm{i}\varphi}$, the n solutions located at the circle around the origin with radius $\sqrt[n]{r}$ are

$$z_k = \sqrt[n]{r}\,\mathrm{e}^{\mathrm{i}\dfrac{\varphi + 2k\pi}{n}}, \quad k = 0, 1, \ldots, n-1\,.$$

The angles between the real axis and the radiant of these numbers are

$$\frac{\varphi + 2k\pi}{n}, \qquad k = 0, 1, \ldots, n-1\,.$$

Intersection of the unit circle

In the figure the unit circle $|z| = 1$ is divided into 6 segments by the solutions of the equation

$$z^6 = 1$$

yielding the points

$$z_1 = \mathrm{e}^0, \quad z_2 = \mathrm{e}^{\mathrm{i}\frac{\pi}{3}}, \quad z_3 = \mathrm{e}^{\mathrm{i}\frac{2\pi}{3}},$$

$$z_4 = \mathrm{e}^{\mathrm{i}\pi}, \quad z_5 = \mathrm{e}^{\mathrm{i}\frac{4\pi}{3}}, \quad z_6 = \mathrm{e}^{\mathrm{i}\frac{5\pi}{3}}.$$

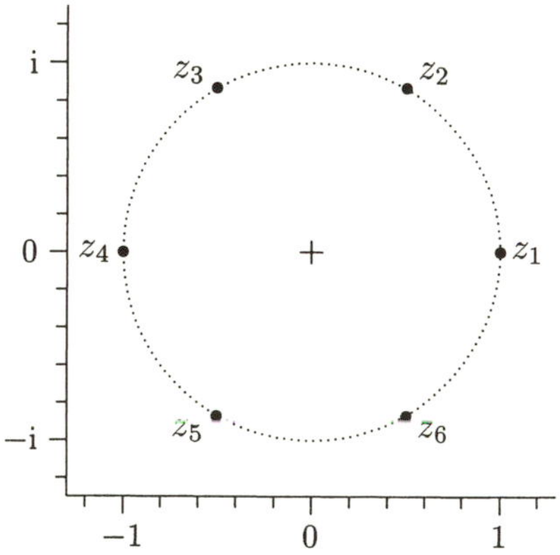

Combinatorial Analysis

Permutations

• For n given elements an arbitrary arrangement of all elements is called a *permutation*. If among the n elements there are p groups of the same elements, then one speaks about permutations *with repetition*. Let the number of elements in the i-th group be n_i, where it is assumed that $n_1+n_2+\ldots+n_p=n$.

	without repetition	with repetition
number of different permutations	$P_n = n!$	$P_{n_1,\ldots,n_p} = \dfrac{n!}{n_1!\,n_2!\cdot\ldots\cdot n_p!}$ $n_1+n_2+\ldots+n_p=n$

The permutations of 1,2,3,4 ($n=4$):

1 2 3 4	2 1 3 4	3 1 2 4	4 1 2 3	
1 2 4 3	2 1 4 3	3 1 4 2	4 1 3 2	
1 3 2 4	2 3 1 4	3 2 1 4	4 2 1 3	
1 3 4 2	2 3 4 1	3 2 4 1	4 2 3 1	$4! = 24$
1 4 2 3	2 4 1 3	3 4 1 2	4 3 1 2	
1 4 3 2	2 4 3 1	3 4 2 1	4 3 2 1	

The permutations of 1,2,3,4 with repetition ($n=4$, $n_1=1$, $n_2=2$, $n_3=1$):

1 2 2 3	2 1 2 3	2 2 3 1	3 1 2 2	
1 2 3 2	2 1 3 2	2 3 1 2	3 2 1 2	$\dfrac{4!}{1!\cdot 2!\cdot 1!} = 12$
1 3 2 2	2 2 1 3	2 3 2 1	3 2 2 1	

Arrangements

• Given n different elements and k places, an arbitrary assignment of the elements to the places is called an *arrangement (without repetition)*; this corresponds to a sampling of k out of n elements **taking into account the order**, $1 \le k \le n$. If any of the n elements occurs arbitrarily often so that it can be chosen several times, then one speaks about *arrangements with repetition*.

	without repetition	with repetition
number of different arrangements	$V_n^k = \dfrac{n!}{(n-k)!}$ $1 \le k \le n$	$\overline{V}_n^k = n^k$

The arrangements of 1,2,3,4 to 2 places ($n = 4,\ k = 2$):

1 2	2 1	3 1	4 1	
1 3	2 3	3 2	4 2	$\frac{4!}{2!} = 12$
1 4	2 4	3 4	4 3	

The arrangements of 1,2,3,4 to 2 places with repetition ($n = 4,\ k = 2$):

1 1	2 1	3 1	4 1	
1 2	2 2	3 2	4 2	
1 3	2 3	3 3	4 3	$4^2 = 16$
1 4	2 4	3 4	4 4	

Combinations

• If there are chosen k out of n different elements, where $1 \le k \le n$ and **one does not take into account the order**, then one speaks about a *combination (without repetition)*. If any of the n different elements occurs several times, then one speaks about a *combination with repetition*.

	without repetition	with repetition
number of different combinations	$C_n^k = \binom{n}{k}$ $1 \le k \le n$	$\overline{C}_n^k = \binom{n+k-1}{k}$

The combinations of 1,2,3,4 to 2 places ($n = 4,\ k = 2$):

1 2	2 3	3 4	
1 3	2 4		$\binom{4}{2} = 6$
1 4			

The combinations of 1,2,3,4 to 2 places with repetition ($n = 4,\ k = 2$):

1 1	2 2	3 3	4 4	
1 2	2 3	3 4		$\binom{4+2-1}{2} = 10$
1 3	2 4			
1 4				

Sequences and Series

Sequences of numbers

A mapping $a : K \to \mathbb{R}$, $K \subset \mathbb{N}$, is called a *sequence (of numbers)* and denoted by $\{a_n\}$. For $K = \mathbb{N}$ it consists of the *elements (terms)* $a_n = a(n)$, $n = 1, 2, \ldots$ The sequence is said to be *finite* or *infinite* depending on whether the set K is finite or infinite.

Notions

explicit sequence	–	formation rule $a_n = a(n)$ given
recursive sequence	–	$a_{n+1} = a(a_n, a_{n-1}, \ldots, a_{n-k})$
bounded sequence	–	$\exists\ C \in \mathbb{R}:\ \ \lvert a_n\rvert \le C\ \ \forall n \in K$
increasing sequence	–	$a_{n+1} \ge a_n \quad \forall n \in \mathbb{N}$
strictly increasing sequence	–	$a_{n+1} > a_n \quad \forall n \in \mathbb{N}$
decreasing sequence	–	$a_{n+1} \le a_n \quad \forall n \in \mathbb{N}$
strictly decreasing sequence	–	$a_{n+1} < a_n \quad \forall n \in \mathbb{N}$
convergent sequence (to the limit g)	–	The number g is called *limit* of the sequence $\{a_n\}$ if to any number $\varepsilon > 0$ there exists an index $n(\varepsilon)$ such that $\lvert a_n - g\rvert < \varepsilon$ for all $n \ge n(\varepsilon)$. Notation: $\lim\limits_{n\to\infty} a_n = g$ or $a_n \to g$ for $n \to \infty$.
divergent sequence	–	sequence not having a limit
properly divergent sequence (to the improper limit $+\infty$ and $-\infty$, resp.)	–	sequence for which to any number c there is an index $n(c)$ such that $a_n > c$ ($a_n < c$, resp.) for all $n \ge n(c)$
improperly divergent sequence	–	sequence which does neither converge nor improperly diverge
null sequence	–	sequence tending to the limit $g = 0$
alternating sequence	–	sequence the terms of which are alternatingly positive and negative
arithmetic sequence	–	$a_{n+1} - a_n = d \ \ \forall n \in \mathbb{N},\ \ d = \text{const}$
geometric sequence	–	$\dfrac{a_{n+1}}{a_n} = q \ \ \forall n \in \mathbb{N},\ \ q = \text{const}$

- A number a is called a *limit point* of the sequence $\{a_n\}$ if to any number $\varepsilon > 0$ there are infinitely many elements a_n such that $\lvert a_n - a\rvert < \varepsilon$.

Convergence theorems

- A sequence can have at most one limit.
- A monotone sequence converges if and only if it is bounded.
- A bounded sequence has at least one limit point.
- If a is a limit point of the sequence $\{a_n\}$, then $\{a_n\}$ has a subsequence converging to a.

Convergence properties

Let $\lim\limits_{n\to\infty} a_n = a$, $\lim\limits_{n\to\infty} b_n = b$ and $\alpha, \beta \in \mathbb{R}$. Then:

$$\lim_{n\to\infty}(\alpha a_n + \beta b_n) = \alpha a + \beta b \qquad \lim_{n\to\infty} a_n b_n = ab$$

$$\lim_{n\to\infty}\frac{a_n}{b_n} = \frac{a}{b} \quad \text{if } b, b_n \neq 0 \qquad \lim_{n\to\infty}|a_n| = |a|$$

$$\lim_{n\to\infty}\sqrt[k]{a_n} = \sqrt[k]{a} \quad \text{for } a, a_n \geq 0,\ k = 1, 2, \ldots$$

$$\lim_{n\to\infty}\frac{1}{n}(a_1 + \ldots + a_n) = a \qquad A \leq a_n \leq B \Longrightarrow A \leq a \leq B$$

Limits of special sequences

$$\lim_{n\to\infty}\frac{1}{n} = 0 \qquad \lim_{n\to\infty}\frac{n}{n+\alpha} = 1, \quad \alpha \in \mathbb{R}$$

$$\lim_{n\to\infty}\sqrt[n]{\lambda} = 1 \quad \text{for } \lambda > 0 \qquad \lim_{n\to\infty}\left(1 + \frac{1}{n}\right)^n = \mathrm{e}$$

$$\lim_{n\to\infty}\left(1 - \frac{1}{n}\right)^n = \frac{1}{\mathrm{e}} \qquad \lim_{n\to\infty}\left(1 + \frac{\lambda}{n}\right)^n = \mathrm{e}^\lambda, \quad \lambda \in \mathbb{R}$$

Sequences of functions

Sequences of the form $\{f_n\}$, $n \in \mathbb{N}$, the terms f_n of which are real-valued functions defined on an interval $D \subset \mathbb{R}$ are called *function sequences.* All values $x \in D$ for which the sequence $\{f_n(x)\}$ has a limit form the *domain of convergence* of the function sequence (it will be assumed that it coincides with D).

- The *limit function* f of the sequence of functions $\{f_n\}$ is defined by

$$f(x) = \lim_{n\to\infty} f_n(x), \quad x \in D.$$

Uniform convergence

• The function sequence $\{f_n\}$, $n \in \mathbb{N}$, converges *uniformly in D* to the limit function f if for any real number $\varepsilon > 0$ there is a number $n(\varepsilon)$ independent of x such that for all $n \geq n(\varepsilon)$ and all $x \in D$ one has: $|f(x) - f_n(x)| < \varepsilon$.

• The function sequence $\{f_n\}$, $n \in \mathbb{N}$, is uniformly convergent in the interval $D \subset \mathbb{R}$ if and only if for any real number $\varepsilon > 0$ there exists a number $n(\varepsilon)$ independent of x such that for all $n \geq n(\varepsilon)$ and all $m \in \mathbb{N}$ one has:

$$|f_{n+m}(x) - f_n(x)| < \varepsilon \qquad \text{for all } x \in D$$

Cauchy condition

Infinite series

$$a_1 + a_2 + a_3 + \ldots = \sum_{k=1}^{\infty} a_k$$

partial sums:

$$\begin{aligned} s_1 &= a_1 \\ s_2 &= a_1 + a_2 \\ &\cdots\cdots \\ s_n &= a_1 + a_2 + \ldots + a_n \end{aligned}$$

• The infinite series $\sum\limits_{k=1}^{\infty} a_k$ is called *convergent* if the sequence $\{s_n\}$ of partial sums converges. The limit s of the sequence $\{s_n\}$ of partial sums is called the *sum* of the series (provided it exists):

$$\lim_{n\to\infty} s_n = s = \sum_{k=1}^{\infty} a_k$$

• If the sequence $\{s_n\}$ of partial sums diverges, then the series $\sum\limits_{k=1}^{\infty} a_k$ is said to be *divergent*.

Criteria of convergence for alternating series

The series $\sum\limits_{n=1}^{\infty} a_n$ is called *alternating* if the sign changes from term to term. An alternating series is convergent if for its terms a_n one has

$$|a_n| \geq |a_{n+1}| \text{ for } n = 1, 2, \ldots \text{ and } \lim_{n\to\infty} |a_n| = 0\,.$$

Leibniz's alternating series test

Criteria of convergence for series of nonnegative terms

A series of nonnegative terms a_n converges if and only if the sequence $\{s_n\}$ of its partial sums is bounded above.

Let $0 \leq a_n \leq b_n$, $n = 1, 2, \ldots$

If $\sum\limits_{n=1}^{\infty} b_n$ is convergent, then $\sum\limits_{n=1}^{\infty} a_n$ is also convergent.

If $\sum\limits_{n=1}^{\infty} a_n$ is divergent, then $\sum\limits_{n=1}^{\infty} b_n$ is also divergent.

comparison test

If $\frac{a_{n+1}}{a_n} \leq q$, $n = 1, 2, \ldots$, with $0<q<1$ or $\lim_{n\to\infty} \frac{a_{n+1}}{a_n} < 1$, then the series $\sum_{n=1}^{\infty} a_n$ converges;

if $\frac{a_{n+1}}{a_n} \geq 1$, $n = 1, 2, \ldots$ or $\lim_{n\to\infty} \frac{a_{n+1}}{a_n} > 1$, then it diverges.

ratio test

If $\sqrt[n]{a_n} \leq \lambda$, $n = 1, 2, \ldots$ with $0 < \lambda < 1$ or $\lim_{n\to\infty} \sqrt[n]{a_n} < 1$, then the series $\sum_{n=1}^{\infty} a_n$ converges;

if $\sqrt[n]{a_n} \geq 1$, $n = 1, 2, \ldots$ or $\lim_{n\to\infty} \sqrt[n]{a_n} > 1$, then it diverges.

Cauchy's root test

Series of arbitrary terms

- If the series $\sum_{n=1}^{\infty} a_n$ converges, then $\boxed{\lim_{n\to\infty} a_n = 0}$ **necessary criterion of convergence**

- The series $\sum_{n=1}^{\infty} a_n$ is convergent if and only if for every real number $\varepsilon > 0$ there is a number $n(\varepsilon) \in \mathbb{N}$ such that for all $n > n(\varepsilon)$ and for any number $m \in \mathbb{N}$ one has:

$$|a_n + a_{n+1} + \ldots + a_{n+m}| < \varepsilon$$

Cauchy condition

- A series $\sum_{n=1}^{\infty} a_n$ is said to be *absolutely convergent* if the series $\sum_{n=1}^{\infty} |a_n|$ converges.
- The series $\sum_{n=1}^{\infty} a_n$ is convergent if it is absolutely convergent.

Transformation of series

- If finitely many terms of a series are removed or added, then the convergence behaviour does not change.
- Convergent series remain convergent if they are termwise added, subtracted or multiplied by a constant:

$$\sum_{n=1}^{\infty} a_n = a, \quad \sum_{n=1}^{\infty} b_n = b \quad \Longrightarrow \quad \sum_{n=1}^{\infty} (a_n \pm b_n) = a \pm b, \quad \sum_{n=1}^{\infty} c \cdot a_n = c \cdot a$$

- In an absolutely convergent series the order of the terms can be arbitrarily changed. In doing so, the series is still convergent and the sum remains the same.

Sums of special series

$$1-\frac{1}{2}+\frac{1}{3}\mp\ldots+\frac{(-1)^{n+1}}{n}+\ldots=\ln 2$$

$$1+\frac{1}{2}+\frac{1}{4}+\ldots+\frac{1}{2^n}+\ldots=2$$

$$1-\frac{1}{3}+\frac{1}{5}\mp\ldots+\frac{(-1)^{n+1}}{2n-1}+\ldots=\frac{\pi}{4}$$

$$1-\frac{1}{2}+\frac{1}{4}\mp\ldots+\frac{(-1)^{n}}{2^n}+\ldots=\frac{2}{3}$$

$$1+\frac{1}{2^2}+\frac{1}{3^2}+\ldots+\frac{1}{n^2}+\ldots=\frac{\pi^2}{6}$$

$$1-\frac{1}{2^2}+\frac{1}{3^2}\mp\ldots+\frac{(-1)^{n+1}}{n^2}+\ldots=\frac{\pi^2}{12}$$

$$1+\frac{1}{3^2}+\frac{1}{5^2}+\ldots+\frac{1}{(2n-1)^2}+\ldots=\frac{\pi^2}{8}$$

$$1+\frac{1}{1!}+\frac{1}{2!}+\ldots+\frac{1}{n!}+\ldots=\mathrm{e}$$

$$1-\frac{1}{1!}+\frac{1}{2!}\mp\ldots+\frac{(-1)^n}{n!}+\ldots=\frac{1}{\mathrm{e}}$$

$$\frac{1}{1\cdot 3}+\frac{1}{3\cdot 5}+\ldots+\frac{1}{(2n-1)(2n+1)}+\ldots=\frac{1}{2}$$

$$\frac{1}{1\cdot 2}+\frac{1}{2\cdot 3}+\ldots+\frac{1}{n(n+1)}+\ldots=1$$

$$\frac{1}{1\cdot 3}+\frac{1}{2\cdot 4}+\ldots+\frac{1}{n(n+2)}+\ldots=\frac{3}{4}$$

Function and power series

Function series

An infinite series the terms of which are functions is called *function series*:

$$f_1(x)+f_2(x)+\ldots=\sum_{k=1}^{\infty} f_k(x) \qquad \text{partial sums:} \quad s_n(x)=\sum_{k=1}^{n} f_k(x)$$

• The intersection of all domains of definition of the functions f_k is the *domain* D of the function series. This series is called *convergent* for some value $x \in D$ if the sequence $\{s_n(x)\}$ of partial sums converges to a limit $s(x)$, otherwise it is called *divergent*. All $x \in D$ for which the function series converges form the *domain of convergence* of the function series (it is assumed that the latter is equal to D).

• The *limit function* of the sequence $\{s_n\}$ is the function $s\colon D \to \mathbb{R}$ defined by the relation

$$\lim_{n\to\infty} s_n(x) = s(x) = \sum_{k=1}^{\infty} f_k(x)$$

• The function series $\sum\limits_{k=1}^{\infty} f_k(x)$ is said to be *uniformly convergent in D* if the sequence $\{s_n\}$ of partial sums converges uniformly ▶ function sequences.

Weierstrass comparison test

The function series $\sum\limits_{n=1}^{\infty} f_n(x)$ converges uniformly in D if there exists a convergent series $\sum\limits_{n=1}^{\infty} a_n$ such that $\forall\, n \in \mathbb{N}$ and $\forall\, x \in D$: $|f_n(x)| \le a_n$.

• If all functions f_n, $n \in \mathbb{N}$, are continuous at the point x_0 and if the series $\sum\limits_{n=1}^{\infty} f_n(x)$ is uniformly convergent in D, then the limit function $s(x)$ is also continuous at x_0.

Power series

Function series the terms of which are of the form $f_n(x) = a_n(x - x_0)^n$, $n \in \mathbb{N}_0$, are called *power series* with *centre* at x_0. After the transformation $x := x - x_0$ one gets power series with centre at zero, this is assumed in the following. In its domain of convergence the power series is a function s:

$$s(x) = a_0 + a_1 x + a_2 x^2 + \ldots = \sum_{n=0}^{\infty} a_n x^n$$

If this power series is neither divergent for all $x \neq 0$ nor convergent for all x, then there exists one and only one number $r > 0$ called the *radius of convergence* such that the power series converges for $|x| < r$ and diverges for $|x| > r$. For $|x| = r$ a general statement cannot be made. (We agree to set $r = 0$ if the power series converges only for $x = 0$ and to set $r = \infty$ if it converges for all $x \in \mathbb{R}$.)

Determination of the domain of convergence

Let $b_n = \left|\frac{a_n}{a_{n+1}}\right|$ and $c_n = \sqrt[n]{|a_n|}$. Then:

$\{b_n\}$ is convergent	$\Longrightarrow$	$r = \lim\limits_{n\to\infty} b_n$
$\{b_n\}$ is properly divergent to $+\infty$	$\Longrightarrow$	$r = \infty$
$\{c_n\}$ is convergent to zero	$\Longrightarrow$	$r = \infty$
$\{c_n\}$ is convergent to $c \neq 0$	$\Longrightarrow$	$r = \frac{1}{c}$
$\{c_n\}$ is properly divergent to $+\infty$	$\Longrightarrow$	$r = 0$

Properties of power series (radius of convergence $r > 0$)

- A power series is absolutely convergent for every number $x \in (-r, r)$. It converges uniformly in any closed interval $I \subset (-r, r)$.
- The sum $s(x)$ of a power series is arbitrarily often differentiable in the interval $(-r, r)$. The derivatives can be obtained by termwise differentiation.
- In $[0, t]$ and $[t, 0]$, resp., with $|t| < r$ the power series can also be integrated termwise:

$$s(x) = \sum_{n=0}^{\infty} a_n x^n \Longrightarrow s'(x) = \sum_{n=1}^{\infty} n a_n x^{n-1} \quad \text{and} \quad \int_0^t s(x)\,\mathrm{d}x = \sum_{n=0}^{\infty} a_n \frac{t^{n+1}}{n+1}$$

- If the power series $\sum\limits_{n=0}^{\infty} a_n x^n$ and $\sum\limits_{n=0}^{\infty} b_n x^n$ converge in the same interval $(-v, v)$ and have the same sums there, then the two power series are identical: $a_n = b_n \ \forall\, n = 0, 1, \ldots$

Taylor series

If the function $f : D \to \mathbb{R}$, $D \subset \mathbb{R}$ is arbitrarily often differentiable at $x_0 \in D$, then the following power series is said to be the *Taylor series* formed at the point x_0:

$$\sum_{n=0}^{\infty} \frac{f^{(n)}(x_0)}{n!}(x - x_0)^n, \quad f^{(0)}(x) = f(x)$$

Taylor series

- If f is arbitrarily often differentiable in a neighbourhood U of the point x_0 and if the remainder in ▶ Taylor's formula converges to zero for all $x \in U$, then the Taylor series has a radius of convergence $r > 0$ and for x satisfying $|x - x_0| < r$ one has:

$$f(x) = \sum_{n=0}^{\infty} \frac{f^{(n)}(x_0)}{n!}(x - x_0)^n$$

Taylor expansion

Tables of power series

Domain of convergence: $|x| \le 1$

function	power series, Taylor series
$(1+x)^\alpha$	$1+\alpha x+\frac{\alpha(\alpha-1)}{2!}x^2+\frac{\alpha(\alpha-1)(\alpha-2)}{3!}x^3+\ldots \quad (\alpha>0)$
$\sqrt{1+x}$	$1+\frac{1}{2}x-\frac{1\cdot 1}{2\cdot 4}x^2+\frac{1\cdot 1\cdot 3}{2\cdot 4\cdot 6}x^3-\frac{1\cdot 1\cdot 3\cdot 5}{2\cdot 4\cdot 6\cdot 8}x^4\pm\ldots$
$\sqrt[3]{1+x}$	$1+\frac{1}{3}x-\frac{1\cdot 2}{3\cdot 6}x^2+\frac{1\cdot 2\cdot 5}{3\cdot 6\cdot 9}x^3-\frac{1\cdot 2\cdot 5\cdot 8}{3\cdot 6\cdot 9\cdot 12}x^4\pm\ldots$

Domain of convergence: $|x| < 1$

function	power series, Taylor series
$\frac{1}{(1+x)^\alpha}$	$1-\alpha x+\frac{\alpha(\alpha+1)}{2!}x^2-\frac{\alpha(\alpha+1)(\alpha+2)}{3!}x^3\pm\ldots \quad (\alpha>0)$
$\frac{1}{1+x}$	$1-x+x^2-x^3+x^4-x^5\pm\ldots$
$\frac{1}{(1+x)^2}$	$1-2x+3x^2-4x^3+5x^4-6x^5\pm\ldots$
$\frac{1}{(1+x)^3}$	$1-\frac{1}{2}\left(2\cdot 3x-3\cdot 4x^2+4\cdot 5x^3-5\cdot 6x^4\pm\ldots\right)$
$\frac{1}{\sqrt{1+x}}$	$1-\frac{1}{2}x+\frac{1\cdot 3}{2\cdot 4}x^2-\frac{1\cdot 3\cdot 5}{2\cdot 4\cdot 6}x^3+\frac{1\cdot 3\cdot 5\cdot 7}{2\cdot 4\cdot 6\cdot 8}x^4\mp\ldots$
$\frac{1}{\sqrt[3]{1+x}}$	$1-\frac{1}{3}x+\frac{1\cdot 4}{3\cdot 6}x^2-\frac{1\cdot 4\cdot 7}{3\cdot 6\cdot 9}x^3+\frac{1\cdot 4\cdot 7\cdot 10}{3\cdot 6\cdot 9\cdot 12}x^4\mp\ldots$
$\arcsin x$	$x+\frac{1}{2\cdot 3}x^3+\frac{1\cdot 3}{2\cdot 4\cdot 5}x^5+\ldots+\frac{1\cdot 3\cdot\ldots\cdot(2n-1)}{2\cdot 4\cdot\ldots\cdot 2n\cdot(2n+1)}x^{2n+1}+\ldots$
$\arccos x$	$\frac{\pi}{2}-x-\frac{1}{2\cdot 3}x^3-\ldots-\frac{1\cdot 3\cdot\ldots\cdot(2n-1)}{2\cdot 4\cdot\ldots\cdot 2n\cdot(2n+1)}x^{2n+1}-\ldots$
$\arctan x$	$x-\frac{1}{3}x^3+\frac{1}{5}x^5-\frac{1}{7}x^7\pm\ldots+(-1)^n\frac{1}{2n+1}x^{2n+1}\pm\ldots$

Domain of convergence: $|x| \leq \infty$

function	power series, Taylor series
$\sin x$	$x - \frac{1}{3!}x^3 + \frac{1}{5!}x^5 - \frac{1}{7!}x^7 \pm \ldots + (-1)^n \frac{1}{(2n+1)!}x^{2n+1} \pm \ldots$
$\cos x$	$1 - \frac{1}{2!}x^2 + \frac{1}{4!}x^4 - \frac{1}{6!}x^6 \pm \ldots + (-1)^n \frac{1}{(2n)!}x^{2n} \pm \ldots$
e^x	$1 + \frac{1}{1!}x + \frac{1}{2!}x^2 + \ldots + \frac{1}{n!}x^n + \ldots$
a^x	$1 + \frac{\ln a}{1!}x + \frac{\ln^2 a}{2!}x^2 + \ldots + \frac{\ln^n a}{n!}x^n + \ldots$
$\sinh x$	$x + \frac{1}{3!}x^3 + \frac{1}{5!}x^5 + \ldots + \frac{1}{(2n+1)!}x^{2n+1} + \ldots$
$\cosh x$	$1 + \frac{1}{2!}x^2 + \frac{1}{4!}x^4 + \ldots + \frac{1}{(2n)!}x^{2n} + \ldots$

Domain of convergence: $-1 < x \leq 1$

function	power series, Taylor series
$\ln(1+x)$	$x - \frac{1}{2}x^2 + \frac{1}{3}x^3 - \frac{1}{4}x^4 \pm \ldots + (-1)^{n+1}\frac{1}{n}x^n \pm \ldots$

Fourier series

Series of the form

$$s(x) = a_0 + \sum_{k=1}^{\infty} \left(a_k \cos \frac{k\pi x}{l} + b_k \sin \frac{k\pi x}{l} \right)$$

are called trigonometric series or Fourier series. To represent a given function $f(x)$ by a Fourier series, it is necessary that $f(x)$ is a periodic function, i. e. $f(x+2l) = f(x)$, and that the so-called Fourier coefficients a_k, b_k are equal to

$$a_0 = \frac{1}{2l} \int f(x)\,\mathrm{d}x, \quad a_k = \frac{1}{l} \int f(x) \cos \frac{k\pi x}{l}\,\mathrm{d}x, \quad b_k = \frac{1}{l} \int f(x) \sin \frac{k\pi x}{l}\,\mathrm{d}x.$$

Symmetric functions

f even function, i. e. $f(-x) = f(x) \implies b_k = 0$ for $k = 1, 2, \ldots$
f odd function, i. e. $f(-x) = -f(x) \implies a_k = 0$ for $k = 0, 1, 2, \ldots$

Table of some Fourier series

The functions are defined on an interval of the length 2π and continued with the period 2π.

$$y = \begin{cases} x & \text{for} \quad -\pi < x < \pi \\ 0 & \text{for} \quad x = \pi \end{cases}$$

$$= 2\left(\frac{\sin x}{1} - \frac{\sin 2x}{2} + \frac{\sin 3x}{3} \pm \dots\right)$$

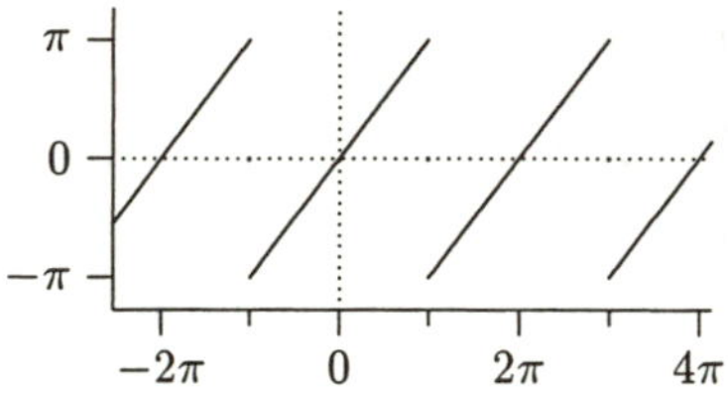

$$y = \begin{cases} x & \text{for } -\frac{\pi}{2} \le x \le \frac{\pi}{2} \\ \pi - x & \text{for } \frac{\pi}{2} \le x \le \frac{3\pi}{2} \end{cases}$$

$$= \frac{4}{\pi}\left(\frac{\sin x}{1^2} - \frac{\sin 3x}{3^2} + \frac{\sin 5x}{5^2} \mp \dots\right)$$

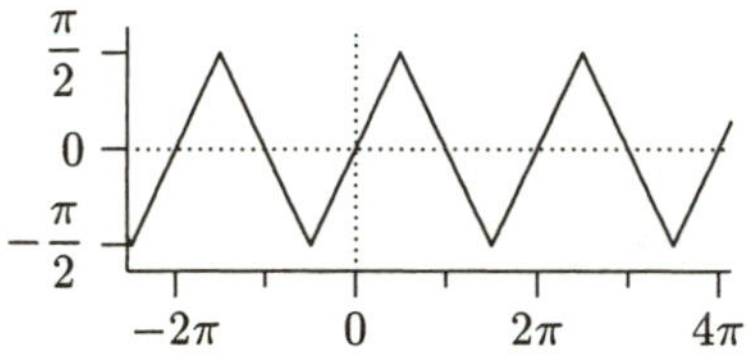

$$y = |x| \quad \text{for} \quad -\pi \le x \le \pi$$

$$= \frac{\pi}{2} - \frac{4}{\pi}\left(\frac{\cos x}{1^2} + \frac{\cos 3x}{3^2} + \frac{\cos 5x}{5^2} + \dots\right)$$

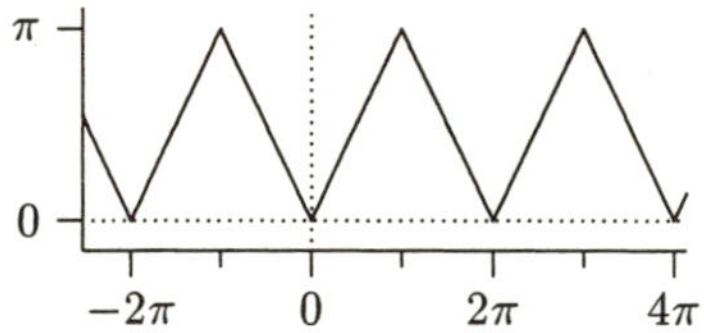

$$y = \begin{cases} -\alpha & \text{for} \quad -\pi < x < 0 \\ \alpha & \text{for} \quad 0 < x < \pi \\ 0 & \text{for} \quad x = 0, \pi \end{cases}$$

$$= \frac{4\alpha}{\pi}\left(\frac{\sin x}{1} + \frac{\sin 3x}{3} + \frac{\sin 5x}{5} + \dots\right)$$

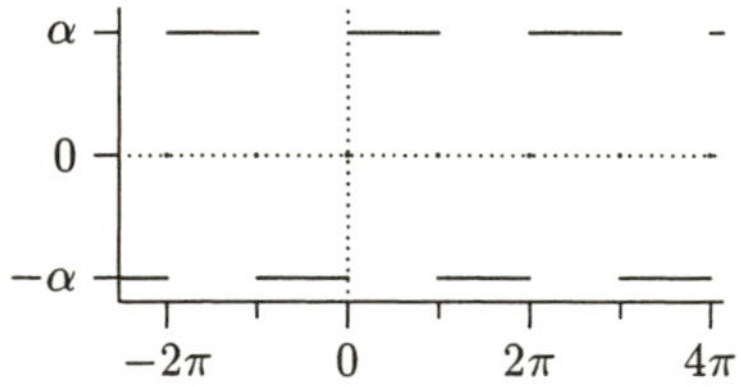

$$y = |\sin x| \quad \text{for} \quad -\pi \le x \le \pi$$

$$= \frac{2}{\pi} - \frac{4}{\pi}\left(\frac{\cos 2x}{1 \cdot 3} + \frac{\cos 4x}{3 \cdot 5} + \frac{\cos 6x}{5 \cdot 7} + \dots\right)$$

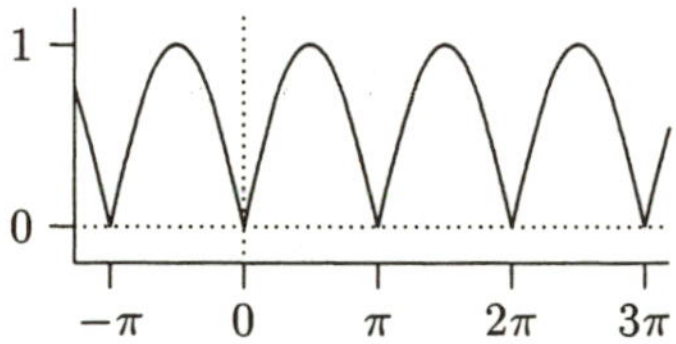

Mathematics of Finance

Simple interest

Notations

p	–	interest rate per conversion period (in percent)
t	–	time in units that correspond to the rate, moment
K_0	–	opening capital, original principal, present value
K_t	–	amount, capital at the moment t
Z_t	–	simple interest earned in the term t
i	–	interest rate: $i = \frac{p}{100}$
T	–	number of days

• The most frequently period considered is the year, but a half-year, quarter, month etc. can be used either. The number of days per year or month differs from country to country. Usual usances are $\frac{30}{360}$, $\frac{\text{act}}{360}$, $\frac{\text{act}}{\text{act}}$, where act means the actual number of days. In what follows, in all formulas containing the quantity T the underlying period is the year with 360 days, each month having 30 days (i. e., the first usance is used).

Basic interest formulas

$T = 30 \cdot (m_2 - m_1) + d_2 - d_1$	–	number of days for which interest is paid; m_1, m_2 – months; d_1, d_2 – days
$Z_t = K_0 \cdot \frac{p}{100} \cdot t = K_0 \cdot i \cdot t$	–	simple interest
$Z_T = \frac{K_0 \cdot i \cdot T}{360} = \frac{K_0 \cdot p \cdot T}{100 \cdot 360}$	–	simple interest on a day basis
$K_0 = \frac{100 \cdot Z_t}{p \cdot t} = \frac{Z_t}{i \cdot t}$	–	capital (at $t = 0$)
$p = \frac{100 \cdot Z_t}{K_0 \cdot t}$	–	interest rate (in percent)
$i = \frac{Z_t}{K_0 \cdot t}$	–	interest rate
$t = \frac{100 \cdot Z_t}{K_0 \cdot p} = \frac{Z_t}{K_0 \cdot i}$	–	term, time

Capital at the moment t

$K_t = K_0(1 + i \cdot t) = K_0\left(1 + i \cdot \frac{T}{360}\right)$	– amount, capital at the moment t
$K_0 = \frac{K_t}{1 + i \cdot t} = \frac{K_t}{1 + i \cdot \frac{T}{360}}$	– present value
$i = \frac{K_n - K_0}{K_0 \cdot t} = 360 \cdot \frac{K_n - K_0}{K_0 \cdot T}$	– interest rate
$t = \frac{K_n - K_0}{K_0 \cdot i}$	– term, time
$T = 360 \cdot \frac{K_n - K_0}{K_0 \cdot i}$	– number of days for which interest is paid

Periodical payments

• Dividing the original period into m parts of length $\frac{1}{m}$ and assuming periodical payments of size r at the beginning (annuity due) and at the end (ordinary annuity), respectively, of each payment interval, the following amount results:

$R = r\left(m + \frac{m+1}{2} \cdot i\right)$ – annuity due

$R = r\left(m + \frac{m-1}{2} \cdot i\right)$ – ordinary annuity

Especially $m = 12$ (monthly payments and annual interest):

$R = r(12 + 6,5i)$ – annuity due; $R = r(12 + 5,5i)$ – ordinary annuity

Different methods for computing interest

Let $t_i = D_i M_i Y_i$ be day, month and year of the i-th date ($i = 1$: begin, $i = 2$: end); let $t = t_2 - t_1$ describe the actual number of days between begin and end; let T_i denote the number of days in the 'broken' year i; basis i = 365 oder 366.

method	formula
30/360	$t = [360 \cdot (Y_2 - Y_1) + 30 \cdot (M_2 - M_1) + D_2 - D_1]/360$
act/360	$t = (t_2 - t_1)/360$
act/act	$t = \frac{T_1}{\text{basis 1}} + Y_2 - Y_1 - 1 + \frac{T_2}{\text{basis 2}}$ *

* If the term considered lies within one year, only the first summand remains.

Compound interest

When considering several conversion periods, one speaks about *compound interest* if interest earned is added to the capital (usually at the end of every conversion period) and yields again interest.

Notations

p	–	rate of interest (in percent) per period
n	–	number of conversion periods
K_0	–	opening capital, present value
K_n	–	capital after n periods, amount, final value
i	–	(nominal) interest rate per conversion period: $i = \frac{p}{100}$
q	–	accumulation factor (for 1 period): $q = 1 + i$
q^n	–	accumulation factor (for n periods)
m	–	number of parts of the period
d	–	discount factor
$i_m, \hat{i}_m$	–	interest rates belonging to each of the m parts of the period
δ	–	intensity of interest

Conversion table of basic quantities

	p	i	q	d	δ
p	p	$100i$	$100(q-1)$	$100\frac{d}{1-d}$	$100(e^\delta - 1)$
i	$\frac{p}{100}$	i	$q-1$	$\frac{d}{1-d}$	$e^\delta - 1$
q	$1 + \frac{p}{100}$	$1+i$	q	$\frac{1}{1-d}$	e^δ
d	$\frac{p}{100+p}$	$\frac{i}{1+i}$	$\frac{q-1}{q}$	d	$1 - e^{-\delta}$
δ	$\ln\left(1 + \frac{p}{100}\right)$	$\ln(1+i)$	$\ln q$	$\ln\left(\frac{1}{1-d}\right)$	δ

Basic formulas

$K_n = K_0 \cdot (1+i)^n = K_0 \cdot q^n$	– compound amount formula
$K_0 = \dfrac{K_n}{(1+i)^n} = \dfrac{K_n}{q^n}$	– present value at compound interest, amount at time $t = 0$
$p = 100\left(\sqrt[n]{\dfrac{K_n}{K_0}} - 1\right)$	– rate of interest (in percent)
$n = \dfrac{\log K_n - \log K_0}{\log q}$	– term, time
$n \approx \dfrac{69}{p}$	– approximate formula for the time within which a capital doubles
$K_n = K_0 \cdot q_1 \cdot q_2 \cdot \ldots \cdot q_n$	– final value under changing rates of interest p_j, $j=1,\ldots,n$ (with $q_j = \frac{p_j}{100}$)
$p_r = 100\left(\dfrac{1+i}{1+r} - 1\right) \approx 100(i-r)$	– real rate of interest considering a rate of inflation r

Mixed, partly simple and partly compound interest

$K_t = K_0(1+it_1)(1+i)^N(1+it_2)$	– capital after time t

- Here N denotes the integral number of conversion periods, and t_1, t_2 are the lengths of parts of the conversion period where simple interest is paid.
- To simplify calculations, in mathematics of finance usually the compound amount formula with noninteger exponent is used instead of the formula of mixed interest, i. e. $K_t = K_0(1+i)^t$, where $t = t_1 + N + t_2$.

Anticipative interest (discount)

In this case the rate of interest is determined as part of the **final** value (▶ discount factor p. 33).

$d = \dfrac{K_1 - K_0}{K_1} = \dfrac{K_t - K_0}{K_t \cdot t}$	– (discount) rate of interest under anticipatice compounding
$K_n = \dfrac{K_0}{(1-d)^n}$	– final value
$K_0 = K_n(1-d)^n$	– present value

More frequently compounding

$K_{n,m} = K_0 \cdot \left(1 + \frac{i}{m}\right)^{n \cdot m}$	–	amount after n years when interest rate is converted m times per year
$i_m = \frac{i}{m}$	–	relative rate per period
$\hat{i}_m = \sqrt[m]{1+i} - 1$	–	equivalent rate per period
$i_{\text{eff}} = (1 + i_m)^m - 1$	–	effective rate of interest per year
$p_{\text{eff}} = 100\left[(1 + \frac{p}{100m})^m - 1\right]$	–	effective rate of interest per year (in percent)

- Instead of one year one can take any other period as the original one.
- Compounding interest m times per year with the equivalent rate per period $\hat{i}_m$ leads to the same final value as compounding once per year with the nominal rate i; compounding interest m times per year with the relative rate per period i_m leads to that (greater) final value, which results when compounding once per year with the effective rate i_{eff}.

Continuous compounding

$K_{n,\infty} = K_0 \cdot e^{i \cdot n}$	–	amount at continuous compounding
$\delta = \ln(1+i)$	–	intensity of interest (equivalent to the interest rate i)
$i = e^\delta - 1$	–	nominal rate (equivalent to the intensity δ)

Average date of payment

Problem: At which date of payment t_m equivalently the total debt $K_1 + K_2 + \ldots + K_k$ has to be payed?

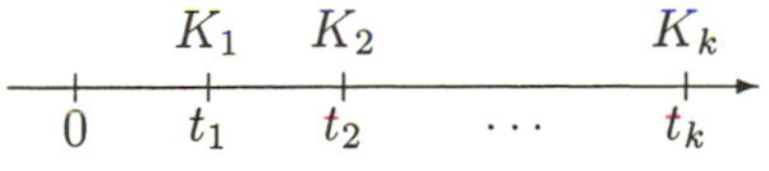

liabilities to pay

simple interest:

$$t_m = \frac{K_1 + K_2 + \ldots + K_k - K_0}{i}, \quad \text{where} \quad K_0 = \frac{K_1}{1 + it_1} + \ldots + \frac{K_k}{1 + it_k}$$

compound interest:

$$t_m = \frac{\ln(K_1 + \ldots + K_k) - \ln K_0}{\ln q}, \quad \text{where} \quad K_0 = \frac{K_1}{q^{t_1}} + \ldots + \frac{K_k}{q^{t_k}}$$

continuous compounding:

$$t_m = \frac{\ln(K_1 + \ldots + K_k) - \ln K_0}{\delta}, \quad \text{where} \quad K_0 = K_1 e^{-\delta t_1} + \ldots + K_k e^{-\delta t_k}$$

Annuities

Notations

p	–	rate of interest
n	–	term, number of payment intervals or rent periods
R	–	periodic rent, size of each payment
q	–	accumulation factor: $q = 1 + \frac{p}{100}$

Basic formulas

Basic assumption: Conversion and rent periods are equal to each other.

$F_n^{\text{due}} = R \cdot q \cdot \dfrac{q^n - 1}{q - 1}$	–	amount of an annuity due, final value
$P_n^{\text{due}} = \dfrac{R}{q^{n-1}} \cdot \dfrac{q^n - 1}{q - 1}$	–	present value of an annuity due
$F_n^{\text{ord}} = R \cdot \dfrac{q^n - 1}{q - 1}$	–	amount of an ordinary annuity, final value
$P_n^{\text{ord}} = \dfrac{R}{q^n} \cdot \dfrac{q^n - 1}{q - 1}$	–	present value of an ordinary annuity
$P_\infty^{\text{due}} = \dfrac{Rq}{q - 1}$	–	present value of a perpetuity, payments at the beginning of each period
$P_\infty^{\text{ord}} = \dfrac{R}{q - 1}$	–	present value of a perpetuity, interest used as earned

$$n = \frac{1}{\log q} \cdot \log \left(F_n^{\text{ord}} \cdot \frac{q-1}{R} + 1 \right) = \frac{1}{\log q} \cdot \log \frac{R}{R - P_n^{\text{ord}}(q-1)} \qquad \text{– term}$$

Factors describing the amount of 1 per period

	due	ordinary
amount of 1 per period	$\ddot{s}_{\overline{n}\rceil} = q \cdot \dfrac{q^n - 1}{q - 1}$	$s_{\overline{n}\rceil} = \dfrac{q^n - 1}{q - 1}$
present worth of 1 per period	$\ddot{a}_{\overline{n}\rceil} = \dfrac{q^n - 1}{q^{n-1}(q - 1)}$	$a_{\overline{n}\rceil} = \dfrac{q^n - 1}{q^n(q - 1)}$

Conversion period > rent period

If m periodic payments (rents) are made per conversion period, then in the above formulas the payments R are to be understood as $R = r\left(m + \frac{m+1}{2} \cdot i\right)$ (annuities due) and $R = r\left(m + \frac{m-1}{2} \cdot i\right)$ (ordinary annuities), resp. These amounts R arise at the end of the conversion period, so with respect to R one always has to use formulas belonging to ordinary annuities.

Basic quantities

$a_{\overline{n}\vert}$	–	present value of 1 per period (ordinary annuity)
$\ddot{a}_{\overline{n}\vert}$	–	present value of 1 per period (annuity due)
$s_{\overline{n}\vert}$	–	final value (amount) of 1 per period (ordinary annuity)
$\ddot{s}_{\overline{n}\vert}$	–	final value (amount) of 1 per period (annuity due)
$a_{\overline{\infty}\vert}$	–	present value of 1 per period (perpetuity, payments at the beginning of each period)
$\ddot{a}_{\overline{\infty}\vert}$	–	present value of 1 per period (perpetuity, interest used as earned)

Factors for amount and present value

$$a_{\overline{n}\vert} = \frac{1}{q} + \frac{1}{q^2} + \frac{1}{q^3} + \ldots + \frac{1}{q^n} = \frac{q^n - 1}{q^n(q-1)}$$

$$\ddot{a}_{\overline{n}\vert} = 1 + \frac{1}{q} + \frac{1}{q^2} + \ldots + \frac{1}{q^{n-1}} = \frac{q^n - 1}{q^{n-1}(q-1)}$$

$$s_{\overline{n}\vert} = 1 + q + q^2 + \ldots + q^{n-1} = \frac{q^n - 1}{q - 1}$$

$$\ddot{s}_{\overline{n}\vert} = q + q^2 + q^3 + \ldots + q^n = q \cdot \frac{q^n - 1}{q - 1}$$

$$a_{\overline{\infty}\vert} = \frac{1}{q} + \frac{1}{q^2} + \frac{1}{q^3} + \ldots = \frac{1}{q - 1}$$

$$\ddot{a}_{\overline{\infty}\vert} = 1 + \frac{1}{q} + \frac{1}{q^2} + \ldots = \frac{q}{q - 1}$$

Conversion table

	$a_{\overline{n}\vert}$	$\ddot{a}_{\overline{n}\vert}$	$s_{\overline{n}\vert}$	$\ddot{s}_{\overline{n}\vert}$	q^n
$a_{\overline{n}\vert}$	$a_{\overline{n}\vert}$	$\frac{\ddot{a}_{\overline{n}\vert}}{q}$	$\frac{s_{\overline{n}\vert}}{1+is_{\overline{n}\vert}}$	$\frac{\ddot{s}_{\overline{n}\vert}}{q(1+d\ddot{s}_{\overline{n}\vert})}$	$\frac{q^n-1}{q^n i}$
$\ddot{a}_{\overline{n}\vert}$	$qa_{\overline{n}\vert}$	$\ddot{a}_{\overline{n}\vert}$	$\frac{qs_{\overline{n}\vert}}{1+is_{\overline{n}\vert}}$	$\frac{\ddot{s}_{\overline{n}\vert}}{1+d\ddot{s}_{\overline{n}\vert}}$	$\frac{q^n-1}{q^n d}$
$s_{\overline{n}\vert}$	$\frac{a_{\overline{n}\vert}}{1-ia_{\overline{n}\vert}}$	$\frac{\ddot{a}_{\overline{n}\vert}}{q(1-d\ddot{a}_{\overline{n}\vert})}$	$s_{\overline{n}\vert}$	$\frac{\ddot{s}_{\overline{n}\vert}}{q}$	$\frac{q^n-1}{i}$
$\ddot{s}_{\overline{n}\vert}$	$\frac{qa_{\overline{n}\vert}}{1-ia_{\overline{n}\vert}}$	$\frac{\ddot{a}_{\overline{n}\vert}}{1-d\ddot{a}_{\overline{n}\vert}}$	$qs_{\overline{n}\vert}$	$\ddot{s}_{\overline{n}\vert}$	$\frac{q^n-1}{d}$
q^n	$\frac{1}{1-ia_{\overline{n}\vert}}$	$\frac{1}{1-d\ddot{a}_{\overline{n}\vert}}$	$1+is_{\overline{n}\vert}$	$1+d\ddot{s}_{\overline{n}\vert}$	q^n

Dynamic annuities

Arithmetically increasing dynamic annuity

Cash flows (increases proportional to the rent R with factor δ):

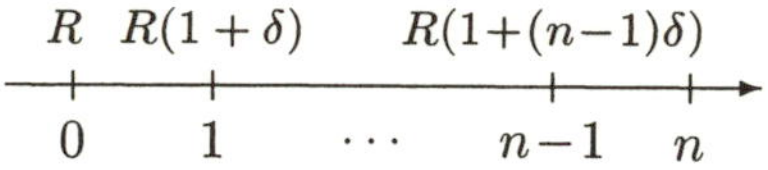

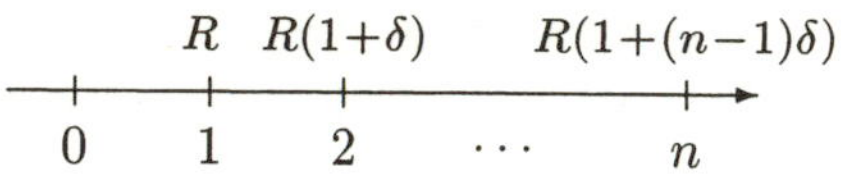

$$F_n^{\text{due}} = \frac{Rq}{q-1}\left[q^n - 1 + \delta\left(\frac{q^n-1}{q-1} - n\right)\right]$$

$$P_n^{\text{due}} = \frac{R}{q^{n-1}(q-1)}\left[q^n - 1 + \delta\left(\frac{q^n-1}{q-1} - n\right)\right]$$

$$F_n^{\text{ord}} = \frac{R}{q-1}\left[q^n - 1 + \delta\left(\frac{q^n-1}{q-1} - n\right)\right]$$

$$P_n^{\text{ord}} = \frac{R}{q^n(q-1)}\left[q^n - 1 + \delta\left(\frac{q^n-1}{q-1} - n\right)\right]$$

$$P_\infty^{\text{due}} = \frac{Rq}{q-1}\left(1 + \frac{\delta}{q-1}\right), \qquad P_\infty^{\text{ord}} = \frac{R}{q-1}\left(1 + \frac{\delta}{q-1}\right)$$

Geometrically increasing dynamic annuity

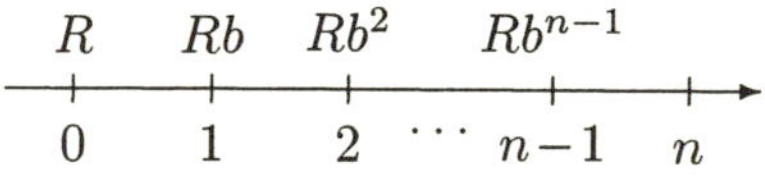

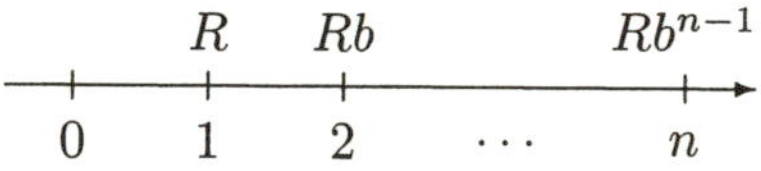

The constant quotient $b = 1 + \frac{s}{100}$ of succeeding terms is characterized by the *rate of increase* s.

$$F_n^{\text{due}} = Rq \cdot \frac{q^n - b^n}{q-b}, \quad b \neq q; \qquad F_n^{\text{due}} = Rnq^n, \quad b = q$$

$$P_n^{\text{due}} = \frac{R}{q^{n-1}} \cdot \frac{q^n - b^n}{q-b}, \quad b \neq q; \qquad P_n^{\text{due}} = Rn, \quad b = q$$

$$F_n^{\text{ord}} = R \cdot \frac{q^n - b^n}{q-b}, \quad b \neq q; \qquad F_n^{\text{ord}} = Rnq^{n-1}, \quad b = q$$

$$P_n^{\text{ord}} = \frac{R}{q^n} \cdot \frac{q^n - b^n}{q-b}, \quad b \neq q; \qquad P_n^{\text{ord}} = \frac{Rn}{q}, \quad b = q$$

$$P_\infty^{\text{due}} = \frac{Rq}{q-b}, \quad b < q; \qquad P_\infty^{\text{ord}} = \frac{R}{q-b}, \quad b < q$$

Amortization calculus

Notations

p	–	interest rate (in percent)
n	–	number of repayment periods
i	–	interest rate: $i = \frac{p}{100}$
q	–	accumulation factor: $q = 1 + i$
S_0	–	loan, original debt
S_k	–	outstanding principal after k periods
T_k	–	payoff in the k-th period
Z_k	–	interest in the k-th period
A_k	–	total payment in the k-th period

Kinds of amortization

- *Constant payoffs*: repayments constant: $T_k = T = \dfrac{S_0}{n}$, interest decreasing
- *Constant annuities*: total payments constant: $A_k = A = \text{const}$, interest decreasing, payoffs increasing
- *Amortization of a debt due at the end of the payback period*: $A_k = S_0 \cdot i$, $k = 1, \ldots, n-1$; $A_n = S_0 \cdot (1 + i)$
- In an *amortization schedule* all relevant quantities (interest, payoffs, total payment, outstanding principal, etc.) are clearly arranged in a table.

Basic formula for the total payment

$A_k = T_k + Z_k$	–	total payment (annuity) consisting of payoff and interest

Constant payoffs (conversion period = payment period)

$T_k = \dfrac{S_0}{n}$	–	payoff in the k-th period
$Z_k = S_0 \cdot \left(1 - \dfrac{k-1}{n}\right) i$	–	interest in the k-th period
$A_k = \dfrac{S_0}{n}\,[1 - (n - k + 1)i]$	–	total payment in the k-th period
$S_k = S_0 \cdot \left(1 - \dfrac{k}{n}\right)$	–	outstanding principal after k periods
$P = \dfrac{S_0 i}{n}\left[(n+1)a_{\overline{n}\rvert} - \dfrac{1}{q^n}\left(q\dfrac{q^n - 1}{(q-1)^2} - \dfrac{n}{q-1}\right)\right]$	–	present value of all interest payments

Constant annuities (conversion period = payment period)

$A = S_0 \cdot \frac{q^n(q-1)}{q^n-1}$	– (total) payment, annuity
$S_0 = \frac{A(q^n-1)}{q^n(q-1)}$	– original debt
$T_k = T_1 q^{k-1} = (A - S_0 \cdot i)q^{k-1}$	– payoff, repayment
$S_k = S_0 q^k - A\frac{q^k-1}{q-1} = S_0 - T_1\frac{q^k-1}{q-1}$	– outstanding principal
$Z_k = S_0 i - T_1(q^{k-1}-1) = A - T_1 q^{k-1}$	– interest
$n = \frac{1}{\log q}\left[\log A - \log(A - S_0 i)\right]$	– length of payback period, period of full repayment

More frequently payments

In every period m constant annuities $A^{(m)}$ are payed.

$A^{(m)} = \frac{A}{m + \frac{m-1}{2}i}$	– payment at the end of each period
$A^{(m)} = \frac{A}{m + \frac{m+1}{2}i}$	– payment at the beginning of each period

Especially: Monthly payments, conversion period = 1 year ($m = 12$)

$A_{\text{mon}} = \frac{A}{12 + 5,5i}$	– payment at the end of every month
$A_{\text{mon}} = \frac{A}{12 + 6,5i}$	– payment at the beginning of every month

Amortization with agio

In an amortization with additional agio (redemption premium) of α percent on the payoff the quantity T_k has to be replaced by $\hat{T}_k = T_k \cdot \left(1 + \frac{\alpha}{100}\right) = T_k \cdot f_\alpha$. When considering amortization by constant annuities with included agio, the quantities $S_\alpha = S_0 \cdot f_\alpha$ (*fictitious debt*), $i_\alpha = \frac{i}{f_\alpha}$ (*fictitious rate of interest*) and $q_\alpha = 1 + i_\alpha$, resp., are to be used in the above formulas.

Price calculus

Notations

P	–	price, quotation (in percent)
K_{nom}	–	nominal capital or value
K_{real}	–	real capital, market value
n	–	(remaining) term, payback period
p, p_{eff}	–	nominal (effective, resp.) rate of interest
$b_{n,\text{nom}}$; $b_{n,\text{real}}$	–	present worth of 1 per period (ordinary annuity)
$a = C - 100$	–	agio for price above par
$d = 100 - C$	–	disagio for price below par
R	–	return at the end of the payback period
$q_{\text{eff}} = 1 + \frac{p_{\text{eff}}}{100}$	–	accumulation factor (effective interest rate)

Price formulas

$$P = 100 \cdot \frac{K_{\text{real}}}{K_{\text{nom}}}$$

– price as quotient of real and nominal capital

$$P = 100 \cdot \frac{b_{n,\text{real}}}{b_{n,\text{nom}}} = 100 \cdot \frac{\sum\limits_{k=1}^{n} \frac{1}{q_{\text{eff}}^k}}{\sum\limits_{k=1}^{n} \frac{1}{q^k}}$$

– price of a debt repayed by constant annuities

$$P = \frac{100}{n}\left[n \cdot \frac{p}{p_{\text{eff}}} + b_{n,\text{real}}\left(1 - \frac{p}{p_{\text{eff}}}\right)\right]$$

– price of a debt repayed by constant payoffs

$$P = \frac{1}{q_{\text{eff}}^n} \cdot \left(p \cdot \frac{q_{\text{eff}}^n - 1}{q_{\text{eff}} - 1} + R\right)$$

– price of a debt due at the end of the payback period

$$P = p \cdot (p_{\text{eff}})^{-1}$$

– price of a perpetuity

$$p_s = \frac{100}{C}\left(p - \frac{a}{n}\right) = \frac{100}{C}\left(p + \frac{d}{n}\right)$$

– simple yield-to-maturity;

= approximate effective interest rate of a debt due at the end of the payback period (price above and below par, resp.)

- Securities, shares (or stocks) are evaluated at the market by the price. For given price C in general the effective rate of interest (yield-to-maturity, redemption yield) can be obtained from the above equations by solving (approximately) a polynomial equation of higher degree (▶ p. 44).

Investment analysis

Multi-period capital budgeting techniques (discounted cash flow methods) are methods for estimating investment profitability. The most known are: *capital* (or *net present) value method, method of internal rate of return, annuity method.* Future income and expenses are prognostic values.

Notations

I_i	–	income at moment i
E_i	–	expenses, investments at moment i
C_i	–	net income, cash flow at moment i: $C_i = I_i - E_i$
K_I	–	present value of income
K_E	–	present value of expenses
C	–	net present value, capital value of the investment
n	–	number of periods
p	–	conventional (or minimum acceptable) rate of interest
q	–	accumulation factor: $q = 1 + \frac{p}{100}$

Capital value method

$K_I = \sum\limits_{i=0}^{n} \frac{I_i}{q^i}$	–	present value of income; sum of all present values of future income
$K_E = \sum\limits_{i=0}^{n} \frac{E_i}{q^i}$	–	present value of expenses; sum of all present values of future expenses
$C = K_I - K_E = \sum\limits_{i=0}^{n} \frac{C_i}{q^i}$	–	capital value of net income, net present value

- For $C = 0$ the investment corresponds to the given conventional rate of interest p, for $C > 0$ its maturity yield is higher. If several possibilities of investments are for selection, then that with the highest net present value is preferred.

Method of internal rate of return

The *internal rate of return (yield-to-maturity)* is that quantity for which the net present value of the investment is equal to zero. If several investments are possible, then that with the highest internal rate of return is chosen.

Annuity method

$F_A = \frac{q^n \cdot (q-1)}{q^n - 1}$	–	annuity (or capital recovery) factor
$A_I = K_I \cdot F_A$	–	income annuity
$A = K_E \cdot F_A$	–	expenses annuity
$A_P = A_I - A$	–	net income (profit) annuity

- For $A_I = A$ the maturity yield of the investment is equal to p, for $A_I > A$ the maturity yield is higher than the conventional rate of interest p.

Depreciations

Depreciations describe the reduction in value of capital goods or items of equipment. The difference between original value (cost price, production costs) and depreciation yields the *book-value*.

n	–	term of utilization (in years)
A	–	original value
w_k	–	depreciation (write-down) in the k-th year
R_k	–	book-value after k years (R_n – remainder, final value)

Linear (straight-line) depreciation

$w_k = w = \dfrac{A - R_n}{n}$	–	annual depreciation
$R_k = A - k \cdot w$	–	book-value after k years

Arithmetically degressive depreciation (reduction by d each year)

$w_k = w_1 - (k-1) \cdot d$	–	depreciation in the k-th year
$d = 2 \cdot \dfrac{nw_1 - (A - R_n)}{n(n-1)}$	–	amount of reduction
Sum-of-the-years digits method (as a special case): $w_n = d$		
$w_k = (n - k + 1) \cdot d$	–	depreciation in the k-th year
$d = \dfrac{2 \cdot (A - R_n)}{n(n+1)}$	–	amount of reduction

Geometrically degressive (double-declining balance) depreciation (reduction by s percent of the last year's book value in each year)

$R_k = A \cdot \left(1 - \dfrac{s}{100}\right)^k$	–	book-value after k years
$s = 100 \cdot \left(1 - \sqrt[n]{\dfrac{R_n}{A}}\right)$	–	rate of depreciation
$w_k = A \cdot \dfrac{s}{100} \cdot \left(1 - \dfrac{s}{100}\right)^{k-1}$	–	depreciation in the k-th year

Transition from degressive to linear depreciation

Under the assumption $R_n = 0$ it makes sense to write down geometrically degressive until the year $\lceil k \rceil$ with $k = n + 1 - \frac{100}{s}$ and after that to write down linearly.

Numerical methods for the determination of zeros

Task: Find a zero x^* of the continuous function $f(x)$; let ε be the accuracy bound for stopping the iteration process.

Table of values

For chosen values x find the corresponding function values $f(x)$. Then one obtains a rough survey on the graph of the function and the location of zeros.

Interval bisection

Given x_L with $f(x_L) < 0$ and x_R with $f(x_R) > 0$.

1. Calculate $x_M = \frac{1}{2}(x_L + x_R)$ and $f(x_M)$.
2. If $|f(x_M)| < \varepsilon$, then stop and take x_M as an approximation of x^*.
3. If $f(x_M) < 0$, then set $x_L := x_M$ (x_R unchanged), if $f(x_M) > 0$, then set $x_R := x_M$ (x_L unchanged), go to 1.

Method of false position (linear interpolation, regula falsi)

Given x_L with $f(x_L) < 0$ and x_R with $f(x_R) > 0$.

1. Calculate $x_S = x_L - \dfrac{x_R - x_L}{f(x_R) - f(x_L)} f(x_L)$ and $f(x_S)$.
2. If $|f(x_S)| < \varepsilon$, then stop and take x_S as an approximation of x^*.
3. If $f(x_S) < 0$, then set $x_L := x_S$ (x_R unchanged), if $f(x_M) > 0$, then set $x_R := x_S$ (x_L unchanged), go to 1.

- For $f(x_L) > 0$, $f(x_R) < 0$ the methods can be adapted in an obvious way.

Newton's method

Given $x_0 \in U(x^*)$; let the function f be differentiable.

1. Calculate $x_{k+1} = x_k - \dfrac{f(x_k)}{f'(x_k)}$.
2. If $|f(x_{k+1})| < \varepsilon$, then stop and take x_{k+1} as an approximation of x^*.
3. Set $k := k + 1$, go to 1.

- If $f'(x_k) = 0$ for some k, then restart the iteration process with another starting point x_0.
- Other stopping rule: $|x_L - x_R| < \varepsilon$ or $|x_{k+1} - x_k| < \varepsilon$.

Descartes' rule of signs. *The number of positive zeros of the polynomial* $\sum\limits_{k=0}^{n} a_k x^k$ *is equal to* w *or* $w-2$, $w-4$, ... , *where* w *is the number of changes in sign of the coefficients* a_k *(not considering zeros).*

Functions of one Independent Variable

Basic notions

A real function f of one independent variable $x \in \mathbb{R}$ is a mapping (rule of assignment) $y = f(x)$ which relates to every number x of the domain $D_f \subset \mathbb{R}$ one and only one number $y \in \mathbb{R}$. Notation: $f\colon D_f \to \mathbb{R}$.

range	–	$W_f = \{y \in \mathbb{R} \mid \exists\, x \in D_f \text{ with } y = f(x)\}$
one-to-one function	–	for any $y \in W_f$ there is one and only one $x \in D_f$ such that $y = f(x)$
inverse function, reciprocal function	–	if f is a one-to-one mapping, then the mapping $y \to x$ with $y = f(x)$ is also a one-to-one mapping called the inverse function to f; notation $f^{-1}\colon W_f \to \mathbb{R}$

Growth (monotony), symmetry, periodicity

increasing function	–	$f(x_1) \le f(x_2)\ \ \forall\, x_1, x_2 \in D_f,\ x_1 < x_2$
decreasing function	–	$f(x_1) \ge f(x_2)\ \ \forall\, x_1, x_2 \in D_f,\ x_1 < x_2$
strictly increasing function	–	$f(x_1) < f(x_2)\ \ \forall\, x_1, x_2 \in D_f,\ x_1 < x_2$
strictly decreasing function	–	$f(x_1) > f(x_2)\ \ \forall\, x_1, x_2 \in D_f,\ x_1 < x_2$
even function	–	$f(-x) = f(x)\ \ \forall\, x \in (-a, a) \cap D_f,\ a > 0$
odd function	–	$f(-x) = -f(x)\ \forall\, x \in (-a, a) \cap D_f, a > 0$
periodic function (period p)	–	$f(x + p) = f(x)\ \ \forall x, x + p \in D_f$

- ε-neighbourhood of the point x^* (= set of all points having a distance from x^* smaller than ε): $U_\varepsilon(x^*) = \{x \in \mathbb{R} : |x - x^*| < \varepsilon\}, \quad \varepsilon > 0$

Boundedness

bounded from above function	–	$\exists\, K\colon f(x) \le K\ \ \forall\, x \in D_f$
bounded from below function	–	$\exists\, K\colon f(x) \ge K\ \ \forall\, x \in D_f$
bounded function	–	$\exists\, K\colon |f(x)| \le K\ \ \forall\, x \in D_f$

Extrema

supremum	– smallest upper bound K; $\sup_{x\in D_f} f(x)$
infimum	– largest lower bound K; $\inf_{x\in D_f} f(x)$
global maximum point	– $x^*\in D_f$ such that $f(x^*)\geq f(x)\ \forall x\in D_f$
global maximum	– $f(x^*)=\max_{x\in D_f} f(x)$
local maximum point	– $x^*\in D_f$ such that $f(x^*)\geq f(x)\ \ \forall x\in D_f\cap U_\varepsilon(x^*)$
global minimum point	– $x^*\in D_f$ such that $f(x^*)\leq f(x)\ \forall x\in D_f$
global minimum	– $f(x^*)=\min_{x\in D_f} f(x)$
local minimum point	– $x^*\in D_f$ such that $f(x^*)\leq f(x)\ \ \forall\, x\in D_f\cap U_\varepsilon(x^*)$

Curvature properties

convex function	–	$f(\lambda x_1+(1-\lambda)x_2)\leq \lambda f(x_1)+(1-\lambda)f(x_2)$
strictly convex function	–	$f(\lambda x_1+(1-\lambda)x_2)< \lambda f(x_1)+(1-\lambda)f(x_2)$
concave function	–	$f(\lambda x_1+(1-\lambda)x_2)\geq \lambda f(x_1)+(1-\lambda)f(x_2)$
strictly concave function	–	$f(\lambda x_1+(1-\lambda)x_2)> \lambda f(x_1)+(1-\lambda)f(x_2)$

- The inequalities are true for any $x_1,x_2\in D_f$ and arbitrary numbers $\lambda\in(0,1)$. Under convexity and concavity the inequalities hold also for $\lambda=0$ and $\lambda=1$.

Representation of real functions

zero	–	a number $x_0\in D_f$ satisfying $f(x_0)=0$
graph of a function	–	visualization of the points $(x,y)=(x,f(x))$ associated with f in the plane $\mathbb{R}^2$, using a Cartesian system of co-ordinates in general
Cartesian co-ordinate system	–	system in the plane consisting of two co-ordinate axes orthogonal to each other; horizontal axis *(of abszissae)* usually x, vertical axis *(of ordinates-)* usually y; the axes are provided with (possibly different) scales

Linear functions

Let $a, b, \lambda \in \mathbb{R}$.

linear function	– $y = f(x) = ax$
affine linear function	– $y = f(x) = ax + b$

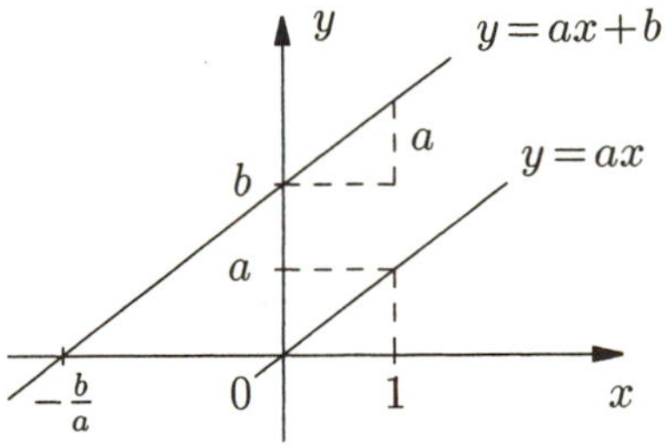

Properties of linear functions

$$f(x_1 + x_2) = f(x_1) + f(x_2) \qquad f(\lambda x) = \lambda f(x) \qquad f(0) = 0$$

Properties of affine linear functions

$$\frac{f(x_1) - f(x_2)}{x_1 - x_2} = a \qquad f\left(-\frac{b}{a}\right) = 0, \quad a \neq 0 \qquad f(0) = b$$

- Affine linear functions are often simply denoted as linear functions.
- In an x, y-system of co-ordinates with uniformly scaled axes the graph of a linear or affine linear function is a straight line.

Quadratic functions $y = f(x) = ax^2 + bx + c \quad (a \neq 0)$

Discriminant: $D = p^2 - 4q$

with $p = \frac{b}{a}$, $q = \frac{c}{a}$

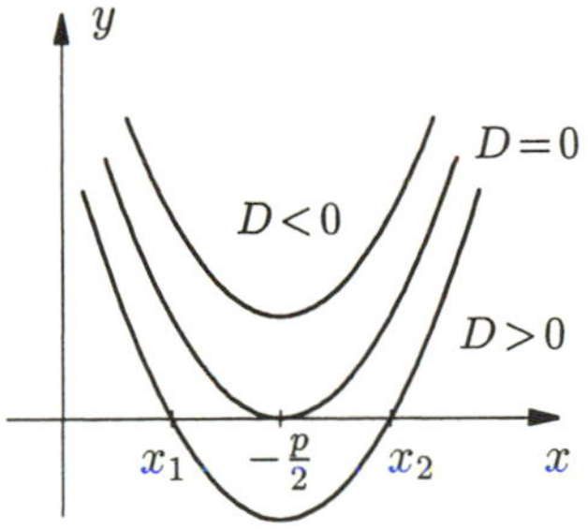

Zeros

$D > 0:$	$x_{1,2} = \frac{1}{2}\left(-p \pm \sqrt{D}\right)$	two real zeros
$D = 0:$	$x_1 = x_2 = -\frac{p}{2}$	one double zero
$D < 0:$		no zero

Extremal points

$a > 0:$	one minimum point	$x_{\min} = -\frac{p}{2}$
$a < 0:$	one maximum point	$x_{\max} = -\frac{p}{2}$

• For $a > 0$ ($a < 0$) the function f is strictly convex (concave) and the graph of f is a parabola opened above (below) with vertex $\left(-\frac{p}{2}, -\frac{aD}{4}\right)$.

Polynomials

Functions $y = p_n(x)\colon \mathbb{R} \to \mathbb{R}$ of the kind

$$p_n(x) = a_n x^n + a_{n-1}x^{n-1} + \ldots + a_1 x + a_0, \quad a_n \neq 0, \quad a_i \in \mathbb{R}, \quad n \in \mathbb{N}_0$$

are called *entire rational functions* or *polynomials of degree* n.

• According to the fundamental theorem of algebra every polynomial of degree n can be represented in the form

$$p_n(x) = a_n(x - x_1)(x - x_2)\ldots(x - x_{n-1})(x - x_n)$$

product representation

The numbers x_i are the real or complex zeros of the polynomial. Complex zeros always occur pairwise in conjugate complex form. The zero x_i is a zero of order p if the factor $(x - x_i)$ in the product representation occurs p times. Function values of a polynomial as well as the values of its derivatives can be calculated as follows:

$$b_{n-1} := a_n, \quad b_i := a_{i+1} + ab_{i+1}, \quad i = n-2, \ldots, 0, \quad p_n(a) = a_0 + ab_0$$

$$c_{n-2} := b_{n-1}, \quad c_i := b_{i+1} + ac_{i+1}, \quad i = n-3, \ldots, 0, \quad p_n'(a) = b_0 + ac_0$$

Horner's scheme

	a_n	a_{n-1}	a_{n-2}	$\ldots$	a_2	a_1	a_0
a	$-$	ab_{n-1}	ab_{n-2}	$\ldots$	ab_2	ab_1	ab_0
	b_{n-1}	b_{n-2}	b_{n-3}	$\ldots$	b_1	b_0	$p_n(a)$
a	$-$	ac_{n-2}	ac_{n-3}	$\ldots$	ac_1	ac_0	
	c_{n-2}	c_{n-3}	c_{n-4}	$\ldots$	c_0	$p_n'(a)$	

The following relation holds:

$$p_n(x) = p_n(a) + (x - a)\cdot(b_{n-1}x^{n-1} + b_{n-2}x^{n-2} + \cdots + b_1 x + b_0)$$

Fractional rational functions, partial fraction decomposition

Functions of the kind $y = r(x)$,

$$r(x) = \frac{p_m(x)}{q_n(x)} = \frac{a_m x^m + a_{m-1}x^{m-1} + \cdots + a_1 x + a_0}{b_n x^n + b_{n-1}x^{n-1} + \cdots + b_1 x + b_0}, \quad a_m \neq 0, \; b_n \neq 0$$

are called *fractional rational* functions, especially *proper* rational functions for $m < n$ and *improper* rational functions for $m \geq n$.

• An *improper* fractional rational function can be rewritten in the form $r(x) = p(x) + s(x)$ by means of *polynomial division*, where $p(x)$ is a polynomial (*asymptote*) and $s(x)$ is an *improper* fractional rational function (▶ product representation of a polynomial).

zeros of $r(x)$	–	all zeros of the polynomial in the numerator, which are not zeros of the denominator
poles of $r(x)$	–	all zeros of the polynomial in the denominator, which are not zeros of the numerator as well as all common zeros of the numerator and the denominator, the multiplicity of which in the numerator is less then its mutiplicity in the denominator
gaps of $r(x)$	–	all common zeros of the polynomials in the numerator and the denominator, the multiplicity of which in the numerator is greater or equal to its mutliplicity in the denominator

Partial fraction decomposition of proper fractional rational functions

1. Representation of the denominator polynomial $q_n(x)$ as a product of linear and quadratic polynomials with real coefficients, where the quadratic polynomials have conjugate complex zeros:

   $q_n(x) = (x-a)^\alpha (x-b)^\beta \ldots (x^2 + cx + d)^\gamma \ldots$

2. Trial solution

$$r(x) = \frac{A_1}{x-a} + \frac{A_2}{(x-a)^2} + \ldots + \frac{A_\alpha}{(x-a)^\alpha} + \frac{B_1}{(x-b)} + \frac{B_2}{(x-b)^2}$$
$$+ \cdots + \frac{B_\beta}{(x-b)^\beta} + \ldots + \frac{C_1 x + D_1}{x^2 + cx + d} + \cdots + \frac{C_\gamma x + D_\gamma}{(x^2 + cx + d)^\gamma} + \ldots$$

3. Determination of the (real) coefficients $A_i, B_i, C_i, D_i, \ldots$:
   a) Find the least common denominator and
   b) multiply by the least common denominator.
   c) The substitution of $x = a, x = b, \ldots$ yields $A_\alpha, B_\beta, \ldots$
   d) The comparison of coefficients leads to linear equations for the remaining unknown coefficients.

Exponential functions

$y = a^x$	–	exponential function, $a \in \mathbb{R},\ a > 0$
a	–	base
x	–	exponent
Special case $a = \mathrm{e}$:		
$y = \mathrm{e}^x = \exp(x)$	–	exponential function to the base e

Domain: $D_f = \mathbb{R}$

Range: $W_f = \mathbb{R}^+ = \{y \mid y > 0\}$

- The inverse function of the exponential function $y = a^x$ is the logarithmic function $y = \log_a x$ (▶ p. 51).
- Rules of operation ▶ powers (p. 15)
- The growth of an exponential function with $a > 1$ is stronger as the growth of any power function $y = x^n$.

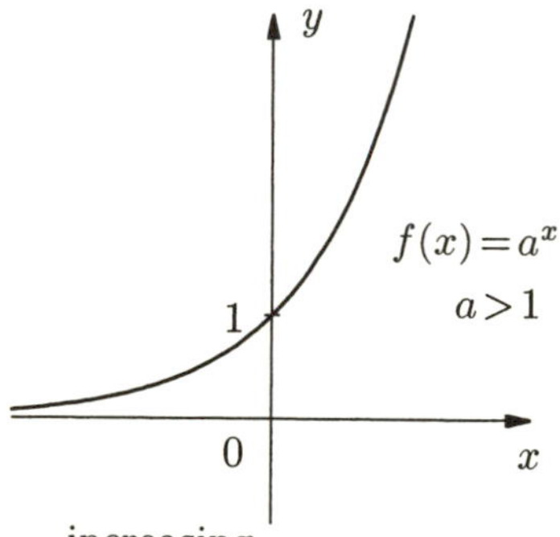

increasing exponential function

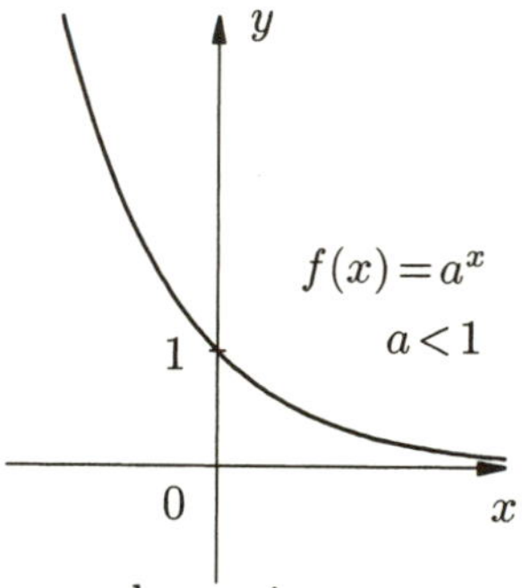

decreasing exponential function

Negative power

Using the transformation

$$a^{-x} = \left(\frac{1}{a}\right)^x, \qquad a > 0,$$

the function values for negative (positive) powers can be obtained via function values with positive (negative) powers.

Base a, $0 < a < 1$

Using the rule

$$a^{-x} = b^x \quad \text{with} \quad b = \frac{1}{a},$$

an exponential function to the base a, $0 < a < 1$ can be transformed into an exponential function to the base b, $b > 1$.

Logarithmic functions

$y = \log_a x$	– logarithmic function, $a \in \mathbb{R},\ a > 1$
x	– argument
a	– base
Special case $a = \mathrm{e}$:	
$y = \ln x$	– function of the natural logarithm
Special case $a = 10$:	
$y = \lg x$	– function of the decimal (Briggsian) logarithm

Domain: $D_f = \mathbb{R}^+ = \{x \in \mathbb{R} \mid x > 0\}$

Range: $W = \mathbb{R}$

- The value $y = \log_a x$ is defined by the relation $x = a^y$.
- Rules of operation ▶ logarithms (p. 15).

• The inverse function of the logarithmic function $y = \log_a x$ is the exponential function (▶ p. 50). Using the same scale on both the x- and the y-axis, the graph of the function $y = a^x$ is obtained as reflection of the graph of $y = \log_a x$ with respect to the bisectrix $y = x$.

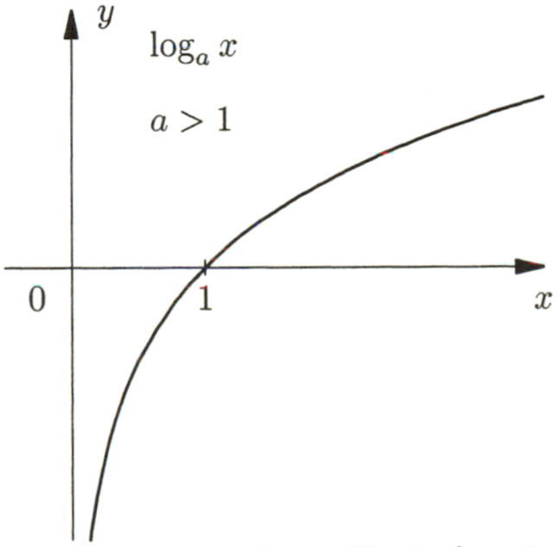

logarithmic function, increasing

Base a, $0 < a < 1$

Using the rule

$$\log_a x = -\log_b x \quad \text{with} \quad b = \frac{1}{a}$$

a logarithmic function to the base a, $0 < a < 1$, can be transformed into a logarithmic function to the base b, $b > 1$.

Trigonometric functions

Due to the intercept theorems in congruent triangles the relations between sides are equal. In right-angled triangles these relations are uniquely defined by one of the non-right angles. By definition

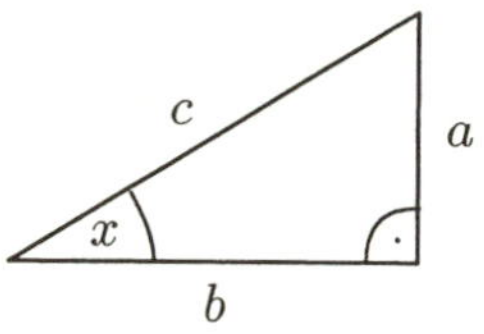

$$\sin x = \frac{a}{c}, \qquad \cos x = \frac{b}{c},$$

$$\tan x = \frac{a}{b}, \qquad \cot x = \frac{b}{a}.$$

For angles x between $\frac{\pi}{2}$ and 2π the line segments a, b are provided with signs according to their location in a Cartesian co-ordinate system.

Translation and reflection properties

$\sin\left(\frac{\pi}{2}+x\right)=\sin\left(\frac{\pi}{2}-x\right)=\cos x$	$\sin(\pi+x)=-\sin x$
$\cos\left(\frac{\pi}{2}+x\right)=-\cos\left(\frac{\pi}{2}-x\right)=-\sin x$	$\cos(\pi+x)=-\cos x$
$\tan\left(\frac{\pi}{2}+x\right)=-\tan\left(\frac{\pi}{2}-x\right)=-\cot x$	$\tan(\pi+x)=\tan x$
$\cot\left(\frac{\pi}{2}+x\right)=-\cot\left(\frac{\pi}{2}-x\right)=-\tan x$	$\cot(\pi+x)=\cot x$
$\sin\left(\frac{3\pi}{2}+x\right)=-\cos x$	$\cos\left(\frac{3\pi}{2}+x\right)=\sin x$
$\tan\left(\frac{3\pi}{2}+x\right)=-\cot x$	$\cot\left(\frac{3\pi}{2}+x\right)=-\tan x$

Periodicity

$\sin(x+2\pi)=\sin x$	$\cos(x+2\pi)=\cos x$
$\tan(x+\pi)=\tan x$	$\cot(x+\pi)=\cot x$

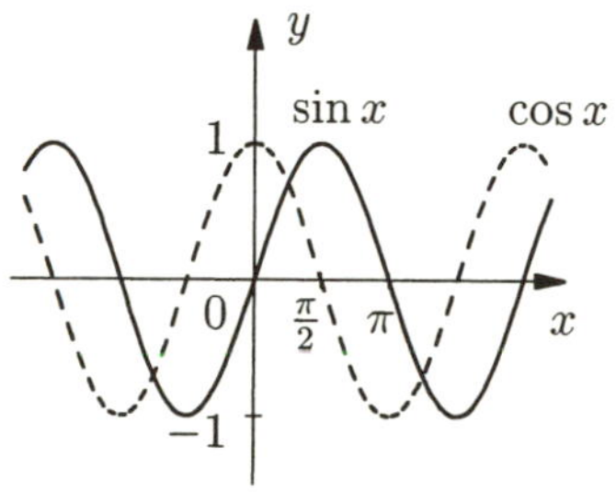

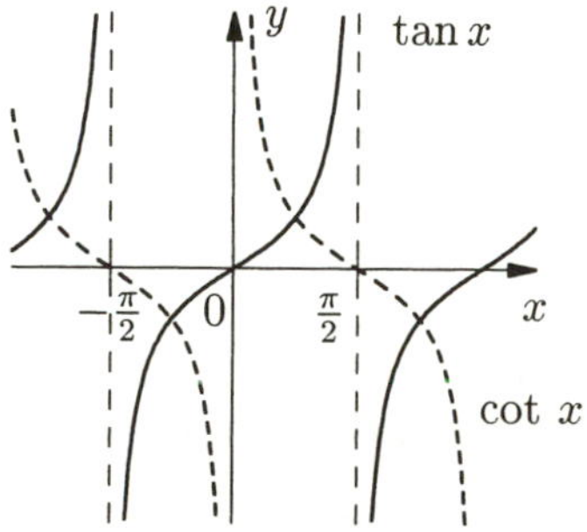

Special function values

Radian measure	0	$\frac{\pi}{6}$	$\frac{\pi}{4}$	$\frac{\pi}{3}$	$\frac{\pi}{2}$
Measure in degree	$0°$	$30°$	$45°$	$60°$	$90°$
$\sin x$	0	$\frac{1}{2}$	$\frac{1}{2}\sqrt{2}$	$\frac{1}{2}\sqrt{3}$	1
$\cos x$	1	$\frac{1}{2}\sqrt{3}$	$\frac{1}{2}\sqrt{2}$	$\frac{1}{2}$	0
$\tan x$	0	$\frac{1}{3}\sqrt{3}$	1	$\sqrt{3}$	–
$\cot x$	–	$\sqrt{3}$	1	$\frac{1}{3}\sqrt{3}$	0

Transformation of trigonometric functions $(0 \le x \le \frac{\pi}{2})$

	$\sin x$	$\cos x$	$\tan x$	$\cot x$
$\sin x$	–	$\sqrt{1-\cos^2 x}$	$\frac{\tan x}{\sqrt{1+\tan^2 x}}$	$\frac{1}{\sqrt{1+\cot^2 x}}$
$\cos x$	$\sqrt{1-\sin^2 x}$	–	$\frac{1}{\sqrt{1+\tan^2 x}}$	$\frac{\cot x}{\sqrt{1+\cot^2 x}}$
$\tan x$	$\frac{\sin x}{\sqrt{1-\sin^2 x}}$	$\frac{\sqrt{1-\cos^2 x}}{\cos x}$	–	$\frac{1}{\cot x}$
$\cot x$	$\frac{\sqrt{1-\sin^2 x}}{\sin x}$	$\frac{\cos x}{\sqrt{1-\cos^2 x}}$	$\frac{1}{\tan x}$	–

$$\sin^2 x + \cos^2 x = 1, \qquad \tan x = \frac{\sin x}{\cos x}\ (\cos x \neq 0), \qquad \cot x = \frac{\cos x}{\sin x}\ (\sin x \neq 0)$$

Addition theorems

$$\sin(x \pm y) = \sin x \cos y \pm \cos x \sin y \qquad \cos(x \pm y) = \cos x \cos y \mp \sin x \sin y$$

$$\tan(x \pm y) = \frac{\tan x \pm \tan y}{1 \mp \tan x \tan y} \qquad \cot(x \pm y) = \frac{\cot x \cot y \mp 1}{\cot y \pm \cot x}$$

Double-angle formulas

$$\sin 2x = 2\sin x \cos x = \frac{2\tan x}{1+\tan^2 x} \qquad \cos 2x = \cos^2 x - \sin^2 x = \frac{1-\tan^2 x}{1+\tan^2 x}$$

$$\tan 2x = \frac{2\tan x}{1-\tan^2 x} = \frac{2}{\cot x - \tan x} \qquad \cot 2x = \frac{\cot^2 x - 1}{2\cot x} = \frac{\cot x - \tan x}{2}$$

Half-angle formulas (for $0 < x < \pi$)

$$\sin\frac{x}{2} = \sqrt{\frac{1-\cos x}{2}} \qquad \tan\frac{x}{2} = \sqrt{\frac{1-\cos x}{1+\cos x}} = \frac{\sin x}{1+\cos x} = \frac{1-\cos x}{\sin x}$$

$$\cos\frac{x}{2} = \sqrt{\frac{1+\cos x}{2}} \qquad \cot\frac{x}{2} = \sqrt{\frac{1+\cos x}{1-\cos x}} = \frac{\sin x}{1-\cos x} = \frac{1+\cos x}{\sin x}$$

Powers of trigonometric functions

$$\sin^2 x = \frac{1}{2}(1-\cos 2x) \qquad \cos^2 x = \frac{1}{2}(1+\cos 2x)$$

$$\sin^3 x = \frac{1}{4}(3\sin x - \sin 3x) \qquad \cos^3 x = \frac{1}{4}(3\cos x + \cos 3x)$$

$$\sin^4 x = \frac{1}{8}(3 - 4\cos 2x + \cos 4x) \qquad \cos^4 x = \frac{1}{8}(3 + 4\cos 2x + \cos 4x)$$

Inverse trigonometric functions

• The inverse trigonometric functions are also denoted as *arctrigonometric* or *cyclometric* functions. For example, from the relation $x = \sin y$ we get the function $y = \arcsin x$ (arc sine or inverse sine).

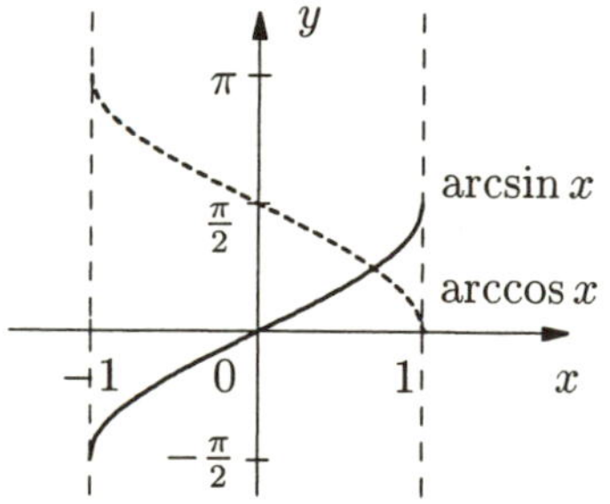

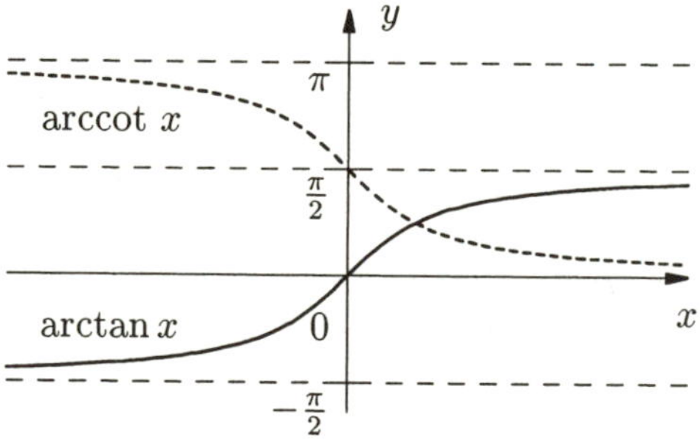

Domains and ranges

inverse trigonometric function	domain	range
$y = \arcsin x$	$-1 \le x \le 1$	$-\frac{\pi}{2} \le y \le \frac{\pi}{2}$
$y = \arccos x$	$-1 \le x \le 1$	$0 \le y \le \pi$
$y = \arctan x$	$-\infty < x < \infty$	$-\frac{\pi}{2} < y < \frac{\pi}{2}$
$y = \operatorname{arccot} x$	$-\infty < x < \infty$	$0 < y < \pi$

Hyperbolic functions

$y = \sinh x = \frac{1}{2}(e^x - e^{-x})$	–	hyperbolic sine, $D_f = \mathbb{R}$, $W_f = \mathbb{R}$
$y = \cosh x = \frac{1}{2}(e^x + e^{-x})$	–	hyperbolic cosine, $D_f = \mathbb{R}$, $W_f = [1, \infty)$
$y = \tanh x = \frac{e^x - e^{-x}}{e^x + e^{-x}}$	–	hyperbolic tangent, $D_f = \mathbb{R}$, $W_f = (-1, 1)$
$y = \coth x = \frac{e^x + e^{-x}}{e^x - e^{-x}}$	–	hyperbolic cotangent $D_f = \mathbb{R} \setminus \{0\}$, $W_f = (-\infty, -1) \cup (1, \infty)$

Area-hyperbolic functions

The inverse functions to hyperbolic sine, tangent, cotangent and to the right part of hyperbolic cosine are called the *area-hyperbolic functions*.

$y = \operatorname{arsinh} x$	–	area-hyperbolic sine, $D_f = \mathbb{R}$, $W_f = \mathbb{R}$
$y = \operatorname{arcosh} x$	–	area-hyperbolic cosine, $D_f = [1, \infty)$, $W_f = [0, \infty)$
$y = \operatorname{artanh} x$	–	are-hyperbolic tangent, $D_f = (-1, 1)$, $W_f = \mathbb{R}$
$y = \operatorname{arcoth} x$	–	area-hyperbolic cotangent, $D_f = (-\infty, -1) \cup (1, \infty)$, $W_f = \mathbb{R} \setminus \{0\}$

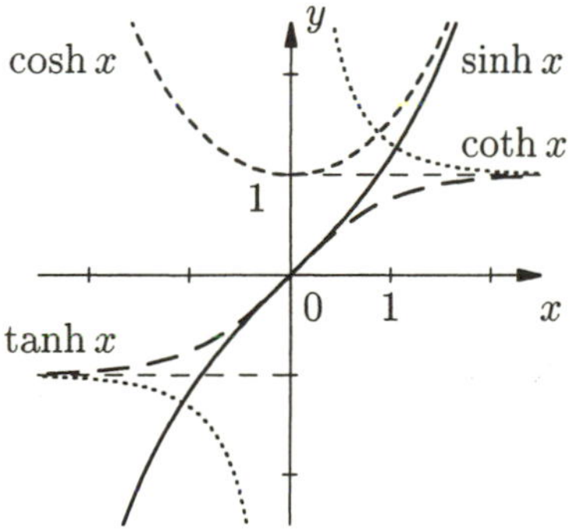

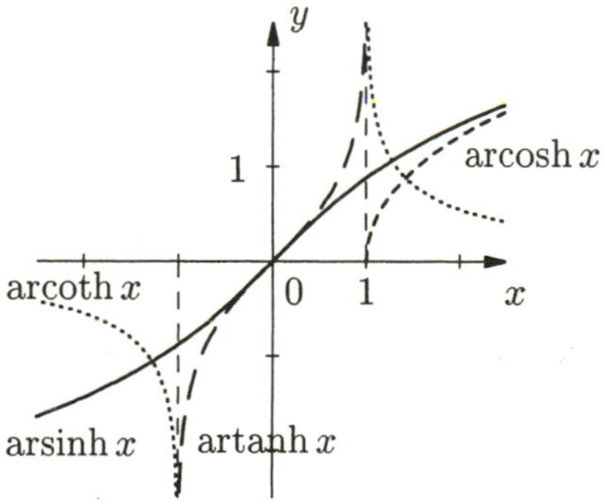

Some economic functions

Notation

x	–	quantity of a good (in units)
p	–	price of a good (in units of money per unit of quantity)
E	–	national income, national product (in units of money per unit of time)

Microeconomic and macroeconomic functions

$x = x(p)$	–	demand function (price-response function); in general decreasing; x – quantity demanded and sold, resp.
$p = p(x)$	–	supply function, in general increasing; x – quantity supplied
$U(p) = x(p) \cdot p$	–	turnover function (return function, revenue function); dependend on price p
$K(x) = K_f + K_v(x)$	–	cost function as the sum of fixed and quantity (or employment) dependent variable share of the costs
$k(x) = \dfrac{K(x)}{x}$	–	(total) average costs; costs per unit
$k_f(x) = \dfrac{K_f}{x}$	–	average fixed costs; fixed costs per unit
$k_v(x) = \dfrac{K_v(x)}{x}$	–	average variable costs; variable costs per unit
$G(x) = U(x) - K(x)$	–	profit (operating profit)
$D(x) = U(x) - K_v(x)$	–	(total) contribution margin
$g(x) = \dfrac{G(x)}{x}$	–	average profit; profit per unit
$C = C(E)$	–	(macroeconomic) consumption function, expenses for consumer goods; in general increasing (E – see above)
$S(E) = E - C(E)$	–	(macroeconomic) savings function

• The value of the *average function* $\bar{f}(x) = \frac{f(x)}{x}$ belonging to the function f is equal to the ascent of the ray running from the origin to the point $(x, f(x))$. It describes that share of the function value which belongs to **one unit** of x.

• A point x satisfying the equation $G(x) = 0$, i. e. $U(x) = K(x)$, is called the *break-even point*. Apart from trivial cases, its determination (*break-even analysis*) is usually accomplished by means of numerical approximation methods.

• The profit per unit is equal to the difference of price per unit and costs per unit: $g(x) = p(x) - k(x)$. The *contribution margin per unit* is the difference of price and variable costs per unit.

Logistic function (saturation process)

$$y = f(t) = \frac{a}{1 + b \cdot e^{-ct}},$$

$$a, b, c > 0$$

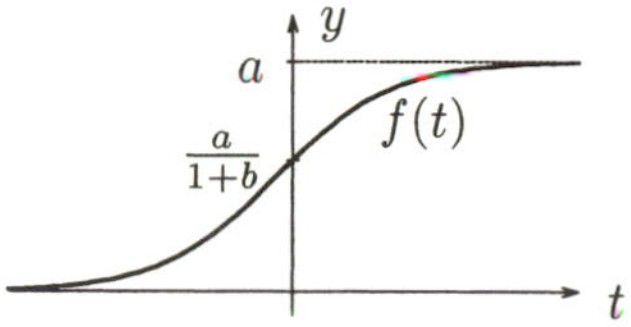

This function satisfies the relations $\varrho_f(t) = \frac{y'}{y} = p(a-y)$ and $y' = py(a-y)$ (▶ differential equations), where p – proportionality factor, y – impulse factor, $(a-y)$ – brake factor.

• The rate of increase $\varrho_f(t)$ is at an arbitrary moment t directly proportional to the distance from the level of saturation a. The increase of the function f is proportional to the product of impulse and brake factor.

Stock function ("saw-tooth function")

$$y = f(t) = iS - \frac{S}{T}t,$$

$$(i-1)T \le t < iT,$$

$$T > 0, \quad i = 1, 2, \ldots$$

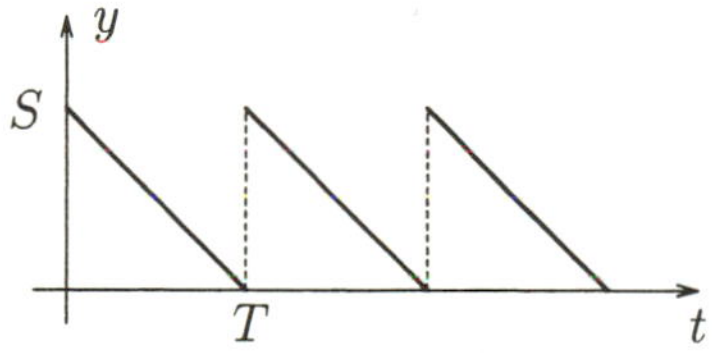

• At the moments iT, $i = 0, 1, 2, \ldots$, the warehouse is filled up, while in the intervals $[(i-1)T, iT)$ the delivery takes place with constant in time intensity.

Gompertz-Makeham's function (mortality law)

$$y = f(t) = a \cdot b^t \cdot c^{d^t}, \quad a, b, c \in \mathbb{R}, \; d > 0$$

• This function satisfies the relation $y' = p(t)y$ (▶ differential equations) with proportionality factor (mortality intensity) $p(t) = p_1 + p_2 \cdot d^t = \ln|b| + \ln|c| \cdot \ln d \cdot d^t$. The reduction in the number of quicks of a population within the interval $[t, t + \mathrm{d}t]$ is proportional to the number of still living persons $y = f(t)$ at the age of t.

Trend function with periodic fluctuations

$$y = f(t) = a + bt + c \cdot \sin dt,$$
$$a, b, c, d \in \mathbb{R}$$

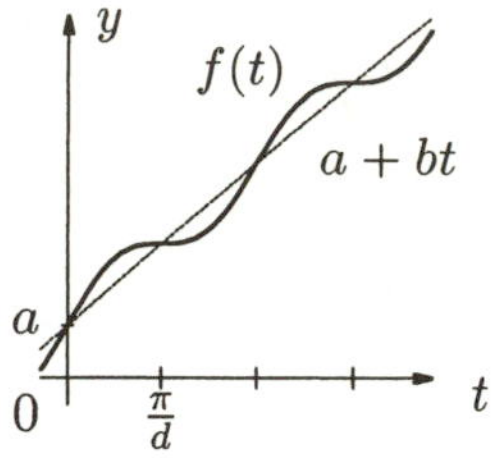

• The linear trend function $a+bt$ is overlapped by the periodic function $\sin dt$ describing (annual) seasonal fluctuations.

Continuous (exponential) growth

The function

$$y = f(t) = a_0 \cdot q^{\alpha t}$$

describes the time-dependent growth behaviour (population, money stock etc.); a_0 – initial value at the moment $t = 0$, α – growth intensity.

Generalized exponential growth

$$y = f(t) = a + b \cdot q^t,$$
$$a, b > 0, \quad q > 1$$

• Both the function and its rate of change (rate of increase) $\varrho_f(t) = \frac{y'}{y}$ (▶ p. 66) are increasing; moreover $\lim_{t\to\infty} \varrho_f(t) = \ln q$.

Cobb-Douglas production function (one input factor)

The *isoelastic* (i. e. having a constant elasticity ▶ p. 66) function

$$x = f(r) = c \cdot r^\alpha, \quad c, \alpha > 0$$

describes the connection between the factor input r of a production (in units of quantity) and the output (produce; in may be different units of quantity; ▶ p. 112).

Limitational production function (one input factor)

$$x = f(r) = \begin{cases} a \cdot r & \text{if } r \le \hat{r} \\ b & \text{if } r > \hat{r}, \end{cases} \qquad a, b > 0$$

• The mentioned production functions arise from production functions involving several input factors by keeping all but one factor fixed (*partial factor variation*).

Differential Calculus for Functions of one Variable

Limit of a function

If $\{x_n\}$ is an **arbitrary** sequence of points converging to the point x_0 such that $x_n \in D_f$, then the number $a \in \mathbb{R}$ is called the *limit* of the function f at the point x_0 if $\lim\limits_{n\to\infty} f(x_n) = a$. Notation: $\lim\limits_{x\to x_0} f(x) = a$ (or $f(x) \to a$ for $x \to x_0$).

• If in addition to the above conditions the restricting requirement $x_n > x_0$ ($x_n < x_0$) is true, then one speaks about the *limit from the right* (*from the left*). Notation: $\lim\limits_{x\downarrow x_0} f(x) = a$ ($\lim\limits_{x\uparrow x_0} f(x) = a$). For the existence of the limit of a function the limits from the right and the left must agree.

• If the sequence $\{f(x_n)\}$ fails to converge, then the function f is said to have no limit at the point x_0. If the function values increase (decrease) without any bound (*improper* limit), then the notation $\lim\limits_{x\to x_0} f(x) = \infty$ (resp. $-\infty$) is used.

Rules of operation for limits

If both the limits $\lim\limits_{x\to x_0} f(x) = a$ and $\lim\limits_{x\to x_0} g(x) = b$ exist, then:

$$\lim_{x\to x_0} (f(x) \pm g(x)) = a \pm b, \qquad \lim_{x\to x_0} (f(x) \cdot g(x)) = a \cdot b,$$

$$\lim_{x\to x_0} \frac{f(x)}{g(x)} = \frac{a}{b}, \quad \text{if} \quad g(x) \neq 0, \quad b \neq 0.$$

L'Hospital's rules for $\frac{0}{0}$ and $\frac{\infty}{\infty}$

Let f and g be differentiable in a neighbourhood of x_0, let exist $\lim\limits_{x\to x_0} \frac{f'(x)}{g'(x)} = K$ (as finite or infinite value), and let $g'(x) \neq 0$, $\lim\limits_{x\to x_0} f(x) = 0$, $\lim\limits_{x\to x_0} g(x) = 0$ or $\lim\limits_{x\to x_0} |f(x)| = \lim\limits_{x\to x_0} |g(x)| = \infty$. Then the relation $\lim\limits_{x\to x_0} \frac{f(x)}{g(x)} = K$ holds.

• The case $x \to \pm\infty$ is possible as well.

• Terms of the form $0 \cdot \infty$ or $\infty - \infty$ can be transformed into the form $\frac{0}{0}$ or $\frac{\infty}{\infty}$. Expressions of the kind 0^0, ∞^0 or 1^∞ can be rewritten in the form $0 \cdot \infty$ by means of the transformation $f(x)^{g(x)} = e^{g(x) \ln f(x)}$.

Important limits

$\lim\limits_{x\to\pm\infty} \frac{1}{x} = 0,$	$\lim\limits_{x\to\infty} \mathrm{e}^x = \infty,$	$\lim\limits_{x\to-\infty} \mathrm{e}^x = 0,$
$\lim\limits_{x\to\infty} x^n = \infty \;\; (n \geq 1),$	$\lim\limits_{x\to\infty} \ln x = \infty,$	$\lim\limits_{x\downarrow 0} \ln x = -\infty,$
$\lim\limits_{x\to\infty} \frac{x^n}{\mathrm{e}^{\alpha x}} = 0 \quad (\alpha \in \mathbb{R},\ \alpha > 0,\ n \in \mathbb{N}),$		$\lim\limits_{x\to\infty} q^x = 0 \;\; (0 < q < 1),$
$\lim\limits_{x\to\infty} q^x = \infty \;\; (q > 1),$		$\lim\limits_{x\to\infty} \left(1+\frac{\alpha}{x}\right)^x = \mathrm{e}^\alpha \;\; (\alpha \in \mathbb{R})$

Continuity

A function $f : D_f \to \mathbb{R}$ is called *continuous at the point* $x_0 \in D_f$ if

$$\lim_{x\to x_0} f(x) = f(x_0).$$

- Alternative formulation: f is *continuous at the point* x_0 if to any (arbitrarily small) number $\varepsilon > 0$ there exists a number $\delta > 0$ such that $|f(x) - f(x_0)| < \varepsilon$ if $|x - x_0| < \delta$.
- If a function is continuous $\forall x \in D_f$, then it is said to be *continuous*.

Kinds of discontinuity

finite jump	–	$\lim\limits_{x\downarrow x_0} f(x) \neq \lim\limits_{x\uparrow x_0} f(x)$
infinite jump	–	one of the two one-sided limits is infinite
pole	–	$\left\| \lim\limits_{x\downarrow x_0} f(x) \right\| = \left\| \lim\limits_{x\uparrow x_0} f(x) \right\| = \infty$
pole of order $p \in \mathbb{N}$	–	point x_0 for which the limit $\lim\limits_{x\to x_0} (x - x_0)^p f(x)$ exists, is finite and different from zero
gap = removable discontinuity	–	$\lim\limits_{x\to x_0} f(x) = a$ exists, but f is not defined for $x = x_0$ or $f(x_0) \neq a$

- A fractional rational function has poles at the zeros of its denominator provided that at these points the numerator is different from zero (▶ fractional rational functions, p. 49).

Properties of continuous functions

- If the functions f and g are continuous on their domains D_f and D_g, respectively, then the functions $f + g$, $f - g$, $f \cdot g$ and $\frac{f}{g}$ (the latter for $g(x) \neq 0$) are continuous on $D_f \cap D_g$.

- If the function f is continuous on the closed interval $[a, b]$, then it attains its greatest value $f_{\max}$ and its smallest value $f_{\min}$ on this interval. Every number between $f_{\min}$ and $f_{\max}$ is attained as a function value at least once.

Rules of operation for limits of continuous functions

If f is continuous, then $\lim\limits_{x \to x_0} f(g(x)) = f\left(\lim\limits_{x \to x_0} g(x)\right)$.

Special cases:

$$\lim_{x \to x_0} (f(x))^n = \left(\lim_{x \to x_0} f(x)\right)^n, \qquad \lim_{x \to x_0} a^{f(x)} = a^{\left(\lim\limits_{x \to x_0} f(x)\right)}, \quad a > 0$$

$$\lim_{x \to x_0} \ln f(x) = \ln\left(\lim_{x \to x_0} f(x)\right), \qquad \text{if } f(x) > 0$$

Differentiation

Difference and differential quotient

$$\frac{\Delta y}{\Delta x} = \frac{f(x + \Delta x) - f(x)}{\Delta x} = \tan \beta$$

$$\frac{\mathrm{d}y}{\mathrm{d}x} = \lim_{\Delta x \to 0} \frac{f(x + \Delta x) - f(x)}{\Delta x} = \tan \alpha$$

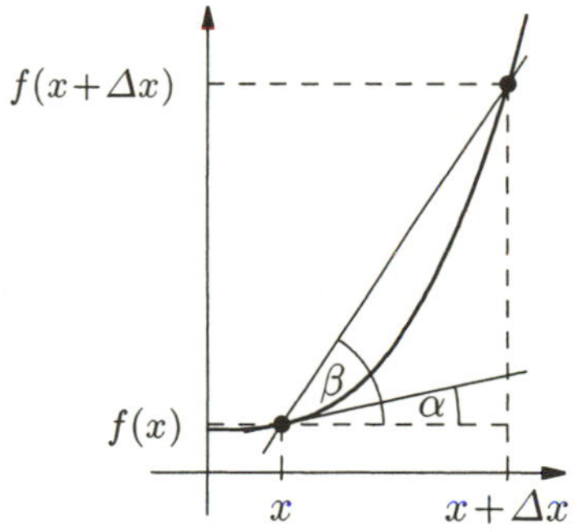

If the latter limit exists, then the function f is called *differentiable at the point* x. In this case, it is also continuous there. If f is differentiable $\forall x \in D_f$, then it is referred to as *differentiable* on D_f.

The limit is called *differential quotient* or *derivative* and denoted by $\frac{\mathrm{d}y}{\mathrm{d}x}$ (or $\frac{\mathrm{d}f}{\mathrm{d}x}$, $y'(x)$, $f'(x)$). The *difference quotient* $\frac{\Delta y}{\Delta x}$ describes the angular coefficient of the secant through the points $(x, f(x))$ and $(x + \Delta x, f(x + \Delta x))$. The differential quotient is the angular coefficient of the tangent to the graph of f at the point $(x, f(x))$.

Rules of differentiation

	function	derivative
constant factor	$a \cdot u(x)$	$a \cdot u'(x)$, a – real
sum rule	$u(x) \pm v(x)$	$u'(x) \pm v'(x)$
product rule	$u(x) \cdot v(x)$	$u'(x) \cdot v(x) + u(x) \cdot v'(x)$
quotient rule	$\dfrac{u(x)}{v(x)}$	$\dfrac{u'(x) \cdot v(x) - u(x) \cdot v'(x)}{[v(x)]^2}$
especially:	$\dfrac{1}{v(x)}$	$-\dfrac{v'(x)}{[v(x)]^2}$
chain rule	$u(v(x))$ (resp. $y = u(z),\ z = v(x)$)	$u'(z) \cdot v'(x)$ $\left(\frac{\mathrm{d}y}{\mathrm{d}x} = \frac{\mathrm{d}y}{\mathrm{d}z} \cdot \frac{\mathrm{d}z}{\mathrm{d}x}\right)$
differentiation by means of the inverse function	$f(x)$	$\dfrac{1}{(f^{-1})'(f(x))}$ $\left(\dfrac{\mathrm{d}y}{\mathrm{d}x} = 1 \Big/ \dfrac{\mathrm{d}x}{\mathrm{d}y}\right)$
logarithmic differentiation	$f(x)$	$(\ln f(x))' \cdot f(x)$
implicit function	$y = f(x)$ given as $F(x, y) = 0$	$f'(x) = -\dfrac{F_x(x,y)}{F_y(x,y)}$
general exponential function	$u(x)^{v(x)}$ $(u > 0)$	$u(x)^{v(x)} \times$ $\times \left(v'(x) \ln u(x) + v(x) \dfrac{u'(x)}{u(x)}\right)$

• Differentiation by means of the inverse function and logarithmic differentiation are used if the inverse function or the function $\ln f(x)$ can be differentiated in an "easier" way as the original functions.

Derivatives of elementary functions

$f(x)$	$f'(x)$	$f(x)$	$f'(x)$
$c = \text{const}$	0	$\ln x$	$\frac{1}{x}$
x	1	$\log_a x$	$\frac{1}{x \cdot \ln a} = \frac{1}{x} \log_a \mathrm{e}$
x^n	$n \cdot x^{n-1}$	$\lg x$	$\frac{1}{x} \lg \mathrm{e}$
$\frac{1}{x}$	$-\frac{1}{x^2}$	$\sin x$	$\cos x$
$\frac{1}{x^n}$	$-\frac{n}{x^{n+1}}$	$\cos x$	$-\sin x$
$\sqrt{x}$	$\frac{1}{2\sqrt{x}}$	$\tan x$	$1 + \tan^2 x = \frac{1}{\cos^2 x}$
$\sqrt[n]{x}$	$\frac{1}{n \sqrt[n]{x^{n-1}}}$	$\cot x$	$-1 - \cot^2 x = -\frac{1}{\sin^2 x}$
x^x	$x^x(\ln x + 1)$	$\arcsin x$	$\frac{1}{\sqrt{1 - x^2}}$
e^x	e^x	$\arccos x$	$-\frac{1}{\sqrt{1 - x^2}}$
a^x	$a^x \ln a$	$\arctan x$	$\frac{1}{1 + x^2}$
$\operatorname{arccot} x$	$-\frac{1}{1 + x^2}$	$\sinh x$	$\cosh x$
$\cosh x$	$\sinh x$	$\tanh x$	$1 - \tanh^2 x$
$\coth x$	$1 - \coth^2 x$	$\operatorname{arsinh} x$	$\frac{1}{\sqrt{1 + x^2}}$
$\operatorname{arcosh} x$	$\frac{1}{\sqrt{x^2 - 1}}$	$\operatorname{artanh} x$	$\frac{1}{1 - x^2}$
$\operatorname{arcoth} x$	$-\frac{1}{x^2 - 1}$		

Differential

For a function f which is differentiable at the point x_0 one has

$$\Delta y = \Delta f(x_0) = f(x_0 + \Delta x) - f(x_0) = f'(x_0) \cdot \Delta x + \mathrm{o}(\Delta x),$$

where the relation $\lim\limits_{\Delta x \to 0} \dfrac{\mathrm{o}(\Delta x)}{\Delta x} = 0$ holds. Here $\mathrm{o}(\cdot)$ ("small o") is the *Landau order symbol.*

The expression

$$\boxed{\mathrm{d}y = \mathrm{d}f(x_0) = f'(x_0) \cdot \Delta x}$$

or

$$\boxed{\mathrm{d}y = f'(x_0) \cdot \mathrm{d}x}$$

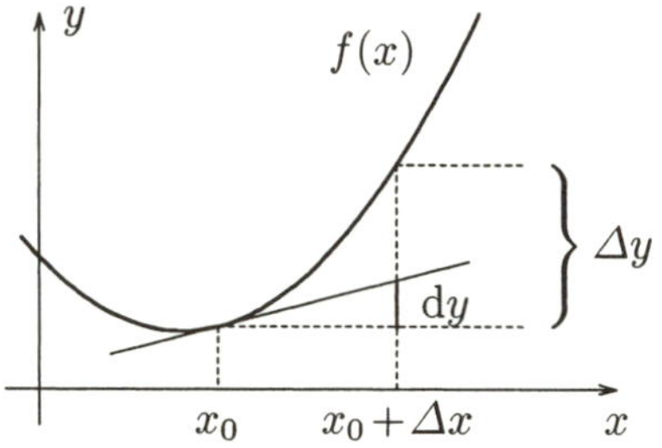

occurring in this relation is called the *differential* of the function f at the point x_0. It describes the main part of the increase of the function value when changing the argument x_0 by Δx:

$$\boxed{\Delta f(x_0) \approx f'(x_0) \cdot \Delta x\,.}$$

Economic interpretation of the first derivative

• In economic applications the first derivative if often called the *marginal function.* It describes **approximately** the increase of the function value when changing the independent variable x by one unit, i. e. $\Delta x = 1$ (▶ differential). The background is the economic notion of the *marginal function* decribing the increase of the function value when changing x by one unit:

$$\boxed{\Delta f(x) = f(x+1) - f(x)\,.}$$

• The investigation of economic problems by means of marginal functions is usually denoted as *marginal analysis.* In doing so, the **units of measure** of the quantities involved are very important:

$$\boxed{\text{unit of measure of } f' \quad = \quad \text{unit of measure of } f \;\; / \;\; \text{unit of measure of } x}$$

Which units of measure do economic functions and their marginal functions have?

u.q. – unit(s) of quantity, u.m. – unit(s) of money, u.t. – unit of time

function $f(x)$	unit of measure of f	unit of measure of x	marginal function $f'(x)$	unit of f'
costs	u.m.	u.q.	marginal costs	$\frac{\text{u.m.}}{\text{u.q.}}$
costs per unit	$\frac{\text{u.m.}}{\text{u.q.}}$	u.q.	marginal costs per unit	$\frac{\text{u.m./u.q.}}{\text{u.q.}}$
turnover (quantity-dependent)	u.m.	u.q.	marginal turnover	$\frac{\text{u.m.}}{\text{u.q.}}$
turnover (price-dependent)	u.m.	$\frac{\text{u.m.}}{\text{u.q.}}$	marginal turnover	$\frac{\text{u.m.}}{\text{u.m./u.q.}}$
production function	u.q.$^{(1)}$	u.q.$^{(2)}$	marginal productivity (marginal return)	$\frac{\text{u.q.}^{(1)}}{\text{u.q.}^{(2)}}$
average return	$\frac{\text{u.q.}^{(1)}}{\text{u.q.}^{(2)}}$	u.q.$^{(2)}$	marginal average return	$\frac{\text{u.q.}^{(1)}/\text{u.q.}^{(2)}}{\text{u.q.}^{(2)}}$
profit	u.m.	u.q.	marginal profit	u.m./u.q.
profit per unit	u.m./u.q.	u.q.	marginal profit per unit	$\frac{\text{u.m./u.q.}}{\text{u.q.}}$
consumption function	u.m./u.t.	$\frac{\text{u.m.}}{\text{u.t.}}$	marginal consumption ratio (marginal propensity to consume)	100 %
savings function	$\frac{\text{u.m.}}{\text{u.t.}}$	$\frac{\text{u.m.}}{\text{u.t.}}$	marginal saving ratio (marginal propensity to save)	100 %

Rates of change and elasticities

Notions

$\dfrac{\Delta x}{x}$	– average relative change of x ($x \neq 0$)
$\dfrac{\Delta f(x)}{\Delta x} = \dfrac{f(x+\Delta x) - f(x)}{\Delta x}$	– average relative change of f (difference quotient)
$R_f(x) = \dfrac{\Delta f(x)}{\Delta x} \cdot \dfrac{1}{f(x)}$	– average rate of change of f at the point x
$E_f(x) = \dfrac{\Delta f(x)}{\Delta x} \cdot \dfrac{x}{f(x)}$	– average elasticity of f at the point x
$\varrho_f(x) = \lim\limits_{\Delta x \to 0} R_f(x) = \dfrac{f'(x)}{f(x)}$	– rate of change of f at the point x; rate of increase, growth rate
$\varepsilon_f(x) = \lim\limits_{\Delta x \to 0} E_f(x) = x \cdot \dfrac{f'(x)}{f(x)}$	– (point) elasticity of f at the point x

• The average elasticity and the elasticity are independent of the chosen units of measure for x and $f(x)$ (dimensionless quantity). The elasticity describes approximately the change of $f(x)$ in percent (relative change) if x increases by 1 %.

• If $y = f(t)$ describes the growth (change) of an economic quantity in dependence on time t, then $\varrho_f(t)$ describes the approximate percentage change of $f(t)$ per unit of time at the moment t.

• A function f is called (at the point x)

elastic	if $\lvert\varepsilon_f(x)\rvert > 1$	$f(x)$ changes relatively stronger than x,
proportionally elastic (1-elastic)	if $\lvert\varepsilon_f(x)\rvert = 1$	approximately equal relative changes of x and $f(x)$,
inelastic	if $\lvert\varepsilon_f(x)\rvert < 1$	$f(x)$ changes relatively less strong than x,
completely inelastic	if $\varepsilon_f(x) = 0$	in linear approximation there is no change of $f(x)$ when x changes.

Rules of operation for elasticities and rates of change

rule	elasticity	rate of change
constant factor	$\varepsilon_{cf}(x) = \varepsilon_f(x) \quad (c \in \mathbb{R})$	$\varrho_{cf}(x) = \varrho_f(x) \quad (c \in \mathbb{R})$
sum	$\varepsilon_{f+g}(x) = \frac{f(x)\varepsilon_f(x)+g(x)\varepsilon_g(x)}{f(x)+g(x)}$	$\varrho_{f+g}(x) = \frac{f(x)\varrho_f(x)+g(x)\varrho_g(x)}{f(x)+g(x)}$
product	$\varepsilon_{f\cdot g}(x) = \varepsilon_f(x) + \varepsilon_g(x)$	$\varrho_{f\cdot g}(x) = \varrho_f(x) + \varrho_g(x)$
quotient	$\varepsilon_{\frac{f}{g}}(x) = \varepsilon_f(x) - \varepsilon_g(x)$	$\varrho_{\frac{f}{g}}(x) = \varrho_f(x) - \varrho_g(x)$
composite function	$\varepsilon_{f\circ g}(x) = \varepsilon_f(g(x)) \cdot \varepsilon_g(x)$	$\varrho_{f\circ g}(x) = g(x)\varrho_f(g(x))\varrho_g(x)$
inverse function	$\varepsilon_{f^{-1}}(y) = \dfrac{1}{\varepsilon_f(x)}$	$\varrho_{f^{-1}}(y) = \dfrac{1}{\varepsilon_f(x) \cdot f(x)}$

Elasticity of the average function

$$\varepsilon_{\bar{f}}(x) = \varepsilon_f(x) - 1$$

$\bar{f}$ – average function $\left(\bar{f}(x) = \dfrac{f(x)}{x},\ x \neq 0\right)$

- If, in particular, $U(p) = p \cdot x(p)$ describes the turnover and $x(p)$ the demand, then due to $\overline{U}(p) = x(p)$ the price elasticity of demand is always less by one than the price elasticity of turnover.

General Amoroso-Robinson equation

$$f'(x) = \bar{f}(x) \cdot \varepsilon_f(x) = \bar{f}(x) \cdot \big(1 + \varepsilon_{\bar{f}}(x)\big)$$

Special Amoroso-Robinson equation

$$V'(y) = x \cdot \left(1 + \frac{1}{\varepsilon_N(x)}\right)$$

x – price,
$y = N(x)$ – demand,
N^{-1} – function inverse to N,
$U(x) = x \cdot N(x) = V(y) = y \cdot N^{-1}(y)$ – turnover,
V' – marginal turnover,
$\varepsilon_N(x)$ – price elasticity of demand

Mean value theorems

Mean value theorem of differential calculus

Let the function f be continuous on $[a, b]$ and differentiable on (a, b). Then there is (at least) one number $\xi \in (a, b)$ such that

$$\boxed{\frac{f(b) - f(a)}{b - a} = f'(\xi)}\;.$$

Generalized mean value theorem of differential calculus

Let the functions f and g be continuous on the interval $[a, b]$ and differentiable on (a, b). Moreover, let $g'(x) \neq 0$ for any $x \in (a, b)$. Then there exists (at least) one number $\xi \in (a, b)$ such that

$$\boxed{\frac{f(b) - f(a)}{g(b) - g(a)} = \frac{f'(\xi)}{g'(\xi)}}\;.$$

Higher derivatives and Taylor expansion

Higher derivatives

The function f is called *n times differentiable* if the derivatives f', $f'' := (f')'$, $f''' := (f'')'$, ..., $f^{(n)} := (f^{(n-1)})'$ exist; $f^{(n)}$ is said to be the *n-th derivative* or the *derivative of n-th order* of f $(n = 1, 2, \ldots)$. in this context $f^{(0)}$ is understood as f.

Taylor's theorem

Let the function f be $n + 1$ times differentiable in a neighbourhood $U_\varepsilon(x_0)$ of the point x_0. Furthermore, let $x \in U_\varepsilon(x_0)$. Then there exists a number ξ ("mean value") located between x_0 and x such that

$$\boxed{\begin{aligned} f(x) = f(x_0) &+ \frac{f'(x_0)}{1!}(x - x_0) + \frac{f''(x_0)}{2!}(x - x_0)^2 + \ldots \\ &+ \frac{f^{(n)}(x_0)}{n!}(x - x_0)^n + \frac{f^{(n+1)}(\xi)}{(n+1)!}(x - x_0)^{n+1}, \end{aligned}}$$

where the last term, called the *remainder* in Lagrange's form, describes the error made if $f(x)$ is replaced by the indicated polynomial of degree n.

- Another notation (expansion at x instead of x_0 using the mean value $x + \zeta h$, $0 < \zeta < 1$) is given by the formula

$$\boxed{f(x+h) = f(x) + \frac{f'(x)}{1!}h + \frac{f''(x)}{2!}h^2 + \ldots + \frac{f^{(n)}(x)}{n!}h^n + \frac{f^{(n+1)}(x+\zeta h)}{(n+1)!}h^{n+1}}$$

- *MacLaurin's form* of the Taylor formula ($x_0=0$, mean value ζx, $0<\zeta<1$):

$$f(x)=f(0)+\frac{f'(0)}{1!}x+\frac{f''(0)}{2!}x^2+\ldots+\frac{f^{(n)}(0)}{n!}x^n+\frac{f^{(n+1)}(\zeta x)}{(n+1)!}x^{n+1}$$

Taylor formulas of elementary functions (with expansion at the point $x_0 = 0$)

function	Taylor polynomial	remainder
e^x	$1+x+\frac{x^2}{2!}+\frac{x^3}{3!}+\ldots+\frac{x^n}{n!}$	$\frac{e^{\zeta x}}{(n+1)!}x^{n+1}$
a^x $(a>0)$	$1+\frac{\ln a}{1!}x+\ldots+\frac{\ln^n a}{n!}x^n$	$\frac{a^{\zeta x}(\ln a)^{n+1}}{(n+1)!}x^{n+1}$
$\sin x$	$x-\frac{x^3}{3!}\pm\ldots+(-1)^{n-1}\frac{x^{2n-1}}{(2n-1)!}$	$(-1)^n\frac{\cos\zeta x}{(2n+1)!}x^{2n+1}$
$\cos x$	$1-\frac{x^2}{2!}+\frac{x^4}{4!}\mp\ldots+(-1)^n\frac{x^{2n}}{(2n)!}$	$(-1)^{n+1}\frac{\cos\zeta x}{(2n+2)!}x^{2n+2}$
$\ln(1+x)$	$x-\frac{x^2}{2}+\frac{x^3}{3}\mp\ldots+(-1)^{n-1}\frac{x^n}{n}$	$(-1)^n\frac{x^{n+1}}{(1+\zeta x)^{n+1}}$
$\frac{1}{1+x}$	$1-x+x^2-x^3\pm\ldots+(-1)^n x^n$	$\frac{(-1)^{n+1}}{(1+\zeta x)^{n+2}}x^{n+1}$
$(1+x)^\alpha$	$1+\binom{\alpha}{1}x+\ldots+\binom{\alpha}{n}x^n$	$\binom{\alpha}{n+1}(1+\zeta x)^{\alpha-n-1}x^{n+1}$

Approximation formulas

For "small" x, i. e. for $|x| \ll 1$, the first summands of the Taylor polynomials with $x_0 = 0$ (linear and quadratic approximation, resp.) yield approximations which are sufficiently exact in many applications. In the table one can find the tolerance limits a, for which in case $|x| \le a$ the error made is $\varepsilon < 0,001$ (► Taylor series).

Table of approximation functions

function and its approximation	tolerance limit a
$\frac{1}{1+x} \approx 1-x$	$0,031$
$\frac{1}{\sqrt[n]{1+x}} \approx 1-\frac{x}{n}$	$0,036\sqrt{n}\ \ (x>0)$
$\sin x \approx x$	0,181
$\tan x \approx x$	0,143
$a^x \approx 1 + x\ln a$	$0,044 \cdot (\ln a)^{-1}$
$\sqrt[n]{1+x} \approx 1+\frac{x}{n}$	
$(1+x)^\alpha \approx 1+\alpha x$	
$\cos x \approx 1-\frac{x^2}{2}$	0,394
$\mathrm{e}^x \approx 1+x$	0,044
$\ln(1+x) \approx x$	0,045

Description of function features by means of derivatives

Monotony

Let the function f be defined and differentiable on the interval $[a,b]$. Then

$f'(x)=0$	$\forall\, x\in[a,b]$	$\Longleftrightarrow$	f is constant on $[a,b]$
$f'(x)\ge 0$	$\forall\, x\in[a,b]$	$\Longleftrightarrow$	f is increasing on $[a,b]$
$f'(x)\le 0$	$\forall\, x\in[a,b]$	$\Longleftrightarrow$	f is decreasing on $[a,b]$
$f'(x)>0$	$\forall\, x\in[a,b]$	$\Longrightarrow$	f is strictly increasing on $[a,b]$
$f'(x)<0$	$\forall\, x\in[a,b]$	$\Longrightarrow$	f is strictly decreasing on $[a,b]$

• The inverse proposition to the last two statements holds only in a weakened form: if f strictly increases (decreases) on $[a,b]$, then one has only $f'(x)\ge 0$ (resp. $f'(x)\le 0$).

Necessary condition for an extremum

If the function f has a (local or global) extremum at the point $x_0 \in (a, b)$ and if f is differentiable at this point, then $\boxed{f'(x_0) = 0\,.}$ Every point x_0 satisfying this equation is called a *stationary* point of the function f.

• The above statement applies only to points where f is differentiable. Boundary points of the domain as well as points where f fails to be differentiable (*breaks*) can be extreme points either.

Sufficient conditions for extrema

If the function f is n times differentiable in $(a, b) \subset D_f$, then f has an extremum at the point $x_0 \in (a, b)$ if the following relations are satisfied, where n is even: $\boxed{f'(x_0) = f''(x_0) = \ldots = f^{(n-1)}(x_0) = 0, \quad f^{(n)}(x_0) \neq 0\,.}$

For $f^{(n)}(x_0) < 0$ the point x_0 yields a maximum, for $f^{(n)}(x_0) > 0$ a minimum.

• Especially:

$$\boxed{\begin{array}{lcl} f'(x_0) = 0 \ \wedge \ f''(x_0) < 0 & \Longrightarrow & f \text{ has a local maximum at } x_0, \\ f'(x_0) = 0 \ \wedge \ f''(x_0) > 0 & \Longrightarrow & f \text{ has a local minimum at } x_0. \end{array}}$$

• If f is continuously differentiable at the boundary points a, b, one has

$$\boxed{\begin{array}{lcl} f'(a) < 0 \ \ (f'(a) > 0) & \Longrightarrow & f \text{ has a local maximum (minimum) at } a, \\ f'(b) > 0 \ \ (f'(b) < 0) & \Longrightarrow & f \text{ has a local maximum (minimum) at } b. \end{array}}$$

• If f is differentiable in the *neighbourhood* $U_\varepsilon(x_0) = \{x \mid |x - x_0| < \varepsilon\}$, $\varepsilon > 0$, of a stationary point x_0 and the sign of f' changes at this point, then x_0 is an extreme point which is a maximum point if $f'(x) > 0$ for $x < x_0$ and $f'(x) < 0$ for $x > x_0$. If the sign of the derivative changes from the negative to the positive, we deal with a local minimum.

• If in $U_\varepsilon(x_0)$ the sign of f' remains constant, then the function f has **no** extremum at x_0. In this case we have a *horizontal inflection point.*

Growth

• If on the interval $[a, b]$ the conditions $f'(x) > 0$ and $f''(x) \geq 0$ are fulfilled, then the function f growths *progressively*, while for $f'(x) > 0$ and $f''(x) \leq 0$ the growth is said to be *degressively*.

Curvature properties of a function

Let the function f be twice differentiable in (a, b). Then

f convex in (a, b)	$\iff f''(x) \geq 0 \quad \forall\, x \in (a, b)$
	$\iff f(y) - f(x) \geq (y - x)f'(x) \quad \forall\, x, y \in (a, b)$
f strict convex in (a, b)	$\Longleftarrow f''(x) > 0 \quad \forall\, x \in (a, b)$
	$\iff f(y) - f(x) > (y - x)f'(x) \quad \forall\, x, y \in (a, b), x \neq y$
f concave in (a, b)	$\iff f''(x) \leq 0 \quad \forall\, x \in (a, b)$
	$\iff f(y) - f(x) \leq (y - x)f'(x) \quad \forall\, x, y \in (a, b)$
f strict convex in (a, b)	$\Longleftarrow f''(x) < 0 \quad \forall\, x \in (a, b)$
	$\iff f(y) - f(x) < (y - x)f'(x) \quad \forall\, x, y \in (a, b), x \neq y$

Curvature

The limit of the change $\Delta\alpha$ of the angle α between the direction of a curve and the x-axis in relation to the covered arc-length Δs for $\Delta s \to 0$ is called the *curvature* of a curve:

$$C = \lim_{\Delta s \downarrow 0} \frac{\Delta\alpha}{\Delta s}.$$

presentation of the curve	curvature C
Cartesian form $y = f(x)$	$\dfrac{f''(x)}{(1 + (f'(x))^2)^{3/2}}$
parametric form $x = x(t)$, $y = y(t)$	$\dfrac{\dot{x}(t)\ddot{y}(t) - \dot{y}(t)\ddot{y}(t)}{(\dot{x}^2(t) + \dot{y}^2(t))^{3/2}}$ with $\dot{x}(t) = \dfrac{\mathrm{d}x}{\mathrm{d}t}, \quad \dot{y}(t) = \dfrac{\mathrm{d}y}{\mathrm{d}t}$

- The curvature C of a curve is equal to the reciprocal of the radius of the circle which contacts the curve $y = f(x)$ at the point $P(x, f(x))$.
- The curvature C is nonnegative if the curve is convex and nonpositive if it is concave.

Necessary conditions for an inflection point

If the function f is twice diffentiable in the interval (a, b) and has a *point of inflection* at x_w (point between intervals of convexity and concavity), then

$$\boxed{f''(x_w) = 0.}$$

Sufficient condition for an inflection point

If f is three times continuously differentiable at (a, b), then sufficient for x_w with $f''(x_w) = 0$ to be a point of reflection is the validity of the relation

$$\boxed{f'''(x_w) \neq 0.}$$

Investigation of economic functions, profit maximization

Notations

$\bar{f}(x) = \dfrac{f(x)}{x}$	–	average function
$f'(x)$	–	marginal function
$K(x) = K_v(x) + K_f$	–	total costs = variable costs + fixed costs
$k(x) = \dfrac{K(x)}{x}$	–	total costs per unit
$k_v(x) = \dfrac{K_v(x)}{x}$	–	variable costs per unit
$G(x) = U(x) - K(x)$	–	profit = turnover – costs
$g(x) = \dfrac{G(x)}{x}$	–	profit per unit

- Due to $\bar{f}(1) = f(1)$, a function and its average function have the same value for $x = 1$.

Average function and marginal function

$$\boxed{\bar{f}'(x) = 0 \quad \Longrightarrow \quad f'(x) = \bar{f}(x)} \qquad \text{(necessary optimality condition)}$$

- An average function may have an extremum only at a point where it is equal to its marginal function.

In particular: $\boxed{K_v'(x_m) = k_v(x_m) = k_{v,\min}}$

• At the point x_m of minimal average variable costs the marginal costs and the variable costs per unit are equal (short-term bottom price, lower price limit).

$$K'(x_0) = k(x_0) = k_{\min}$$

• For minimal total costs per unit the marginal costs and the average costs must be equal to each other (optimum costs; long-term bottom price).

Profit maximization in the polypoly and monopoly

Solve the extreme value problem $G(x) = U(x) - K(x) = p \cdot x - K(x) \to \min$. Let its solution be x^*.

• In the *polypoly* (perfect competition) the market price p of a good is a constant from the viewpoint of suppliers. In the *monopoly (of supply)* a (decreasing) underlying price-response function $p = p(x)$ is assumed to be the total market demand function.

Polypoly; maximization of total profit

$$K'(x^*) = p, \qquad K''(x^*) > 0$$

(sufficient maximum condition)

• A polypolistic supplier obtains maximal profit by that volume of supply x^* for which the marginal costs are equal to the market price. A maximum can exist only in the case if x^* is located within the convex domain of the cost function.

Polypoly; maximization of the profit per unit

$$g'(x_0) = k'(x_0) = 0, \quad g''(x_0) = -k''(x_0) < 0$$

(sufficient maximum condition)

• The maximal profit per unit is located at the point where average costs are minimal (optimum costs).

Polypoly; linear total cost function, capacity limit x_0

$$x^* = x_0$$

• The profit maximum lies at the capacity limit. It is positive provided that the *break-even point* (see p. 57) lies in $(0, x_0)$.

• The minimum of costs per unit and the maximum of profit per unit are both located at the capacity limit.

Monopoly; maximization of total profit

$$K'(x^*) = U'(x^*), \qquad G''(x^*) < 0$$

(sufficient maximum condition)

• At a point of maximal profit marginal turnover and marginal costs are equal to each other (*Cournot's point*).

Monopoly; maximization of profit per unit

$$p'(\hat{x}) = k'(\hat{x}), \qquad g''(\hat{x}) < 0$$

(sufficient maximum condition)

• Maximal profit per unit is achieved at the point $\hat{x}$ where the ascents of the price-response function and the average cost function are equal.

Optimal lot size (optimal order size)

c_s	–	set-up costs (u.m.) per lot
c_i	–	inventory costs (u.m. per u.q. and u.t.)
d	–	demand, inventory decreases (u.q./u.t.)
r	–	production rate, addition to stocks (u.q./u.t.)
T	–	length of a period (u.t.)
x	–	(unknown) lot size (u.q.)

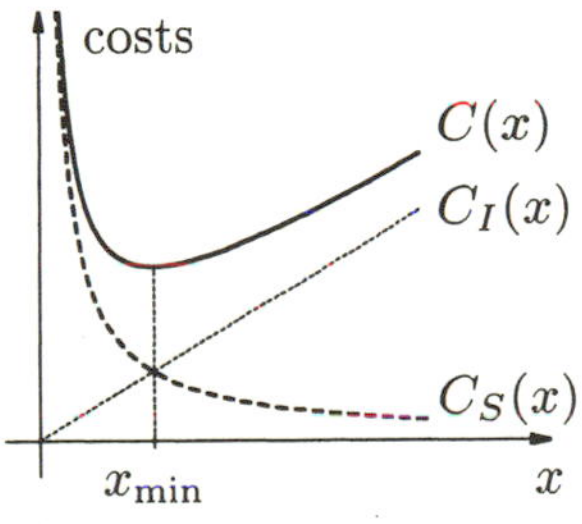

u.m., u.q., u.t. – units of money, quantity and time, resp.

• The rate of inventory decreases d as well as the rate of additions to stock $c > d$ are assumed to be constant. (For $c = d$ from a "theoretical point of view" a stock is not needed.)

• It is to find that lot size x^* for which the total costs per period consisting of set-up and inventory costs will be minimal. The greater the production lot, the lower the relative set-up costs, but the higher the inventory costs (related to the average stock).

• The relevant quantities for the underlying model can be found in the following table.

Relevant quantities

$t_0 = \dfrac{x}{r}$	– production time of a lot
$T_0 = \dfrac{x}{d}$	– length of a production and inventory cycle
$l_{\max} = \left(1 - \frac{d}{r}\right) x$	– maximal inventory level
$\bar{l} = \left(1 - \dfrac{d}{r}\right) \cdot \dfrac{x}{2}$	– average stock
$D = d \cdot T$	– total demand in $[0, T]$
$n = \dfrac{D}{x} = \dfrac{dT}{x}$	– number of lots to be produced in $[0, T]$
$C_S(x) = \dfrac{D}{x} \cdot c_s$	– total set-up costs in $[0, T]$
$C_I(x) = \left(1 - \dfrac{d}{r}\right) \cdot \dfrac{x}{2} \cdot c_i \cdot T$	– total inventory costs in $[0, T]$
$C(x) = C_S(x) + C_I(x)$	– total period costs

Optimal lot size formulas

$$x^* = \sqrt{\frac{2dc_s}{\left(1 - \frac{d}{r}\right) c_i}}$$

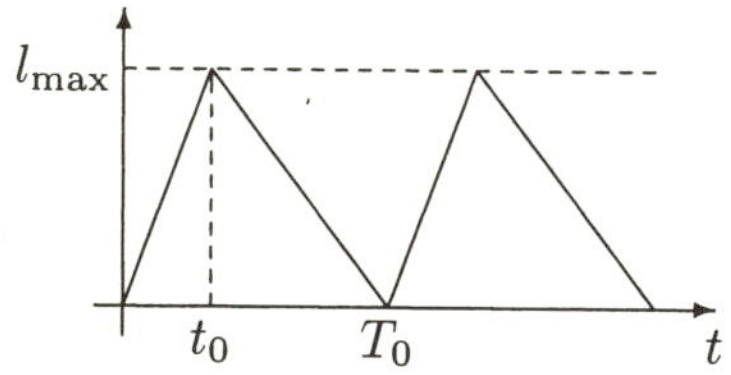

• If the whole addition to stocks takes place immediately at the beginning of the inventory cycle ($r \to \infty$), then $l_{\max} = x$ ("saw-tooth curve", ▶ p. 57), where

$$x^* = \sqrt{\frac{2dc_s}{c_i}}$$

lot size formula of Harris and Wilson

• When buying and storing a commodity being continuously used in a production process, one obtains a similarly structured **problem of optimal order size**: fixed order costs suggest a few, but large orders, while stock-dependent inventory costs suggest more, but smaller orders.

Integral Calculus for Functions of one Variable

Indefinite integral

Every function $F:(a,b)\to\mathbb{R}$ satisfying the relation $F'(x)=f(x)$ for all $x\in(a,b)$ is called a *primitive* of the function $f:(a,b)\to\mathbb{R}$. The set of all primitives $\{F+C\,|\,C\in\mathbb{R}\}$ is said to be the *indefinite integral* of f on (a,b); C is the integration constant. Notation: $\displaystyle\int f(x)\,\mathrm{d}x=F(x)+C$.

Integration rules

constant factor	$\displaystyle\int \lambda f(x)\,\mathrm{d}x=\lambda\int f(x)\,\mathrm{d}x,$	$\lambda\in\mathbb{R}$
sum	$\displaystyle\int [f(x)\pm g(x)]\,\mathrm{d}x=\int f(x)\,\mathrm{d}x\pm\int g(x)\,\mathrm{d}x$	
integration by parts	$\displaystyle\int u(x)v'(x)\,\mathrm{d}x=u(x)v(x)-\int u'(x)v(x)\,\mathrm{d}x$	
integration by substitution	$\displaystyle\int f(g(x))\cdot g'(x)\,\mathrm{d}x=\int f(z)\,\mathrm{d}z,$ (change of variable)	$z=g(x)$
special case $f=\frac{1}{g}$	$\displaystyle\int \frac{g'(x)}{g(x)}\,\mathrm{d}x=\ln\lvert g(x)\rvert+C,$	$g(x)\neq 0$
linear substitution	$\displaystyle\int f(ax+b)\,\mathrm{d}x=\frac{1}{a}F(ax+b)+C,$ (F is a primitive of f)	$a,b\in\mathbb{R}$, $a\neq 0$

Integration of fractional rational functions

$$\int \frac{a_m x^m+a_{m-1}x^{m-1}+\ldots+a_1x+a_0}{b_n x^n+b_{n-1}x^{n-1}+\ldots+b_1x+b_0}\,\mathrm{d}x$$

Polynom division and partial fraction decomposition lead to integrals over polynomials and special *partial fractions.* The partial fractions can be integrated by the use of formulas from the ▶ table of indefinite integrals. The most important are (assumptions: $x-a\neq 0$, $k>1$, $p^2<4q$):

$$\int \frac{\mathrm{d}x}{x-a} = \ln|x-a| + C$$

$$\int \frac{\mathrm{d}x}{(x-a)^k} = -\frac{1}{(k-1)(x-a)^{k-1}} + C$$

$$\int \frac{\mathrm{d}x}{x^2+px+q} = \frac{2}{\sqrt{4q-p^2}} \arctan \frac{2x+p}{\sqrt{4q-p^2}} + C$$

$$\int \frac{Ax+B}{x^2+px+q}\,\mathrm{d}x = \frac{A}{2}\ln(x^2+px+q) + \left(B - \frac{1}{2}Ap\right)\int \frac{\mathrm{d}x}{x^2+px+q}$$

Definite integral

The area A located between the interval $[a,b]$ of the x-axis and the graph of the bounded function f can approximately be calculated by summands of the form $\sum\limits_{i=1}^{n} f(\xi_i^{(n)})\Delta x_i^{(n)}$ with $\Delta x_i^{(n)} = x_i^{(n)} - x_{i-1}^{(n)}$ and $\sum\limits_{i=1}^{n} \Delta x_i^{(n)} = b-a$.

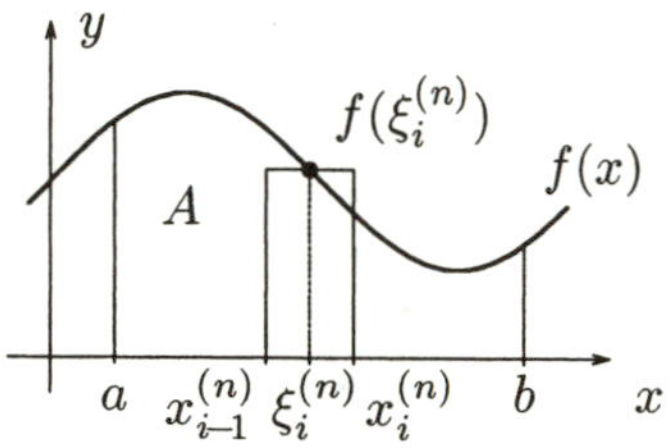

Passing to the limit for $n \to \infty$ and $\Delta x_i^{(n)} \to 0$, under certain assumptions one obtains the *definite (Riemann) integral* of the function f on the interval $[a,b]$, which is equal to the area A: $\displaystyle\int_a^b f(x)\,\mathrm{d}x = A\,.$

Properties and rules of operation

$$\int_a^a f(x)\,\mathrm{d}x = 0$$

$$\int_a^b f(x)\,\mathrm{d}x = -\int_b^a f(x)\,\mathrm{d}x$$

$$\int_a^b [f(x) \pm g(x)]\,\mathrm{d}x = \int_a^b f(x)\,\mathrm{d}x \pm \int_a^b g(x)\,\mathrm{d}x$$

$$\int_a^b \lambda f(x)\,\mathrm{d}x = \lambda \int_a^b f(x)\,\mathrm{d}x, \quad \lambda \in \mathbb{R}$$

$$\int_a^b f(x)\,\mathrm{d}x = \int_a^c f(x)\,\mathrm{d}x + \int_c^b f(x)\,\mathrm{d}x$$

$$\left|\int_a^b f(x)\,\mathrm{d}x\right| \le \int_a^b |f(x)|\,\mathrm{d}x, \quad a < b$$

First mean value theorem of integral calculus

If f is continuous on $[a,b]$, then there exists at least one $\xi \in [a,b]$ such that

$$\int_a^b f(x)\,\mathrm{d}x = (b-a)f(\xi)\,.$$

Generalized first mean value theorem of integral calculus

If f is continuous on $[a,b]$, g is integrable on $[a,b]$ and either $g(x) \geq 0$ for all $x \in [a,b]$ or $g(x) \leq 0$ for all $x \in [a,b]$, then there exists at least one $\xi \in [a,b]$ such that

$$\int_a^b f(x)g(x)\,\mathrm{d}x = f(\xi)\int_a^b g(x)\,\mathrm{d}x\ .$$

If f is continuous on $[a,b]$, then $\displaystyle\int_a^x f(t)\,\mathrm{d}t$ is differentiable for $x \in [a,b]$,

where $$F(x) = \int_a^x f(t)\,\mathrm{d}t \implies F'(x) = f(x)\,.$$

Fundamental theorem of calculus

If f is continuous on $[a,b]$ and F is a primitive of f on $[a,b]$, then

$$\int_a^b f(x)\,\mathrm{d}x = F(b) - F(a)\,.$$

Tables of indefinite integrals

Fundamental integrals (The integration constant is omitted.)

power functions

$$\int x^n\,\mathrm{d}x = \frac{x^{n+1}}{n+1} \qquad (n \in \mathbb{Z},\ n \neq -1,\ x \neq 0 \text{ for } n < 0)$$

$$\int x^\alpha\,\mathrm{d}x = \frac{x^{\alpha+1}}{\alpha+1} \qquad (\alpha \in \mathbb{R},\ \alpha \neq -1,\ x > 0)$$

$$\int \frac{1}{x}\,\mathrm{d}x = \ln|x| \qquad (x \neq 0)$$

exponential and logarithmic functions

$$\int a^x \, dx = \frac{a^x}{\ln a} \qquad (a \in \mathbb{R},\ a > 0,\ a \neq 1)$$

$$\int e^x \, dx = e^x$$

$$\int \ln x \, dx = x \ln x - x \qquad (x > 0)$$

trigonometric functions

$$\int \sin x \, dx = -\cos x$$

$$\int \cos x \, dx = \sin x$$

$$\int \tan x \, dx = -\ln|\cos x| \qquad (x \neq (2k+1)\frac{\pi}{2})$$

$$\int \cot x \, dx = \ln|\sin x| \qquad (x \neq k\pi)$$

inverse trigonometric functions

$$\int \arcsin x \, dx = x \arcsin x + \sqrt{1-x^2} \qquad (|x| \leq 1)$$

$$\int \arccos x \, dx = x \arccos x - \sqrt{1-x^2} \qquad (|x| \leq 1)$$

$$\int \arctan x \, dx = x \arctan x - \frac{1}{2}\ln(1+x^2)$$

$$\int \operatorname{arccot} x \, dx = x \operatorname{arccot} x + \frac{1}{2}\ln(1+x^2)$$

rational functions

$$\int \frac{dx}{1+x^2} = \arctan x$$

$$\int \frac{dx}{1-x^2} = \ln\sqrt{\frac{1+x}{1-x}} \qquad (|x| < 1)$$

$$\int \frac{dx}{x^2-1} = \ln\sqrt{\frac{x-1}{x+1}} \qquad (|x| > 1)$$

irrational functions

$$\int \frac{\mathrm{d}x}{\sqrt{1-x^2}} = \arcsin x \qquad (|x| < 1)$$

$$\int \frac{\mathrm{d}x}{\sqrt{1+x^2}} = \ln(x + \sqrt{x^2+1})$$

$$\int \frac{\mathrm{d}x}{\sqrt{x^2-1}} = \ln(x + \sqrt{x^2-1}) \qquad (|x| > 1)$$

hyperbolic functions

$$\int \sinh x \, \mathrm{d}x = \cosh x$$

$$\int \cosh x \, \mathrm{d}x = \sinh x$$

$$\int \tanh x \, \mathrm{d}x = \ln \cosh x$$

$$\int \coth x \, \mathrm{d}x = \ln |\sinh x| \qquad (x \neq 0)$$

area-hyperbolic functions

$$\int \mathrm{arsinh} x \, \mathrm{d}x = x \, \mathrm{arsinh} x - \sqrt{1+x^2}$$

$$\int \mathrm{arcosh} x \, \mathrm{d}x = x \, \mathrm{arcosh} x - \sqrt{x^2-1} \qquad (x > 1)$$

$$\int \mathrm{artanh} x \, \mathrm{d}x = x \, \mathrm{artanh} x + \frac{1}{2} \ln(1-x^2) \qquad (|x| < 1)$$

$$\int \mathrm{arcoth} x \, \mathrm{d}x = x \, \mathrm{arcoth} x + \frac{1}{2} \ln(x^2-1) \qquad (|x| > 1)$$

Integrals of rational functions

$$\int (ax+b)^n \, \mathrm{d}x = \frac{(ax+b)^{n+1}}{a(n+1)} \qquad (n \neq -1)$$

$$\int \frac{\mathrm{d}x}{ax+b} = \frac{1}{a} \ln |ax+b|$$

$$\int \frac{ax+b}{fx+g}\,\mathrm{d}x = \frac{ax}{f} + \frac{bf-ag}{f^2}\ln|fx+g|$$

$$\int \frac{\mathrm{d}x}{(ax+b)(fx+g)} = \frac{1}{ag-bf}\left(\int \frac{a}{ax+b}\,\mathrm{d}x - \int \frac{f}{fx+g}\,\mathrm{d}x\right)$$

$$\int \frac{\mathrm{d}x}{(x+a)(x+b)(x+c)} = \frac{1}{(b-a)(c-a)}\int \frac{\mathrm{d}x}{x+a} + \frac{1}{(a-b)(c-b)}\int \frac{\mathrm{d}x}{x+b} + \frac{1}{(a-c)(b-c)}\int \frac{\mathrm{d}x}{x+c}$$

$$\int \frac{\mathrm{d}x}{ax^2+bx+c} = \begin{cases} \dfrac{2}{\sqrt{4ac-b^2}}\arctan\dfrac{2ax+b}{4ac-b^2} & \text{for } b^2<4ac \\ \dfrac{1}{\sqrt{b^2-4ac}}\left(\ln(1-\dfrac{2ax+b}{\sqrt{b^2-4ac}}) - \ln(1+\dfrac{2ax+b}{\sqrt{b^2-4ac}})\right) & \text{for } 4ac<b^2 \end{cases}$$

$$\int \frac{\mathrm{d}x}{(ax^2+bx+c)^{n+1}} = \frac{2ax+b}{n(4ac-b^2)(ax^2+bx+c)^n} + \frac{(4n-2)a}{n(4ac-b^2)}\int \frac{\mathrm{d}x}{(ax^2+bx+c)^n}$$

$$\int \frac{x\,\mathrm{d}x}{(ax^2+bx+c)^{n+1}} = \frac{bx+2c}{n(b^2-4ac)(ax^2+bx+c)^n} + \frac{(2n-1)b}{n(b^2-4ac)}\int \frac{\mathrm{d}x}{(ax^2+bx+c)^n}$$

$$\int \frac{\mathrm{d}x}{a^2\pm x^2} = \frac{1}{a}S \text{ with } S = \begin{cases} \arctan\dfrac{x}{a} & \text{for the sign } + \\ \dfrac{1}{2}\ln\dfrac{a+x}{a-x} & \text{for the sign } - \text{ and } |x|<|a| \\ \dfrac{1}{2}\ln\dfrac{x+a}{x-a} & \text{for the sign } - \text{ and } |x|>|a| \end{cases}$$

$(a \neq 0)$

$$\int \frac{\mathrm{d}x}{(a^2\pm x^2)^{n+1}} = \frac{x}{2na^2(a^2\pm x^2)^n} + \frac{2n-1}{2na^2}\int \frac{\mathrm{d}x}{(a^2\pm x^2)^n}$$

$$\int \frac{\mathrm{d}x}{a^3\pm x^3} = \pm\frac{1}{6a^2}\ln\frac{(a\pm x)^2}{a^2\mp ax+x^2} + \frac{1}{a^2\sqrt{3}}\arctan\frac{2x\mp a}{a\sqrt{3}}$$

Integrals of irrational functions

$$\int \sqrt{(ax+b)^n}\,\mathrm{d}x = \frac{2}{a(2+n)}\sqrt{(ax+b)^{n+2}} \qquad (n \neq -2)$$

$$\int \frac{\mathrm{d}x}{x\sqrt{ax+b}} = \begin{cases} \dfrac{1}{\sqrt{b}} \ln \left| \dfrac{\sqrt{ax+b}-\sqrt{b}}{\sqrt{ax+b}+\sqrt{b}} \right| & \text{for} \quad b > 0 \\[2ex] \dfrac{2}{\sqrt{-b}} \arctan \sqrt{\dfrac{ax+b}{-b}} & \text{for} \quad b < 0 \end{cases}$$

$$\int \frac{\sqrt{ax+b}}{x}\,\mathrm{d}x = 2\sqrt{ax+b} + b \int \frac{\mathrm{d}x}{x\sqrt{ax+b}}$$

$$\int \sqrt{a^2-x^2}\,\mathrm{d}x = \frac{1}{2}\left(x\sqrt{a^2-x^2} + a^2 \arcsin\frac{x}{a}\right)$$

$$\int x\sqrt{a^2-x^2}\,\mathrm{d}x = -\frac{1}{3}\sqrt{(a^2-x^2)^3}$$

$$\int \frac{\mathrm{d}x}{\sqrt{a^2-x^2}} = \arcsin\frac{x}{a}$$

$$\int \frac{x\,\mathrm{d}x}{\sqrt{a^2-x^2}} = -\sqrt{a^2-x^2}$$

$$\int \sqrt{x^2+a^2}\,\mathrm{d}x = \frac{1}{2}\left(x\sqrt{x^2+a^2} + a^2 \ln\left(x+\sqrt{x^2+a^2}\right)\right)$$

$$\int x\sqrt{x^2+a^2}\,\mathrm{d}x = \frac{1}{3}\sqrt{(x^2+a^2)^3}$$

$$\int \frac{\mathrm{d}x}{\sqrt{x^2+a^2}} = \ln\left(x+\sqrt{x^2+a^2}\right)$$

$$\int \frac{x\,\mathrm{d}x}{\sqrt{x^2+a^2}} = \sqrt{x^2+a^2}$$

$$\int \sqrt{x^2-a^2}\,\mathrm{d}x = \frac{1}{2}\left(x\sqrt{x^2-a^2} - a^2 \ln\left(x+\sqrt{x^2-a^2}\right)\right)$$

$$\int x\sqrt{x^2-a^2}\,\mathrm{d}x = \frac{1}{3}\sqrt{(x^2-a^2)^3}$$

$$\int \frac{\mathrm{d}x}{\sqrt{x^2-a^2}} = \ln\left(x+\sqrt{x^2-a^2}\right)$$

$$\int \frac{x\,\mathrm{d}x}{\sqrt{x^2-a^2}} = \sqrt{x^2-a^2}$$

$$\int \frac{\mathrm{d}x}{\sqrt{ax^2+bx+c}}$$

$$= \begin{cases} \dfrac{1}{\sqrt{a}} \ln\left|2\sqrt{a}\sqrt{ax^2+bx+c}+2ax+b\right| & \text{for } a>0 \\ -\dfrac{1}{\sqrt{-a}} \arcsin \dfrac{2ax+b}{\sqrt{b^2-4ac}} & \text{for } a<0,\ 4ac<b^2 \end{cases}$$

$$\int \frac{x\,\mathrm{d}x}{\sqrt{ax^2+bx+c}} = \frac{1}{a}\sqrt{ax^2+bx+c} - \frac{b}{2a}\int \frac{\mathrm{d}x}{\sqrt{ax^2+bx+c}}$$

$$\int \sqrt{ax^2+bx+c}\,\mathrm{d}x = \frac{2ax+b}{4a}\sqrt{ax^2+bx+c} + \frac{4ac-b^2}{8a}\int \frac{\mathrm{d}x}{\sqrt{ax^2+bx+c}}$$

Integrals of trigonometric functions

$$\int \sin ax\,\mathrm{d}x = -\frac{1}{a}\cos ax$$

$$\int \sin^2 ax\,\mathrm{d}x = \frac{1}{2}x - \frac{1}{4a}\sin 2ax$$

$$\int \sin^n ax\,\mathrm{d}x = -\frac{1}{na}\sin^{n-1} ax\cos ax + \frac{n-1}{n}\int \sin^{n-2} ax\,\mathrm{d}x \qquad (n \in \mathbb{N})$$

$$\int x^n \sin ax\,\mathrm{d}x = -\frac{1}{a}x^n \cos ax + \frac{n}{a}\int x^{n-1}\cos ax\,\mathrm{d}x \qquad (n \in \mathbb{N})$$

$$\int \frac{\mathrm{d}x}{\sin ax} = \frac{1}{a}\ln\left|\tan\frac{ax}{2}\right|$$

$$\int \frac{\mathrm{d}x}{\sin^n ax} = -\frac{\cos ax}{a(n-1)\sin^{n-1} ax} + \frac{n-2}{n-1}\int \frac{\mathrm{d}x}{\sin^{n-2} ax} \qquad (n>1)$$

$$\int \cos ax\,\mathrm{d}x = \frac{1}{a}\sin ax$$

$$\int \cos^2 ax\,\mathrm{d}x = \frac{1}{2}x + \frac{1}{4a}\sin 2ax$$

$$\int \cos^n ax \, \mathrm{d}x = \frac{1}{na} \sin ax \cos^{n-1} ax + \frac{n-1}{n} \int \cos^{n-2} ax \, \mathrm{d}x$$

$$\int x^n \cos ax \, \mathrm{d}x = \frac{1}{a} x^n \sin ax - \frac{n}{a} \int x^{n-1} \sin ax \, \mathrm{d}x$$

$$\int \frac{\mathrm{d}x}{\cos ax} = \frac{1}{a} \ln \left| \tan \left(\frac{ax}{2} + \frac{\pi}{4} \right) \right|$$

$$\int \frac{\mathrm{d}x}{\cos^n ax} = \frac{1}{n-1} \left[\frac{\sin ax}{a \cos^{n-1} ax} + (n-2) \int \frac{\mathrm{d}x}{\cos^{n-2} ax} \right] \qquad (n > 1)$$

$$\int \sin ax \cos ax \, \mathrm{d}x = \frac{1}{2a} \sin^2 ax$$

$$\int \sin ax \cos bx \, \mathrm{d}x = -\frac{\cos(a+b)x}{2(a+b)} - \frac{\cos(a-b)x}{2(a-b)} \qquad (|a| \neq |b|)$$

$$\int \tan ax \, \mathrm{d}x = -\frac{1}{a} \ln |\cos ax|$$

$$\int \tan^n ax \, \mathrm{d}x = \frac{1}{a(n-1)} \tan^{n-1} ax - \int \tan^{n-2} ax \, \mathrm{d}x \qquad (n \neq 1)$$

$$\int \cot ax \, \mathrm{d}x = \frac{1}{a} \ln |\sin ax|$$

$$\int \cot^n ax \, \mathrm{d}x = -\frac{1}{a(n-1)} \cot^{n-1} ax - \int \cot^{n-2} ax \, \mathrm{d}x \qquad (n \neq 1)$$

Integrals of exponential and logarithmic functions

$$\int \mathrm{e}^{ax} \, \mathrm{d}x = \frac{1}{a} \mathrm{e}^{ax}$$

$$\int x^n \mathrm{e}^{ax} \, \mathrm{d}x = \frac{1}{a} x^n \mathrm{e}^{ax} - \frac{n}{a} \int x^{n-1} \mathrm{e}^{ax} \, \mathrm{d}x$$

$$\int \ln ax \, \mathrm{d}x = x \ln ax - x$$

$$\int \frac{\ln^n x}{x} \, \mathrm{d}x = \frac{1}{n+1} \ln^{n+1} x$$

$$\int x^m \ln^n x \, \mathrm{d}x = \frac{x^{m+1} (\ln x)^n}{m+1} - \frac{n}{m+1} \int x^m \ln^{n-1} x \, \mathrm{d}x \qquad (m \neq -1,\, n \neq -1)$$

Improper integrals

Let the function f have a pole at the point $x = b$, and let f be bounded and integrable on any interval $[a, b-\varepsilon]$ such that $0 < \varepsilon < b-a$. If the integral of f on $[a, b-\varepsilon]$ has a limit for $\varepsilon \to 0$, then this limit is called the *improper integral* of f on $[a, b]$:

$$\int_a^b f(x)\,\mathrm{d}x = \lim_{\varepsilon \to +0} \int_a^{b-\varepsilon} f(x)\,\mathrm{d}x \qquad \text{(integrand unbounded)}$$

- If $x = a$ is a pole of f, then analogously:

$$\int_a^b f(x)\,\mathrm{d}x = \lim_{\varepsilon \to +0} \int_{a+\varepsilon}^{b} f(x)\,\mathrm{d}x \qquad \text{(integrand unbounded)}$$

- If $x = c$ is a pole in the interior of $[a, b]$, then the improper integral of f on $[a, b]$ is the sum of the improper integrals of f on $[a, c]$ and $[c, b]$.
- Let the function f be defined for $x \geq a$ and integrable on any interval $[a, b]$. If the limit of the integrals of f on $[a, b]$ exists for $b \to \infty$, then it is called the *improper integral* of f on $[a, \infty)$ (analogously for $a \to -\infty$):

$$\int_a^\infty f(x)\,\mathrm{d}x = \lim_{b \to \infty} \int_a^b f(x)\,\mathrm{d}x, \qquad \int_{-\infty}^b f(x)\,\mathrm{d}x = \lim_{a \to -\infty} \int_a^b f(x)\,\mathrm{d}x$$

(interval unbounded)

Parameter integrals

If for $a \leq x \leq b$, $c \leq t \leq d$ the function $f(x, t)$ is integrable with respect to x on $[a, b]$ for fixed t, then $F(t) = \int\limits_a^b f(x, t)\,\mathrm{d}x$ is a function of t denoted as *parameter integral* (with parameter t).

- If f is partially differentiable with respect to t and the partial derivative f_t is continuous, then the function F is differentiable (with respect to t), and the following relation holds:

$$\dot{F}(t) = \frac{\mathrm{d}F(t)}{\mathrm{d}t} = \int_a^b \frac{\partial f(x, t)}{\partial t}\,\mathrm{d}x\,.$$

- If φ and ψ are two differentiable functions for $c \leq t \leq d$ and if $f(x, t)$ is partially differentiable with respect to t having a continuous partial derivative in the domain defined by $\varphi(t) < x < \psi(t)$, $c \leq t \leq d$, then the parameter integral of f with boundaries $\varphi(t)$ and $\psi(t)$ is differentiable with respect to t for $c \leq t \leq d$, where

$$F(t) = \int_{\varphi(t)}^{\psi(t)} f(x,t)\,\mathrm{d}x \qquad \Longrightarrow$$

$$\dot{F}(t) = \int_{\varphi(t)}^{\psi(t)} \frac{\partial f(x,t)}{\partial t}\,\mathrm{d}x + f(\psi(t),t)\dot{\psi}(t) - f(\varphi(t),t)\dot{\varphi}(t)\,.$$

- Special case: $F(x) = \int_0^x f(\xi)\,\mathrm{d}\xi \quad \Longrightarrow \quad F'(x) = f(x)$

Economic applications of integral calculus

Total profit

$$G(x) = \int_0^x [e(\xi) - k(\xi)]\,\mathrm{d}\xi$$

$k(x)$ – marginal costs for x units of quantity;
$e(x)$ – marginal turnover for x units of quantity

Consumer's surplus (for the equilibrium point (x_0, p_0))

$$K_R(x_0) = E^* - E_0 = \int_0^{x_0} p_N(x)\,\mathrm{d}x - x_0 \cdot p_0$$

$p_N : x \to p(x)$ – decreasing demand function, $p_0 = p_N(x_0)$,
$E_0 = x_0 \cdot p_0$ – actual total turnover,
$E^* = \int_0^{x_0} p_N(x)\,\mathrm{d}x$ – theoretically possible total turnover

- Consumer's surplus is the difference between theoretically possible and actual total turnover. It is (from consumer's point of view) a measure for the profitability of a buy at the equilibrium point (but not before).

Producer's surplus (for the equilibrium point (x_0, p_0))

$$P_R(x_0) = E_0 - E^* = x_0 \cdot p_0 - \int_0^{x_0} p_A(x)\,\mathrm{d}x$$

$p_A : x \to p_A(x)$ – increasing supply function,
$p_N : x \to p_N(x)$ – decreasing demand function,
$p_A(x_0) = p_N(x_0) =: p_0$ defines the market equilibrium point;
E_0, E^* – actual and theoretically possible total turnover, resp.

- Producer's surplus is the difference between actual and theoretically possible total turnover. It is (from producer's point of view) a measure for the profitability of a sale at the equilibrium point (but not before).

Continuous cash flow

$K(t)$ – time-dependent quantity of payment,
$R(t) = K'(t)$ – time-dependent cash flow,
α – continuous rate of interest (intensity)

$K_{[t_1,t_2]} = \int_{t_1}^{t_2} R(t)\,\mathrm{d}t$	– volume of payment in the time interval $[t_1, t_2]$
$K_{[t_1,t_2]}(t_0) = \int_{t_1}^{t_2} \mathrm{e}^{-\alpha(t-t_0)} R(t)\,\mathrm{d}t$	– present value at $t_0 < t_1$
$K_{[t_1,t_2]}(t_0) = \frac{R}{\alpha}\mathrm{e}^{\alpha t_0}\left(\mathrm{e}^{-\alpha t_1} - \mathrm{e}^{-\alpha t_2}\right)$	– present value for $R(t) \equiv R = \mathrm{const}$
$K_{t_1}(t_0) = \int_{t_1}^{\infty} \mathrm{e}^{-\alpha(t-t_0)} R(t)\,\mathrm{d}t$	– present value of a non-restricted in time cash flow $R(t)$ ("perpetuity")
$K_{t_1}(t_0) = \frac{R}{\alpha}\mathrm{e}^{-\alpha(t_1-t_0)}$	– present value of a constant cash flow $R(t) \equiv R$ non-restricted in time

Growth processes

Let some economical characteristic $y = f(t) > 0$ be described by the following features, where the initial value $f(0) = y_0$ is given:

- the absolute growth in a time interval $[0, t]$ is proportional to the length of the interval and the initial value:

$$\Longrightarrow \quad \boxed{y = f(t) = \frac{c}{2}t^2 + y_0} \qquad (c \text{ – factor of proportionality})$$

- the *rate of growth* $\frac{f'(t)}{f(t)}$ is constant, i. e. $\frac{f'(t)}{f(t)} = \gamma$:

$$\Longrightarrow \quad \boxed{y = f(t) = y_0\mathrm{e}^{\gamma t}} \qquad (\gamma \text{ – intensity of growth})$$

special case: continuous compounding of a capital

$$\Longrightarrow \quad \boxed{K_t = K_0\mathrm{e}^{\delta t}}$$

($K_t = K(t)$ – capital at the moment t; K_0 – opening capital; δ - intensity of interest)

- the rate of growth is equal to some specified integrable function $\gamma(t)$, i. e. $\frac{f'(t)}{f(t)} = \gamma(t)$:

$$\Longrightarrow \quad \boxed{y = f(t) = y_0\mathrm{e}^{\int_0^t \gamma(z)\,\mathrm{d}z} = y_0\mathrm{e}^{\bar{\gamma}t},}$$

where $\bar{\gamma} = \frac{1}{t}\int_0^t \gamma(z)\,\mathrm{d}z$ is the *average intensity of growth* in $[0, t]$.

Differential Equations

General form of an n-th order ordinary differential equation

$F(x, y, y', \ldots, y^{(n)}) = 0$	–	implicit form
$y^{(n)} = f(x, y, y', \ldots, y^{(n-1)})$	–	explicit form

- Every n-times continuously differentiable function $y(x)$ satisfying the differential equation for all x, $a \leq x \leq b$ is called a *(special) solution* of the differential equation in the interval $[a, b]$. The set of all solutions of a differential equation or a system of differential equations is said to be the *general solution.*

- If at the point $x = a$ additional conditions are imposed on the solution, then an *initial value problem* is given. If additional conditions are to be observed at the points a and b, then one speaks about a *boundary value problem.*

First-order differential equations

$$y' = f(x, y) \quad \text{or} \quad P(x, y) + Q(x, y)y' = 0 \quad \text{or} \quad P(x, y)\,\mathrm{d}x + Q(x, y)\,\mathrm{d}y = 0$$

- Assigning to every point in the x, y-plane the tangential direction of the solution curves given by $f(x, y)$ one obtains the *direction field.* The curves of the direction field having equal directions are the *isoclines.*

Separable differential equations

If a differential equation is of the form

$$y' = r(x)s(y) \quad \text{or} \quad P(x) + Q(y)y' = 0 \quad \text{or} \quad P(x)\,\mathrm{d}x + Q(y)\,\mathrm{d}y = 0,$$

then it can always be rewritten in the form $\boxed{R(x)\,\mathrm{d}x = S(y)\,\mathrm{d}y}$ by means of *separation of variables.* This means the substitution of y' by $\frac{\mathrm{d}y}{\mathrm{d}x}$ and rearrangement of the equation. After "formal integration" one thus gets the general solution:

$$\int R(x)\mathrm{d}x = \int S(y)\mathrm{d}y \quad \Longrightarrow \quad \varphi(x) = \psi(y) + C$$

First-order linear differential equations

$$y' + a(x)y = r(x)$$

$r(x) \not\equiv 0$ – inhomogeneous differential equation;
$r(x) \equiv 0$ – homogeneous differential equation

• The general solution is the sum of the general solution y_h of the associated homogeneous differential equation and a special solution y_s of the inhomogeneous differential equation:

$$y(x) = y_h(x) + y_s(x)$$

General solution of the homogeneous differential equation

The general solution $y_h(x)$ of $y' + a(x)y = 0$ is obtained by separation of variables from which one gets the result

$$y_h(x) = Ce^{-\int a(x)\,dx}, \qquad C = \text{const}$$

Special solution of the inhomogeneous differential equation

A special solution $y_s(x)$ of $y' + a(x)y = r(x)$ can be obtained by setting $y_s(x) = C(x)e^{-\int a(x)\,dx}$ (*variation of constants*). In doing so, for the function $C(x)$ one gets

$$C(x) = \int r(x)e^{\int a(x)\,dx}\,dx$$

Linear differential equations of n-th order

$$a_n(x)y^{(n)} + \ldots + a_1(x)y' + a_0(x)y = r(x), \quad a_n(x) \not\equiv 0$$

$r(x) \not\equiv 0$ – inhomogeneous differential equation,
$r(x) \equiv 0$ – homogeneous differential eqquation

• The general solution of the inhomogeneous differential equation is the sum of the general solution y_h of the associated homogeneous differential equation and a special solution y_s of the inhomogeneous differential equation:

$$y(x) = y_h(x) + y_s(x)$$

General solution of the homogeneous differential equation

If all coefficient functions a_k are continuous, then there exist n functions y_k, $k = 1, \ldots, n$ (*fundamental system* of functions) such that the general solution $y_h(x)$ of the associated homogeneous differential equation has the following form:

$$y_h(x) = C_1y_1(x) + C_2y_2(x) + \ldots + C_ny_n(x)$$

• The functions $y_1, \ldots, y_n$ form a fundamental system if and only if each of these functions y_k is a solution of the homogeneous differential equation and if there is at least one point $x_0 \in \mathbb{R}$ for which *Wronski's determinant*

$$W(x) = \begin{vmatrix} y_1(x) & y_2(x) & \ldots & y_n(x) \\ y_1'(x) & y_2'(x) & \ldots & y_n'(x) \\ \vdots & \vdots & \ddots & \vdots \\ y_1^{(n-1)}(x) & y_2^{(n-1)}(x) & \ldots & y_n^{(n-1)}(x) \end{vmatrix}$$

is different from zero. They can be obtained by solving the following n initial value problems ($k = 1, \ldots, n$):

$$a_n(x)y_k^{(n)} + \ldots + a_1(x)y_k' + a_0(x)y_k = 0,$$

$$y_k^{(i)}(x_0) = \begin{cases} 0, & i \neq k-1 \\ 1, & i = k-1 \end{cases} \qquad i = 0, 1, \ldots, n-1$$

• (*Lowering of the order*). If a special solution $\bar{y}$ of the homogeneous differential equation of the n-th order is known, then the substitution $y(x) = \bar{y}(x)\int z(x)\,dx$ leads from the linear (homogeneous or inhomogeneous) differential equation of the n-th order to an equation of the $(n-1)$-th order.

Special solution of the inhomogeneous differential equation

If $\{y_1, \ldots, y_n\}$ is a fundamental system, then using the approach

$$y_s(x) = C_1(x)y_1(x) + \ldots + C_n(x)y_n(x)$$ **variation of constants**

one gets a special solution of the inhomogeneous differential equation by determining the derivatives of the functions $C_1, \ldots, C_n$ as solutions of the linear system of equations

$$\begin{array}{ccccccccc} y_1C_1' & + & y_2C_2' & + & \ldots & + & y_nC_n' & = & 0 \\ y_1'C_1' & + & y_2'C_2' & + & \ldots & + & y_n'C_n' & = & 0 \\ \multicolumn{9}{c}{\cdots\cdots\cdots\cdots\cdots\cdots\cdots\cdots\cdots\cdots} \\ y_1^{(n-2)}C_1' & + & y_2^{(n-2)}C_2' & + & \ldots & + & y_n^{(n-2)}C_n' & = & 0 \\ y_1^{(n-1)}C_1' & + & y_2^{(n-1)}C_2' & + & \ldots & + & y_n^{(n-1)}C_n' & = & \dfrac{r(x)}{a_n(x)} \end{array}$$

Now the functions $C_1, \ldots, C_n$ can be calculated by integration.

Euler's differential equation

If in the general linear differential equation of n-th order the coefficient functions are of the form $a_k(x) = a_k x^k$, $a_k \in \mathbb{R}$, $k = 0, 1, \ldots, n$, then one obtains

$$a_n x^n y^{(n)} + \ldots + a_1 x y' + a_0 y = r(x)$$

• The substitution $x = \mathrm{e}^{\xi}$ (inverse transformation $\xi = \ln x$) leads to a linear differential equation with constant coefficients for the function $y(\xi)$. Its *characteristic equation* is

$$a_n\lambda(\lambda-1)\dots(\lambda-n+1)+\dots+a_2\lambda(\lambda-1)+a_1\lambda+a_0=0$$

Linear differential equations with constant coefficients

$$a_n y^{(n)}+\dots+a_1y'+a_0=r(x), \qquad a_0,\dots,a_n\in\mathbb{R}$$

• The general solution is the sum of the general solution of the associated homogeneous differential equation and any special solution of the inhomogeous differential equation:

$$y(x)=y_h(x)+y_s(x)$$

General solution of the homogeneous differential equation

The n functions y_k of the fundamental system are determined by setting $y=\mathrm{e}^{\lambda x}$ (the *trial solution*). Let the n values λ_k be the zeros of the characteristic polynomial, i. e. solutions of the *characteristic equation*

$$a_n\lambda^n+\dots+a_1\lambda+a_0=0$$

The n functions of the fundamental system associated with the n zeros λ_k of the characteristic equation can be determined according to the following table:

kind of the zero	order of the zero	functions of the fundamental system
λ_k real	simple	$\mathrm{e}^{\lambda_k x}$
	p-fold	$\mathrm{e}^{\lambda_k x},\ x\mathrm{e}^{\lambda_k x},\dots,\ x^{p-1}\mathrm{e}^{\lambda_k x}$
$\lambda_k=a\pm bi$ conjugate complex	simple	$\mathrm{e}^{ax}\sin bx,\ \mathrm{e}^{ax}\cos bx$
	p-fold	$\mathrm{e}^{ax}\sin bx,\ x\mathrm{e}^{ax}\sin bx,\ \dots,\ x^{p-1}\mathrm{e}^{ax}\sin bx,$ $\mathrm{e}^{ax}\cos bx,\ x\mathrm{e}^{ax}\cos bx,\ \dots,\ x^{p-1}\mathrm{e}^{ax}\cos bx$

The general solution y_h of the homogeneous differential equation is

$$y_h(x)=C_1y_1(x)+C_2y_2(x)+\dots+C_ny_n(x)$$

Special solution of the inhomogeneous differential equation

If the inhomogeneity r has a simple structure, then y_s can be determined by means of an approach described in the following table:

$r(x)$	trial solution $y_s(x)$	trial solution in the case of *resonance*
$A_m x^m + \ldots + A_1 x + A_0$	$b_m x^m + \ldots + b_1 x + b_0$	If a summand of the trial solution solves the homogeneous differential equation, then the trial solution is multiplied by x so many times until no summand is a solution of the homogeneous differential equation.
$Ae^{\alpha x}$	$ae^{\alpha x}$	
$A \sin \omega x$ $B \cos \omega x$ $A \sin \omega x + B \cos \omega x$	$a \sin \omega x + b \cos \omega x$	
combination of these functions	corresponding combination of different trial solutions	The above rule can be applied only to that part of the set-up which contains the case of resonance.

First-order linear systems with constant coefficients

$$\begin{array}{rcccccccc} y_1' & = & a_{11}y_1 & + & \ldots & + & a_{1n}y_n & + & r_1(x) \\ \multicolumn{9}{c}{\dotfill} \\ y_n' & = & a_{n1}y_1 & + & \ldots & + & a_{nn}y_n & + & r_n(x) \end{array} \qquad a_{ij} \in \mathbb{R}$$

Vector notation

$\boldsymbol{y}' = \boldsymbol{A}\boldsymbol{y} + \boldsymbol{r}$ with

$$\boldsymbol{y} = \begin{pmatrix} y_1 \\ \vdots \\ y_n \end{pmatrix}, \quad \boldsymbol{y}' = \begin{pmatrix} y_1' \\ \vdots \\ y_n' \end{pmatrix}, \quad \boldsymbol{r} = \begin{pmatrix} r_1(x) \\ \vdots \\ r_n(x) \end{pmatrix}, \qquad \boldsymbol{A} = \begin{pmatrix} a_{11} & \ldots & a_{1n} \\ \vdots & \ddots & \vdots \\ a_{n1} & \ldots & a_{nn} \end{pmatrix}$$

- The general solution has the form $\boldsymbol{y}(x) = \boldsymbol{y}_h(x) + \boldsymbol{y}_s(x)$, where $\boldsymbol{y}_h$ is the general solution of the homogeneous system $\boldsymbol{y}' = \boldsymbol{A}\boldsymbol{y}$ and $\boldsymbol{y}_s$ is a special solution of the inhomogeneous system $\boldsymbol{y}' = \boldsymbol{A}\boldsymbol{y} + \boldsymbol{r}$.

General solution of the homogeneous system

Case 1 $\boldsymbol{A}$ is diagonalizable and has only real eigenvalues λ_k, $k = 1, \ldots, n$ (multiple eigenvalues are counted multiply); let $\boldsymbol{v}_k$ be the corresponding real eigenvectors. Then the general solution of the homogeneous system is

$$\boxed{\boldsymbol{y}_h(x) = C_1 e^{\lambda_1 x}\boldsymbol{v}_1 + \ldots + C_n e^{\lambda_n x}\boldsymbol{v}_n}$$

Case 2 $\boldsymbol{A}$ is diagonalizable and has conjugate complex eigenvalues $\lambda_k = \alpha + \beta\mathrm{i}$, $\lambda_{k+1} = \alpha - \beta\mathrm{i}$ with corresponding eigenvectors $\boldsymbol{v}_k = \boldsymbol{a} + \boldsymbol{b}\mathrm{i}$, $\boldsymbol{v}_{k+1} = \boldsymbol{a} - \boldsymbol{b}\mathrm{i}$. Then in the general solution $\boldsymbol{y}_h$ the terms with indices k, $k+1$ are to be replaced as follows:

$$\boxed{\boldsymbol{y}_h(x) = \ldots + C_k e^{\alpha x}(\boldsymbol{a}\cos\beta x - \boldsymbol{b}\sin\beta x) + C_{k+1}e^{\alpha x}(\boldsymbol{a}\sin\beta x + \boldsymbol{b}\cos\beta x) + \ldots}$$

Case 3 $\boldsymbol{A}$ fails to be diagonalizable; let $\boldsymbol{V}$ be the matrix describing the similarity transformation from the matrix $\boldsymbol{A}$ to the Jordan normal form. Paying attention to the dimensions n_k of the Jordan blocks $\boldsymbol{J}(\lambda_k, n_k)$, $k = 1, \ldots, s$, the matrix $\boldsymbol{V}$ can be written column-wise:

$$\boldsymbol{V} = (\boldsymbol{v}_{11}, \ldots, \boldsymbol{v}_{1n_1}, \ldots, \boldsymbol{v}_{k1}, \ldots, \boldsymbol{v}_{kn_k}, \ldots, \boldsymbol{v}_{s1}, \ldots, \boldsymbol{v}_{sn_s}).$$

Then the general solution of the homogeneous system is

$$\boxed{\begin{aligned} \boldsymbol{y}_h(x) = \ldots &+ C_{k1}e^{\lambda_k x}\boldsymbol{v}_{k1} + C_{k2}e^{\lambda_k x}\left[\frac{x}{1!}\boldsymbol{v}_{k1} + \boldsymbol{v}_{k2}\right] + \ldots \\ &+ C_{kn_k}e^{\lambda_k x}\left[\frac{x^{n_k-1}}{(n_k-1)!}\boldsymbol{v}_{k1} + \ldots + \frac{x}{1!}\boldsymbol{v}_{k,n_k-1} + \boldsymbol{v}_{kn_k}\right] + \ldots \end{aligned}}$$

Calculation of the *eigenvectors* $\boldsymbol{v}_{k1}$: $\quad (\boldsymbol{A} - \lambda_k\boldsymbol{E})\boldsymbol{v}_{k1} = \boldsymbol{0}$

Calculation of the *principal vectors* $\boldsymbol{v}_{kj}$: $(\boldsymbol{A} - \lambda_k\boldsymbol{E})\boldsymbol{v}_{kj} = \boldsymbol{v}_{k,j-1}$, where $j = 2, \ldots, n_k$

If complex eigenvalues occur, then one has to act as in Case 2.

Special solution of the inhomogeneous system

A special solution can be obtained by variation of constants or an trial solution (▶ table p. 93), where in **all** components **all** parts of $r(x)$ are to be considered. Under resonance, the original ansatz has to be enlarged with ansatz functions multiplied by x.

Difference Equations

First-order linear difference equations

$$\boxed{\Delta y = a(n)y + b(n)} \qquad (*)$$

A function $y = f(n)$, $D_f \subset \mathbb{N}_0$, is called a *solution* of the difference equation $(*)$ if $\Delta f(n) = a(n)f(n) + b(n) \quad \forall n \in D_f$, where $\Delta y = y(n+1) - y(n) = f(n+1) - f(n)$.

- If $\{a(n)\}$ and $\{b(n)\}$ are sequences of real numbers, then $(*)$ has the solution

$$\boxed{y = f(n) = y_0 \cdot \prod_{k=0}^{n-1}[a(k)+1] + \sum_{k=0}^{n-2} b(k) \cdot \prod_{l=k+1}^{n-1}[a(l)+1] + b(n-1)}$$

Here $f(0) = y_0 \in \mathbb{R}$ can be chosen arbitrarily, while

$$\prod_{k=0}^{n-1}[a(k)+1] := \begin{cases} [a(0)+1] \cdot \ldots \cdot [a(n-1)+1] & \text{if } n = 1, 2, \ldots \\ 1 & \text{if } n = 0 \end{cases}$$

$$\prod_{l=k+1}^{n-1}[a(l)+1] := \begin{cases} [a(k+1)+1] \cdot \ldots \cdot [a(n-1)+1] & \text{if } n = k+2, \ldots \\ 1 & \text{if } n = k+1 \end{cases}$$

In the special case $a(n) \equiv a = \text{const}$, $b(n) \equiv b = \text{const}$ the solution of the difference equation $(*)$ has the form

$$\boxed{y = f(n) = \begin{cases} y_0 \cdot \displaystyle\prod_{k=0}^{n-1}[a(k)+1] & \text{if } \; b(n) \equiv b = 0 \\ y_0(a+1)^n + \displaystyle\sum_{k=0}^{n-1} b(k)(a+1)^{n-1-k} & \text{if } \; a(n) \equiv a \\ y_0(a+1)^n & \text{if } \; a(n) \equiv a, \, b(n) \equiv 0 \\ y_0(a+1)^n + b \cdot \dfrac{(a+1)^n - 1}{a} & \text{if } \; a(n) \equiv a \neq 0, \; b(n) \equiv b \\ y_0 + b \cdot n & \text{if } \; a(n) \equiv 0, \, b(n) \equiv b \end{cases}}$$

Economic models

$y(n)$	–	national income,	$n = 0, 1, 2, \ldots$
$c(n)$	–	consumption,	$n = 0, 1, 2, \ldots$
$s(n)$	–	sum of savings,	$n = 0, 1, 2, \ldots$
$i(n)$	–	investments,	$n = 0, 1, 2, \ldots$

Growth of national income according to Boulding

Model assumptions:

$$y(n) = c(n) + i(n), \qquad c(n) = \alpha + \beta y(n), \qquad \Delta y(n) = \gamma i(n)$$

α – part of consumption independent of income, $\alpha \geq 0$

β – factor of proportionality for income dependent consumption, $0 < \beta < 1$

γ – multiple of investments by which the national income changes, $\gamma > 0$

$$\Delta y(n) = \gamma(1-\beta)y(n) - \alpha\gamma, \quad n = 0, 1, 2, \ldots$$ **Boulding's model**

Solution: $$y = f(n) = \frac{\alpha}{1-\beta} + \left(y_0 - \frac{\alpha}{1-\beta}\right)(1 + \gamma(1-\beta))^n$$

- Under the assumption $y(0) = y_0 > c(0)$ the function $y = f(n)$ is strictly increasing.

Growth of national income according to Harrod

Model assumptions:

$$s(n) = \alpha y(n), \qquad i(n) = \beta \Delta y(n), \qquad i(n) = s(n)$$

$\alpha y(n)$ – saved part of national income, $0 < \alpha < 1$

β – factor of proportionality between investments and increase of national income, $\beta > 0$, $\beta \neq \alpha$

Harrod's model

$$\Delta y(n) = \frac{\alpha}{\beta} y(n), \; y(0) = y_0, \quad n = 1, 2, \ldots$$

This model has the solution: $$y = f(n) = y_0 \cdot \left(\frac{\alpha}{\beta}\right)^n$$

Ezekid's cobweb model

Assumptions:	
$d(n) = \alpha - \beta p(n), \quad d(n) = n$	$d(n)$ – demand,
$q(n+1) = \gamma + \delta p(n)$	$p(n)$ – price
$\alpha > 0,\ \beta > 0,\ \gamma > 0,\ \delta > 0$	$q(n)$ – supply

It is assumed that supply and demand are in equilibrium.

$$\Delta p(n) = \frac{\alpha - \gamma}{\beta} - \left(1 + \frac{\delta}{\beta}\right) p(n), \ p(0) = p_0, \qquad n = 1, 2, \ldots$$ **cobweb model**

Solution: $$y = p(n) = \frac{\alpha - \gamma}{\beta + \delta} + \left(p_0 - \frac{\alpha - \gamma}{\beta + \delta}\right)\left(-\frac{\delta}{\beta}\right)^n$$

- The quantity $p(n)$ oscillates around the constant value $p^* = \dfrac{\alpha - \gamma}{\beta + \delta}$. For $\delta \geq \beta$ the solution diverges, for $\delta < \beta$ the solution converges to the *equilibrium price* p^*.

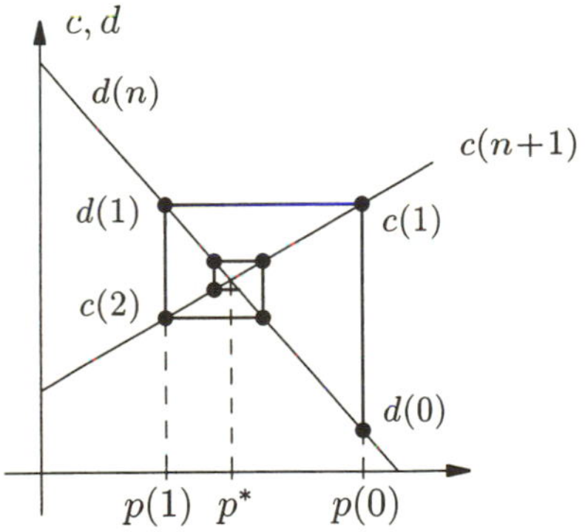

Convergence

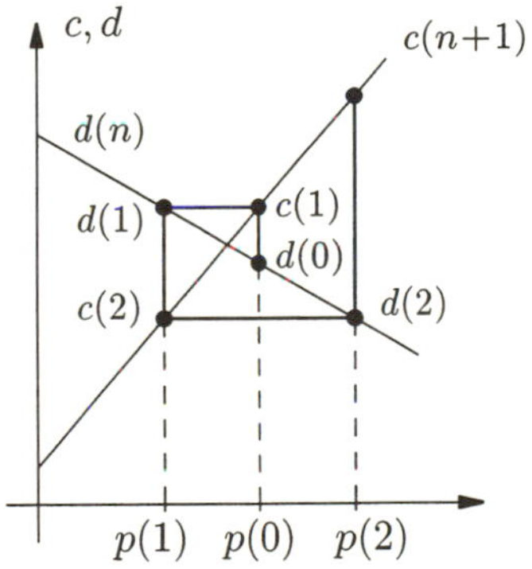

Divergence

Linear second-order difference equations

An equation of the form

$$\Delta^2 y + a\Delta y + by = c(n), \qquad a, b, c \in \mathbb{R} \qquad (*)$$

is called a *linear second-order difference equation with constant coefficients*. The term $\Delta^2 f(n) := f(n+2) - 2f(n+1) + f(n)$ is the *second-order difference*.

• If $c(n) = 0 \ \forall n = 0, 1, 2, \ldots$, then the equation is called *homogeneous*, otherwise it is called *inhomogeneous*.

• A function f with $D_f \subset \{0, 1, 2, \ldots\}$ is said to be a solution of the equation $(*)$ if $\Delta^2 f(n) + a\Delta f(n) + bf(n) = c(n) \ \forall n \in D_f$.

• The general solution of the linear inhomogeneous difference equation $(*)$ is the sum of the general solution of the associated homogeneous difference equation $\Delta^2 y + a\Delta y + by = 0$ and any special solution of $(*)$.

General solution of the second-order homogeneous difference equation

Consider the *characteristic equation* $\boxed{\lambda^2 + a\lambda + b = 0.}$

Its solution is determined from the formula $\lambda_{1,2} = -\frac{a}{2} \pm \frac{1}{2}\sqrt{a^2 - 4b}$. Depending on the discriminant $D = a^2 - 4b$ it can have two real, one real double or two conjugate complex solutions. To represent the general solution of the homogeneous difference equation associated with $(*)$ one has to distinguish between three cases, where C_1, C_2 are arbitrary real constants.

Case 1 $D > 0$: $\quad \lambda_1 = \frac{1}{2}\left(-a + \sqrt{D}\right), \quad \lambda_2 = \frac{1}{2}\left(-a - \sqrt{D}\right)$

Solution: $$\boxed{y = f(n) = C_1(1 + \lambda_1)^n + C_2(1 + \lambda_2)^n}$$

Case 2 $D = 0$: $\quad \lambda_1 = \lambda_2 =: \lambda = -\frac{a}{2}$

Solution: $$\boxed{y = f(n) = C_1(1 + \lambda)^n + C_2 n(1 + \lambda)^n}$$

Case 3 $D < 0$: $\quad \alpha := -\frac{a}{2}, \quad \beta := \frac{1}{2}\sqrt{-D}$

Solution:

$$\boxed{y = f(n) = C_1\left[(1+\alpha)^2 + \beta^2\right]^{\frac{n}{2}} \cos\varphi n + C_2\left[(1+\alpha)^2 + \beta^2\right]^{\frac{n}{2}} \sin\varphi n}$$

where $\tan\varphi = \dfrac{\beta}{1+\alpha} \quad (\alpha \neq -1)$ and $\varphi = \dfrac{\pi}{2} \quad (\alpha = -1)$.

General solution of the second-order inhomogeneous difference equation

The general solution of the inhomogeneous equation is the sum of the general solution of the homogeneous equation and a special solution of the inhomogeneous equation $(*)$. The latter can be obtained e.g. by means of the *ansatz method*, where the corresponding ansatz functions depend on the concrete structure of the right-hand side $c(n)$. The unknown coefficients involved are determined by *comparison of coefficients.*

right-hand side	trial solution
$c(n) = a_k n^k + \ldots + a_1 n + a_0$	$C(n) = A_k n^k + \ldots + A_1 n + A_0$
$c(n) = a \cos \omega n + b \sin \omega n$ ($\alpha \neq 0$ or $\beta \neq \omega$; see Case 3 on p. 98)	$C(n) = A \cos \omega n + B \sin \omega n$

Economic models

$y(n)$ – national income	$c(n)$ – consumption
$i(n)$ – private investments	H – public expenditure

Model assumptions $(n = 0, 1, 2, \ldots)$

$y(n)=c(n)+i(n)+H$	the national income splits up into consumption, private investments and public expenditure
$c(n)=\alpha_1 y(n-1)$	$0 < \alpha_1 < 1$; the consumption is proportional (*multiplicator* α_1) to the national income of the previous period
$i(n)=\alpha_2[c(n)-c(n-1)]$	$\alpha_2 > 0$; the private investments are proportional (*accelerator* α_2) to the increase of the consumption

Samuelson's multiplicator-accelerator model

$$\Delta^2 y + (2 - \alpha_1 - \alpha_1\alpha_2)\Delta y + (1 - \alpha_1)y = H$$

Solution for $\alpha_1 \leq \alpha_2 < 1$:

$$y = f(n) = \frac{H}{1-\alpha_1} + (\alpha_1\alpha_2)^{\frac{n}{2}}(C_1 \cos \varphi n + C_2 \sin \varphi n)$$

- The solution f oscillates with decreasing amplitude around the limit $\frac{H}{1-\alpha_1}$.

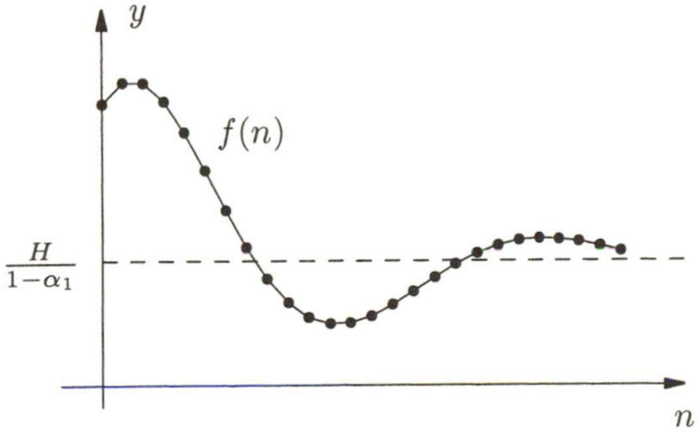

Linear difference equations of n-th order with constant coefficients

$$\boxed{y_{k+n} + a_{n-1}y_{k+n-1} + \ldots + a_1 y_{k+1} + a_0 y_k = c(k)} \qquad (k \in \mathbb{N}) \qquad (1)$$

- A linear difference equation of the form (1) with constant coefficients $a_i \in \mathbb{R}$, $i = 0, 1, \ldots, n-1$, is of *n-th order* if $a_0 \neq 0$.
- The difference equation of n-th order (1) has exactly one solution $y_k = f(k)$ if the initial values for n successive values k are given.
- If $f_1(k), f_2(k), \ldots, f_n(k)$ are arbitrary solutions of the homogeneous linear difference equation

$$\boxed{y_{k+n} + a_{n-1}y_{k+n-1} + \ldots + a_1 y_{k+1} + a_0 y_k = 0,} \qquad (2)$$

then the linear combination

$$\boxed{f(k) = \gamma_1 f_1(k) + \gamma_2 f_2(k) + \ldots + \gamma_n f_n(k)} \qquad (3)$$

with (arbitrary) constants $\gamma_i \in \mathbb{R}$, $i = 1, \ldots, n$, is also a solution of the homogeneous difference equation (2).

- If the n solutions $f_1(k), f_2(k), \ldots, f_n(k)$ of (2) form a *fundamental system*, i. e. $\begin{vmatrix} f_1(0) & f_2(0) & \ldots & f_n(0) \\ \ldots & \ldots & \ldots & \ldots \\ f_1(n-1) & f_2(n-1) & \ldots & f_n(n-1) \end{vmatrix} \neq 0$, then (3) is the general solution of the homogeneous difference equation (2).
- If $y_{k,s}$ is a special solution of the inhomogeneous linear difference equation (1) and $y_{k,h}$ is the general solution of the associated homogeneous linear difference equation (2), then for the general solution of the inhomogeneous linear difference equation (1) the representation $\boxed{y_k = y_{k,h} + y_{k,s}}$ holds.

General solution of the n-th order homogeneous difference equation

Solve the *characteristic equation* $\boxed{\lambda^n + a_{n-1}\lambda^{n-1} + \ldots + a_1\lambda + a_0 = 0\,.}$

Let its solutions be $\lambda_1, \ldots, \lambda_n$. Then the fundamental system consists of n linearly independent solutions $f_1(k), \ldots, f_n(k)$, whose structure depends on the kind of the solutions of the characteristic equation (analogously to ▶ second-order difference equations, p. 97).

Special solution of the n-th order inhomogeneous difference equation

To find a special solution of the inhomogeneous difference equation (1), in many cases the *ansatz method* is successful, where the ansatz function is chosen in such a way that it corresponds to the right-hand side with respect to structure (▶ second-order difference equation, p. 97). The unknown coefficients contained are determined by substituting the ansatz function into (1) and making a *comparison of coefficients.*

Differential Calculus for Functions of Several Variables

Basic notions

Functions in $\mathbb{R}^n$

A one-to-one mapping assigning to any vector $\boldsymbol{x} = (x_1, x_2, \ldots, x_n)^\top \in D_f \subset \mathbb{R}^n$ a real number $f(\boldsymbol{x}) = f(x_1, x_2, \ldots, x_n)$ is called a *real function of several (real) variables*; notation: $f : D_f \to \mathbb{R}$, $D_f \subset \mathbb{R}^n$.

$D_f \;=\; \{\boldsymbol{x} \in \mathbb{R}^n \mid \exists\, y \in \mathbb{R} : y = f(\boldsymbol{x})\}$	–	domain
$W_f \;=\; \{y \in \mathbb{R} \mid \exists\, \boldsymbol{x} \in D_f : y = f(\boldsymbol{x})\}$	–	range

Graphic representation

Functions $y = f(x_1, x_2)$ of two independent variables x_1, x_2 can be visualized in a three-dimensional representation by a (x_1, x_2, y)-system of co-ordinates.

The set of points (x_1, x_2, y) forms a *surface* provided that the function f is continuous. The set of points (x_1, x_2) such that $f(x_1, x_2) = C =$ const is called a *height line* or *level line* of the function f to the height (level) C. These lines are located in the x_1, x_2-plane.

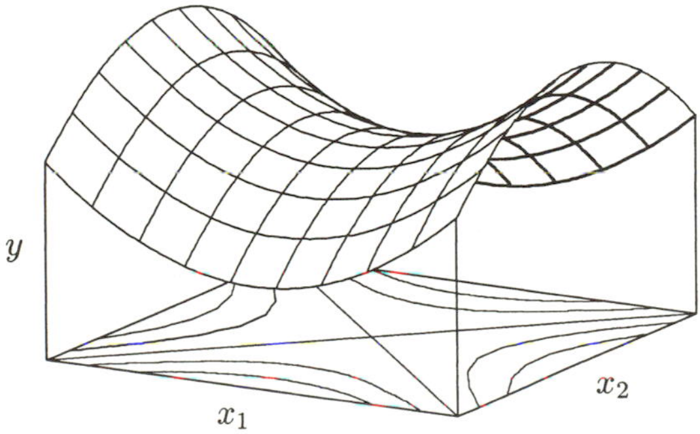

Point sets of the space $\mathbb{R}^n$

Let $\boldsymbol{x}$ and $\boldsymbol{y}$ be points of the space $\mathbb{R}^n$ having the co-ordinates $(x_1, \ldots, x_n)$ and $(y_1, \ldots, y_n)$, respectively. These points can be identified with the fixed vectors $\boldsymbol{x} = (x_1, \ldots, x_n)^\top$ and $\boldsymbol{y} = (y_1, \ldots, y_n)^\top$ directed to them.

$\|\boldsymbol{x}\|_2 = \sqrt{\sum\limits_{i=1}^{n} x_i^2}$	–	Euclidian norm of the vector $\boldsymbol{x}$, also denoted by $|x|$ ▶ vectors, p. 113
$\|\boldsymbol{x}\|_1 = \sum\limits_{i=1}^{n} |x_i|$	–	sum norm of the vector $\boldsymbol{x}$
$\|\boldsymbol{x}\|_\infty = \max\limits_{i=1,\ldots,n} |x_i|$	–	maximum norm of the vector $\boldsymbol{x}$
$\|\boldsymbol{x} - \boldsymbol{y}\|$	–	distance of the points $\boldsymbol{x}, \boldsymbol{y} \in \mathbb{R}^n$
$U_\varepsilon(\boldsymbol{x}) = \{\boldsymbol{y} \in \mathbb{R}^n \mid \|\boldsymbol{y} - \boldsymbol{x}\| < \varepsilon\}$	–	ε-neighbourhood of the point $\boldsymbol{x}$, $\varepsilon > 0$

• For the norms introduced above the inequalities $\|\boldsymbol{x}\|_\infty \le \|\boldsymbol{x}\|_2 \le \|\boldsymbol{x}\|_1$ are valid; $\|\boldsymbol{x}\|$ denotes an arbitrary norm, usually the Euclidian norm $\|\boldsymbol{x}\|_2$.

• A point $\boldsymbol{x}$ is called an *interior point* of the set $M \subset \mathbb{R}^n$ if there exists a neighbourhood $U_\varepsilon(\boldsymbol{x})$ contained in M. The set of all interior points of M is called the *interior* of M and denoted by int M. A point $\boldsymbol{x}$ is called an *accumulation point* of the set M if every neighbourhood $U_\varepsilon(\boldsymbol{x})$ contains points of M different from $\boldsymbol{x}$.

• A set M is said to be *open* if int $M = M$, it is called *closed* if it contains any of its accumulation points.

• A set $M \subset \mathbb{R}^n$ is called *bounded* if there exists a number C such that $\|\boldsymbol{x}\| \le C$ for all $\boldsymbol{x} \in M$.

Limit and continuity

Sequences of points

A *point sequence* $\{\boldsymbol{x}_k\} \subset \mathbb{R}^n$ is a mapping from $\mathbb{N}$ to $\mathbb{R}^n$. The components of the elements $\boldsymbol{x}_k$ of the sequence are denoted by $x_i^{(k)}$, $i = 1, \ldots, n$.

$\boldsymbol{x} = \lim\limits_{k\to\infty} \boldsymbol{x}_k \iff \lim\limits_{k\to\infty} \|\boldsymbol{x}_k - \boldsymbol{x}\| = 0$	– convergence of the point sequence $\{\boldsymbol{x}_k\}$ to the limit point $\boldsymbol{x}$

• A point sequence $\{\boldsymbol{x}_k\}$ converges to the limit point $\boldsymbol{x}$ if and only if any sequence $\{x_i^{(k)}\}$, $i = 1, \ldots, n$, converges to the i-th component x_i of $\boldsymbol{x}$.

Continuity

A number $a \in \mathbb{R}$ is called the *limit* of the function f at the point $\boldsymbol{x}_0$ if for any point sequence $\{\boldsymbol{x}_k\}$ converging to $\boldsymbol{x}_0$ such that $\boldsymbol{x}_k \ne \boldsymbol{x}_0$ and $\boldsymbol{x}_k \in D_f$ the relation $\lim\limits_{k\to\infty} f(\boldsymbol{x}_k) = a$ is true. Notation: $\lim\limits_{\boldsymbol{x}\to\boldsymbol{x}_0} f(\boldsymbol{x}) = a$.

• A function f is called *continuous at the point* $\boldsymbol{x}_0 \in D_f$ if it has a limit at $\boldsymbol{x}_0$ (i. e. if for any point sequence converging to $\boldsymbol{x}_0$ the sequence of corresponding function values converges to one and the same value) and this value is equal to the function value at $\boldsymbol{x}_0$:

$$\lim_{\boldsymbol{x}\to\boldsymbol{x}_0} f(\boldsymbol{x}) = f(\boldsymbol{x}_0) \iff \lim_{k\to\infty} f(\boldsymbol{x}_k) = f(\boldsymbol{x}_0) \;\forall\, \{\boldsymbol{x}_k\} \text{ with } \boldsymbol{x}_k \to \boldsymbol{x}_0$$

• Equivalent formulation: f is *continuous at the point* $\boldsymbol{x}_0$ if, for any number $\varepsilon > 0$, there exists a number $\delta > 0$ such that $|f(\boldsymbol{x}) - f(\boldsymbol{x}_0)| < \varepsilon$ provided that $\|\boldsymbol{x} - \boldsymbol{x}_0\| < \delta$.

• If a function f is continuous for all $\boldsymbol{x} \in D_f$, then it is called *continuous* on D_f.

• If the functions f and g are continuous on their domains D_f and D_g, respectively, then the functions $f \pm g$, $f \cdot g$, and $\frac{f}{g}$ are continuous on $D_f \cap D_g$, the latter being continuous only for values $\boldsymbol{x}$ with $g(\boldsymbol{x}) \neq 0$.

Homogeneous functions

$$f(\lambda x_1, \ldots, \lambda x_n) = \lambda^\alpha \cdot f(x_1, \ldots, x_n) \quad \forall\, \lambda \geq 0$$

– f homogeneous of degree $\alpha \geq 0$

$$f(x_1, \ldots, \lambda x_i, \ldots, x_n) = \lambda^{\alpha_i} f(x_1, \ldots, x_n) \;\forall\, \lambda \geq 0$$

– f partially homogeneous of degree $\alpha_i \geq 0$

$\alpha = 1$: linearly homogeneous
$\alpha > 1$: superlinearly homogeneous
$\alpha < 1$: sublinearly homogeneous

• For linearly homogeneous functions a proportional increase of variables causes a proportional increase of the function value. This is the reason why these functions are also called CES (= constant elasticity of substitution) functions.

Differentiation of functions of several variables

Notion of differentiability

The function $f : D_f \to \mathbb{R}$, $D_f \subset \mathbb{R}^n$, is called *(totally) differentiable* at the point $\boldsymbol{x}_0$ if there exists a vector $\boldsymbol{g}(\boldsymbol{x}_0)$ such that

$$\lim_{\Delta \boldsymbol{x} \to \boldsymbol{0}} \frac{f(\boldsymbol{x}_0 + \Delta \boldsymbol{x}) - f(\boldsymbol{x}_0) - \boldsymbol{g}(\boldsymbol{x}_0)^\top \Delta \boldsymbol{x}}{\|\Delta \boldsymbol{x}\|} = 0$$

• If such a vector $\boldsymbol{g}(\boldsymbol{x}_0)$ exists, then it is called the *gradient* and denoted by $\nabla f(\boldsymbol{x}_0)$ or grad $f(\boldsymbol{x}_0)$. The function f is said to be *differentiable* on D_f if it is differentiable at all points $\boldsymbol{x} \in D_f$.

Partial derivatives

If for $f : D_f \to \mathbb{R}$, $D_f \subset \mathbb{R}^n$, at the point $\boldsymbol{x}_0 = (x_1^0, \ldots, x_n^0)^\top$ there exists the limit

$$\lim_{\Delta x_i \to 0} \frac{f(x_1^0, \ldots, x_{i-1}^0, x_i^0 + \Delta x_i, x_{i+1}^0, \ldots, x_n^0) - f(x_1^0, \ldots, x_n^0)}{\Delta x_i},$$

then it is called the *(first-order) partial derivative* of the function f with respect to the variable x_i at the point $\boldsymbol{x}_0$ and is denoted by $\left.\frac{\partial f}{\partial x_i}\right|_{\boldsymbol{x}=\boldsymbol{x}_0}$, $\frac{\partial y}{\partial x_i}$, $f_{x_i}(\boldsymbol{x}_0)$, or $\partial_{x_i} f$.

• If the function f has partial derivatives with respect to all variables at every point $\boldsymbol{x} \in D_f$, then f is called *partially differentiable.* In the case if all partial derivatives are continuous functions, f is said to be *continuously partially differentiable.*

• When calculating the partial derivatives, all variables to which we do not differentiate are considered as constant. Then the corresponding rules of differentiation for functions of one variable (especially the rules for the differentiation of a constant summand and a constant factor, ▶ p. 62, 63) are to be applied.

Gradient

If the function $f : D_f \to \mathbb{R}$, $D_f \subset \mathbb{R}^n$, is continuously partially differentiable on D_f, then it is also totally differentiable there, where the gradient is the column vector formed from the partial derivatives:

$\nabla f(\boldsymbol{x}) = \left(\frac{\partial f(\boldsymbol{x})}{\partial x_1}, \ldots, \frac{\partial f(\boldsymbol{x})}{\partial x_n}\right)^\top$	– gradient of the function f at the point $\boldsymbol{x}$ (also denoted by $\operatorname{grad} f(\boldsymbol{x})$)

• If the function f is totally differentiable, then for the *directional derivative*

$$f'(\boldsymbol{x};\boldsymbol{r}) = \lim_{t \downarrow 0} \frac{f(\boldsymbol{x}+t\boldsymbol{r}) - f(\boldsymbol{x})}{t}$$

(which exists in this case for arbitrary directions $\boldsymbol{r} \in \mathbb{R}^n$), the representation $f'(\boldsymbol{x};\boldsymbol{r}) = \nabla f(\boldsymbol{x})^\top \boldsymbol{r}$ holds, and $\nabla f(\boldsymbol{x})$ is the direction of steepest ascent of f at the point $\boldsymbol{x}$.

• The gradient $\nabla f(\boldsymbol{x}_0)$ is orthogonal to the level line of f to the level $f(\boldsymbol{x}_0)$, so that (for $n = 2$) the tangent to the level line or (for $n > 2$) the tangential (hyper)plane to the set $\{\boldsymbol{x} \mid f(\boldsymbol{x}) = f(\boldsymbol{x}_0)\}$ at the point $\boldsymbol{x}_0$ has the equation $\nabla f(\boldsymbol{x}_0)^\top(\boldsymbol{x} - \boldsymbol{x}_0) = 0$. Directional derivatives in tangential direction to a level line (for $n = 2$) have the value zero, so that in linear approximation the function value is constant in these directions.

Chain rule

Let the functions $u_k = g_k(x_1, \ldots, x_n)$, $k = 1, \ldots, m$ of n variables as well as the functions f of m variables be totally differentiable at the points $\boldsymbol{x} = (x_1, \ldots, x_n)^\top$ and $\boldsymbol{u} = (u_1, \ldots, u_m)^\top$, respectively. Then the composite function $F(x_1, \ldots, x_n) = f(g_1(x_1, \ldots, x_n), \ldots, g_m(x_1, \ldots, x_n))$ is totally differentiable at the point $\boldsymbol{x}$, where

$$\nabla F(\boldsymbol{x}) = \boldsymbol{G}'(\boldsymbol{x})^\top \nabla f(\boldsymbol{u}) \quad \Longleftrightarrow$$

$$\begin{pmatrix} F_{x_1}(\boldsymbol{x}) \\ \vdots \\ F_{x_n}(\boldsymbol{x}) \end{pmatrix} = \begin{pmatrix} \partial_{x_1} g_1(\boldsymbol{x}) & \ldots & \partial_{x_1} g_m(\boldsymbol{x}) \\ \ldots & \ldots & \ldots \\ \partial_{x_n} g_1(\boldsymbol{x}) & \ldots & \partial_{x_n} g_m(\boldsymbol{x}) \end{pmatrix} \begin{pmatrix} f_{u_1}(\boldsymbol{u}) \\ \vdots \\ f_{u_m}(\boldsymbol{u}) \end{pmatrix}$$

$$\frac{\partial F(\boldsymbol{x})}{\partial x_i} = \sum_{k=1}^{m} \frac{\partial f}{\partial u_k}(g(\boldsymbol{x})) \cdot \frac{\partial g_k}{\partial x_i}(\boldsymbol{x})$$ – componentwise notation

Special case $m = n = 2$; function $f(u, v)$ with $u = u(x, y)$, $v = v(x, y)$:

$$\frac{\partial f}{\partial x} = \frac{\partial f}{\partial u} \cdot \frac{\partial u}{\partial x} + \frac{\partial f}{\partial v} \cdot \frac{\partial v}{\partial x} \qquad \frac{\partial f}{\partial y} = \frac{\partial f}{\partial u} \cdot \frac{\partial u}{\partial y} + \frac{\partial f}{\partial v} \cdot \frac{\partial v}{\partial y}$$

• The matrix $\boldsymbol{G}'(\boldsymbol{x})$ is called the *functional matrix* or *Jacobian matrix* of the system of functions $\{g_1, \ldots, g_m\}$.

Higher partial derivatives

The partial derivatives are again functions and thus have (under suitable assumptions) partial derivatives.

$$\frac{\partial^2 f(\boldsymbol{x})}{\partial x_i \partial x_j} = f_{x_i x_j}(\boldsymbol{x}) = \frac{\partial}{\partial x_j}\left(\frac{\partial f(\boldsymbol{x})}{\partial x_i}\right)$$ – second-order partial derivatives

$$\frac{\partial^3 f(\boldsymbol{x})}{\partial x_i \partial x_j \partial x_k} = f_{x_i x_j x_k}(\boldsymbol{x}) = \frac{\partial}{\partial x_k}\left(\frac{\partial^2 f(\boldsymbol{x})}{\partial x_i \partial x_j}\right)$$ – third-order partial derivatives

Schwarz's theorem (on commutativity of differentiation). If the partial derivatives $f_{x_i x_j}$ and $f_{x_j x_i}$ are continuous in a neighbourhood of the point $\boldsymbol{x}$, then the following relations hold: $f_{x_i x_j}(\boldsymbol{x}) = f_{x_j x_i}(\boldsymbol{x})$.

• Generalization: If the partial derivatives of k-th order exist and are continuous, then the order of differentiation does not play any role when calculating the partial derivatives.

Hessian matrix

$$H_f(\boldsymbol{x}) = \begin{pmatrix} f_{x_1 x_1}(\boldsymbol{x}) & f_{x_1 x_2}(\boldsymbol{x}) & \ldots & f_{x_1 x_n}(\boldsymbol{x}) \\ f_{x_2 x_1}(\boldsymbol{x}) & f_{x_2 x_2}(\boldsymbol{x}) & \ldots & f_{x_2 x_n}(\boldsymbol{x}) \\ \ldots & \ldots & \ldots & \ldots \\ f_{x_n x_1}(\boldsymbol{x}) & f_{x_n x_2}(\boldsymbol{x}) & \ldots & f_{x_n x_n}(\boldsymbol{x}) \end{pmatrix}$$ – Hessian matrix of the twice partially differentiable function f at the point $\boldsymbol{x}$

• Under the assumptions of Schwarz's theorem the Hessian matrix is symmetric.

Total differential

If the function $f : D_f \to \mathbb{R}$, $D_f \subset \mathbb{R}^n$, is totally differentiable at the point $\boldsymbol{x}_0$ (▶ p. 103), then the following relation holds:

$$\Delta f(\boldsymbol{x}_0) = f(\boldsymbol{x}_0 + \Delta\boldsymbol{x}) - f(\boldsymbol{x}_0) = \nabla f(\boldsymbol{x}_0)^\top \Delta\boldsymbol{x} + \mathrm{o}(\|\Delta\boldsymbol{x}\|)$$

Here $\mathrm{o}(\cdot)$ is Landau's symbol with the property $\lim\limits_{\Delta\boldsymbol{x}\to\boldsymbol{0}} \dfrac{\mathrm{o}(\|\Delta\boldsymbol{x}\|)}{\|\Delta\boldsymbol{x}\|} = 0.$

The total differential of the function f at the point $\boldsymbol{x}_0$

$$\nabla f(\boldsymbol{x}_0)^\top \Delta\boldsymbol{x} = \frac{\partial f}{\partial x_1}(\boldsymbol{x}_0)\,\mathrm{d}x_1 + \ldots + \frac{\partial f}{\partial x_n}(\boldsymbol{x}_0)\,\mathrm{d}x_n$$

describes the main increase of the function value if the increment of the n components of the independent variables is $\mathrm{d}x_i$, $i = 1, \ldots, n$ (linear approximation); $\mathrm{d}x_i$ – differentials, Δx_i – (small) finite increments:

$$\Delta f(\boldsymbol{x}) \approx \sum_{i=1}^{n} \frac{\partial f}{\partial x_i}(\boldsymbol{x}) \cdot \Delta x_i$$

Equation of the tangent plane

If the function $f : D_f \to \mathbb{R}$, $D_f \subset \mathbb{R}^n$, is differentiable at the point $\boldsymbol{x}_0$, then its graph possesses a *tangent (hyper)plane* at $(\boldsymbol{x}_0, f(\boldsymbol{x}_0))$ (linear approximation), which has the equation

$$\begin{pmatrix} \nabla f(\boldsymbol{x}_0) \\ -1 \end{pmatrix}^\top \begin{pmatrix} \boldsymbol{x} - \boldsymbol{x}_0 \\ y - f(\boldsymbol{x}_0) \end{pmatrix} = 0 \qquad \text{or} \qquad y = f(\boldsymbol{x}_0) + \nabla f(\boldsymbol{x}_0)^\top (\boldsymbol{x} - \boldsymbol{x}_0).$$

Partial elasticities

If the function $f : D_f \to \mathbb{R}$, $D_f \subset \mathbb{R}^n$, is partially differentiable, then the dimensionless quantity $\varepsilon_{f,x_i}(\boldsymbol{x})$ (*partial elasticity*) describes approximately the relative increase of the function value dependent from the relative increment of the i-th component x_i:

$$\varepsilon_{f,x_i}(\boldsymbol{x}) = f_{x_i}(\boldsymbol{x}) \frac{x_i}{f(\boldsymbol{x})}$$

i-th partial elasticity of the function f at the point x

Relations involving partial elasticities

$\sum\limits_{i=1}^{n} x_i \cdot \dfrac{\partial f(\boldsymbol{x})}{\partial x_i} = \alpha \cdot f(x_1, \ldots, x_n)$	–	Euler's homogeneity relation; f homogeneous of degree α
$\varepsilon_{f,x_1}(\boldsymbol{x}) + \ldots + \varepsilon_{f,x_n}(\boldsymbol{x}) = \alpha$	–	sum of partial elasticities = degree of homogeneity
$\boldsymbol{\varepsilon}(\boldsymbol{x}) = \begin{pmatrix} \varepsilon_{f_1,x_1}(\boldsymbol{x}) & \ldots & \varepsilon_{f_1,x_n}(\boldsymbol{x}) \\ \varepsilon_{f_2,x_1}(\boldsymbol{x}) & \ldots & \varepsilon_{f_2,x_n}(\boldsymbol{x}) \\ \ldots & \ldots & \ldots \\ \varepsilon_{f_m,x_1}(\boldsymbol{x}) & \ldots & \varepsilon_{f_m,x_n}(\boldsymbol{x}) \end{pmatrix}$	–	matrix of elasticities of the functions $f_1, \ldots, f_m$

• The quantities $\varepsilon_{f_i,x_j}(\boldsymbol{x})$ are called *direct elasticities* for $i = j$ and *cross elasticities* for $i \neq j$.

Unconstrained extreme value problems

Given a sufficiently often (partially) differentiable function $f : D_f \to \mathbb{R}$, $D_f \subset \mathbb{R}^n$. Find ▶ local extreme points $\boldsymbol{x}_0$ of f (p. 46); assume that $\boldsymbol{x}_0$ is an interior point of D_f.

Necessary conditions for extrema

$\boldsymbol{x}_0$ local extreme point	$\Longrightarrow$	$\nabla f(\boldsymbol{x}_0) = \mathbf{0} \iff f_{x_i}(\boldsymbol{x}_0) = 0,\ i = 1, \ldots, n$
$\boldsymbol{x}_0$ local minimum point	$\Longrightarrow$	$\nabla f(\boldsymbol{x}_0) = \mathbf{0} \wedge H_f(\boldsymbol{x}_0)$ positive semidefinite
$\boldsymbol{x}_0$ local maximum point	$\Longrightarrow$	$\nabla f(\boldsymbol{x}_0) = \mathbf{0} \wedge H_f(\boldsymbol{x}_0)$ negative semidefinite

• Points $\boldsymbol{x}_0$ with $\nabla f(\boldsymbol{x}_0) = \mathbf{0}$ are called *stationary* points of the function f. If in any neighbourhood of the stationary point $\boldsymbol{x}_0$ there are points $\boldsymbol{x}$, $\boldsymbol{y}$ such that $f(\boldsymbol{x}) < f(\boldsymbol{x}_0) < f(\boldsymbol{y})$, then $\boldsymbol{x}_0$ is said to be a *saddle point* of the function f. A saddle point fails to be an extreme point.

• Boundary points of D_f and points where the function f is nondifferentiable are to be considered separately (e. g. by analysing the function values of points in a neighbourhood of $\boldsymbol{x}_0$). For the notion of (semi-) definiteness of a matrix ▶ p. 119.

Sufficient conditions for extrema

$\nabla f(\boldsymbol{x}_0) = \mathbf{0} \ \wedge\ H_f(\boldsymbol{x}_0)$ positive definite	$\Longrightarrow$	$\boldsymbol{x}_0$ local minimum point
$\nabla f(\boldsymbol{x}_0) = \mathbf{0} \ \wedge\ H_f(\boldsymbol{x}_0)$ negative definite	$\Longrightarrow$	$\boldsymbol{x}_0$ local maximum point
$\nabla f(\boldsymbol{x}_0) = \mathbf{0} \ \wedge\ H_f(\boldsymbol{x}_0)$ indefinite	$\Longrightarrow$	$\boldsymbol{x}_0$ saddle point

Special case $n = 2$

$$f(\boldsymbol{x}) = f(x_1, x_2):$$
$$\nabla f(\boldsymbol{x}_0) = \mathbf{0} \;\wedge\; A > 0 \;\wedge\; f_{x_1x_1}(\boldsymbol{x}_0) > 0 \implies \boldsymbol{x}_0 \text{ local minimum point}$$
$$\nabla f(\boldsymbol{x}_0) = \mathbf{0} \;\wedge\; A > 0 \;\wedge\; f_{x_1x_1}(\boldsymbol{x}_0) < 0 \implies \boldsymbol{x}_0 \text{ local maximum point}$$
$$\nabla f(\boldsymbol{x}_0) = \mathbf{0} \;\wedge\; A < 0 \implies \boldsymbol{x}_0 \text{ saddle point}$$

Here $A = \det H_f(\boldsymbol{x}_0) = f_{x_1x_1}(\boldsymbol{x}_0) \cdot f_{x_2x_2}(\boldsymbol{x}_0) - [f_{x_1x_2}(\boldsymbol{x}_0)]^2$. For $A = 0$ a statement concerning the kind of the stationary point $\boldsymbol{x}_0$ cannot be made.

Constrained extrem value problems

Given the once or twice continuously (partially) differentiable functions $f : D \to \mathbb{R}$, $g_i : D \to \mathbb{R}$, $i = 1, \ldots, m < n$, $D \subset \mathbb{R}^n$, and let $\boldsymbol{x} = (x_1, \ldots, x_n)^\top$. Find the local extreme points of the constrained extreme value problem

$$\begin{array}{ccc} f(\boldsymbol{x}) & \longrightarrow & \max / \min \\ g_1(\boldsymbol{x}) = 0, & \ldots, & g_m(\boldsymbol{x}) = 0 \end{array} \qquad \text{(C)}$$

• The set $G = \{\boldsymbol{x} \in D \,|\, g_1(\boldsymbol{x}) = 0, \ldots, g_m(\boldsymbol{x}) = 0\}$ is called the *set of feasible points* of problem (C).

• Let the *regularity condition* rank $\boldsymbol{G'} = m$ be satisfied, where the $m \times n$-matrix $\boldsymbol{G'}$ denotes the ▶ functional matrix of the system of functions $\{g_1, \ldots, g_m\}$, and the m linearly independent columns of $\boldsymbol{G'}$ are numbered by $i_1, \ldots, i_m$, the remaining columns being $i_{m+1}, \ldots, i_n$.

Elimination method

1. Eliminate the variables x_{i_j}, $j=1, \ldots, m$, from the constraints $g_i(\boldsymbol{x})=0$, $i = 1, \ldots, m$, of the problem (C): $x_{i_j} = \tilde{g}_{i_j}(x_{i_{m+1}}, \ldots, x_{i_n})$.
2. Substitute x_{i_j}, $j=1, \ldots, m$, in the function f: $f(\boldsymbol{x}) = \tilde{f}(x_{i_{m+1}}, \ldots, x_{i_n})$.
3. Find the stationary points of $\tilde{f}$ (having $n - m$ components) and determine the kind of extremum (▶ conditions on p. 107).
4. Calculate the remaining m components x_{i_j}, $j = 1, \ldots, m$, according to 1. in order to obtain stationary points of (C).

• All statements concerning the kind of extrema of $\tilde{f}$ remain in force with respect to problem (C).

Lagrange's method of multipliers

1. Assign to any constraint $g_i(\boldsymbol{x}) = 0$ one (for the time being unknown) *Lagrange multiplier* $\lambda_i \in \mathbb{R}$, $i = 1, \ldots, m$.

2. Write down the *Lagrange function* associated with (C), where $\boldsymbol{\lambda} = (\lambda_1, \ldots, \lambda_m)^\top$:

$$L(\boldsymbol{x}, \boldsymbol{\lambda}) = f(\boldsymbol{x}) + \sum_{i=1}^{m} \lambda_i g_i(\boldsymbol{x}) .$$

3. Find the stationary points $(\boldsymbol{x}_0, \boldsymbol{\lambda}_0)$ of the function $L(\boldsymbol{x}, \boldsymbol{\lambda})$ with respect to variables $\boldsymbol{x}$ and $\boldsymbol{\lambda}$ from the (generally speaking, nonlinear) system of equations

$$L_{x_i}(\boldsymbol{x}, \boldsymbol{\lambda}) = 0, \quad i=1, \ldots, n; \qquad L_{\lambda_i}(\boldsymbol{x}, \boldsymbol{\lambda}) = g_i(\boldsymbol{x}) = 0, \quad i=1, \ldots, m$$

The points $\boldsymbol{x}_0$ are then stationary for (C).

4. If the $n \times n$-matrix $\nabla^2_{\boldsymbol{xx}} L(\boldsymbol{x}_0, \boldsymbol{\lambda}_0)$ (x-part of the Hessian of L) is positive definite over the set $T = \{\boldsymbol{z} \in \mathbb{R}^n \mid \nabla g_i(\boldsymbol{x}_0)^\top \boldsymbol{z} = 0,\ i = 1, \ldots, m\}$, i. e.

$$\boldsymbol{z}^\top \nabla^2_{\boldsymbol{xx}} L(\boldsymbol{x}_0, \boldsymbol{\lambda}_0) \boldsymbol{z} > 0 \quad \forall\, \boldsymbol{z} \in T,\ \boldsymbol{z} \neq \boldsymbol{0},$$

then $\boldsymbol{x}_0$ yields a local minimum point for (C). In case of negative definiteness of $\nabla^2_{\boldsymbol{xx}} L(\boldsymbol{x}_0, \boldsymbol{\lambda}_0)$, $\boldsymbol{x}_0$ is a local maximum point.

Economic interpretation of Lagrange multipliers

Let the extreme point $\boldsymbol{x}_0$ of the (perturbed) problem

$$f(\boldsymbol{x}) \to \max / \min; \qquad g_i(\boldsymbol{x}) - b_i = 0, \quad i = 1, \ldots, m \tag{$C_{\boldsymbol{b}}$}$$

be unique for $\boldsymbol{b} = \boldsymbol{b}_0$, and let $\boldsymbol{\lambda}_0 = (\lambda_1^0, \ldots, \lambda_m^0)^\top$ be the vector of Lagrange multipliers associated with $\boldsymbol{x}_0$. Let, in addition, the regularity condition rank $\boldsymbol{G}' = m$ (see p. 108) be fulfilled. Finally, let $f^*(\boldsymbol{b})$ denote the optimal value of problem ($C_{\boldsymbol{b}}$) depending on the vector of the right-hand side $\boldsymbol{b} = (b_1, \ldots, b_m)^\top$. Then

$$\frac{\partial f^*}{\partial b_i}(\boldsymbol{b}_0) = -\lambda_i^0,$$

i. e., $-\lambda_i^0$ describes (approximately) the influence of the i-th component of the right-hand side on the change of the optimal value of problem ($C_{\boldsymbol{b}}$).

Least squares method

Given the pairs (x_i, y_i), $i = 1, \dots, N$ (x_i – points of measurement or time, y_i – measured values). Find a *trend* (or *ansatz*) function $y = f(x, \boldsymbol{a})$ approximating the measured values as good as possible, where the vector $\boldsymbol{a} = (a_1, \dots, a_M)$ contains the M parameters of the ansatz function to be determined in an optimal manner.

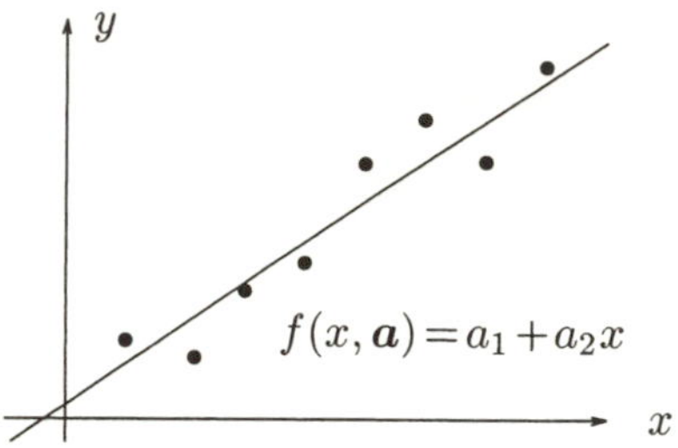

- The symbols $[z_i] = \sum\limits_{i=1}^{N} z_i$ are denoted as *Gaussian brackets.*

$S = \sum\limits_{i=1}^{N} (f(x_i, \boldsymbol{a}) - y_i)^2 \longrightarrow \min$	–	error sum of squares to be minimized
$\sum\limits_{i=1}^{N} (f(x_i, \boldsymbol{a}) - y_i) \cdot \dfrac{\partial f(x_i, \boldsymbol{a})}{\partial a_j} = 0$	–	necessary conditions of minima (normal equations), $j = 1, 2, \dots, M$

- The minimum conditions result from the relations $\frac{\partial S}{\partial a_j} = 0$ and depend on the concrete form of the ansatz function f. More general ansatz functions of the kind $f(\boldsymbol{x}, \boldsymbol{a})$ with $\boldsymbol{x} = (x_1, \dots, x_n)^\top$ lead to analogous equations.

Some types of ansatz functions

$f(x, a_1, a_2) = a_1 + a_2 x$	– linear function
$f(x, a_1, a_2, a_3) = a_1 + a_2 x + a_3 x^2$	– quadratic function
$f(x, \boldsymbol{a}) = \sum\limits_{j=1}^{M} a_j \cdot g_j(x)$	– generalized linear function

- In the above cases a **linear system of normal equations** is obtained:

linear ansatz function	quadratic ansatz function
$a_1 \cdot N + a_2 \cdot [x_i] = [y_i]$	$a_1 \cdot N + a_2 \cdot [x_i] + a_3 \cdot [x_i^2] = [y_i]$
$a_1 \cdot [x_i] + a_2 \cdot [x_i^2] = [x_i y_i]$	$a_1 \cdot [x_i] + a_2 \cdot [x_i^2] + a_3 \cdot [x_i^3] = [x_i y_i]$
	$a_1 \cdot [x_i^2] + a_2 \cdot [x_i^3] + a_3 \cdot [x_i^4] = [x_i^2 y_i]$

Explicit solution for linear ansatz functions

$$a_1 = \frac{[x_i^2] \cdot [y_i] - [x_i y_i] \cdot [x_i]}{N \cdot [x_i^2] - [x_i]^2}, \qquad a_2 = \frac{N \cdot [x_i y_i] - [x_i] \cdot [y_i]}{N \cdot [x_i^2] - [x_i]^2}$$

Simplifications

- By means of the transformation $x_i' = x_i - \frac{1}{N}[x_i]$ the system of normal equations can be simplified since in this case $[x_i'] = 0$.

- For the **exponential ansatz** $y = f(x) = a_1 \cdot e^{a_2 x}$ the transformation $T(y) = \ln y$ leads (for $f(x) > 0$) to a linear system of normal equations.

- For the **logistic function** $f(x) = a \cdot (1 + be^{-cx})^{-1}$ $(a, b, c > 0)$ with known a the transformation $\frac{a}{y} = be^{-cx} \implies Y = \ln \frac{a-y}{y} = \ln b - cx$ leads to a linear system of normal equations, when setting $a_1 = \ln b$, $a_2 = -c$.

Propagation of errors

The propagation of errors investigates the influence of errors of the independent variables of a function on the result of function value calculation.

Notation

exact values	– $y, x_1, \ldots, x_n$ with $y = f(\boldsymbol{x}) = f(x_1, \ldots, x_n)$
approximate values	– $\tilde{y}, \tilde{x}_1, \ldots, \tilde{x}_n$, where $\tilde{y} = f(\tilde{\boldsymbol{x}}) = f(\tilde{x}_1, \ldots, \tilde{x}_n)$
absolute errors	– $\delta y = \tilde{y} - y, \quad \delta x_i = \tilde{x}_i - x_i, \quad i1, \ldots, n$
absolute error bounds Δ	– $\lvert\delta y\rvert \le \Delta y, \quad \lvert\delta x_i\rvert \le \Delta x_i, \quad i = 1, \ldots, n$
relative errors	– $\dfrac{\delta y}{y}, \dfrac{\delta x_i}{x_i}, \quad i = 1, \ldots, n$
relative error bounds	– $\left\lvert\dfrac{\delta y}{y}\right\rvert \le \dfrac{\Delta y}{\lvert y\rvert}, \quad \left\lvert\dfrac{\delta x_i}{x_i}\right\rvert \le \dfrac{\Delta x_i}{\lvert x_i\rvert}, \quad i = 1, \ldots, n$

- If the function f is totally differentiable, then for the propagation of the errors δx_i of the independent variables onto the absolute error of the function f one has:

$$\Delta y \approx \left|\frac{\partial f(\tilde{\boldsymbol{x}})}{\partial x_1}\right| \Delta x_1 + \ldots + \left|\frac{\partial f(\tilde{\boldsymbol{x}})}{\partial x_n}\right| \Delta x_n$$

–bound for the absolute error of $f(\tilde{x})$

$$\frac{\Delta y}{|y|} \approx \left|\frac{\tilde{x}_1}{\tilde{y}} \cdot \frac{\partial f(\tilde{\boldsymbol{x}})}{\partial x_1}\right| \cdot \frac{\Delta x_1}{|x_1|} + \ldots + \left|\frac{\tilde{x}_n}{\tilde{y}} \cdot \frac{\partial f(\tilde{\boldsymbol{x}})}{\partial x_n}\right| \cdot \frac{\Delta x_n}{|x_n|}$$

–bound for the relative error of $f(\tilde{x})$

Economic applications

Cobb-Douglas production function

$y = f(\boldsymbol{x}) = c \cdot x_1^{a_1} \cdot x_2^{a_2} \cdot \ldots \cdot x_n^{a_n}$ $(c, a_i \geq 0)$	x_i – input of the i-th factor y – output

• The Cobb-Douglas function is ▶ homogeneous of degree $r = a_1 + \ldots + a_n$. Due to the relation $f_{x_i}(\boldsymbol{x}) = \frac{a_i}{x_i} f(\boldsymbol{x})$, i. e. $\varepsilon_{f,x_i}(\boldsymbol{x}) = a_i$, the factor powers a_i are also referred to as *(partial) production elasticities.*

Marginal rate of substitution

When considering the ▶ level line to a production function $y = f(x_1, \ldots, x_n)$ with respect to the level y_0 (*isoquant*), one can ask the question by how many units the variable x_i has (approximately) to be changed in order to substitute one unit of the k-th input factor under equal output and unchanged values of the remaining variables. Under certain assumptions an implicit function $x_k = \varphi(x_i)$ is defined (▶ implicit function), the derivative of which is denoted as the *marginal rate of substitution*:

$$\varphi'(x_i) = -\frac{f_{x_i}(\boldsymbol{x})}{f_{x_k}(\boldsymbol{x})}$$

marginal rate of substitution (of the factor k by the factor i)

Sensitivity of the price of a call option

The Black-Scholes formula

$$P_{\text{call}} = P \cdot \Phi(d_1) - S \cdot \mathrm{e}^{-iT} \cdot \Phi(d_2)$$

with $d_1 = \frac{1}{\sigma\sqrt{T}}\left[\ln \frac{P}{S} + T \cdot \left(i + \frac{\sigma^2}{2}\right)\right]$ and $d_2 = d_1 - \sigma\sqrt{T}$ describes the price P_{call} of a call option on a share in dependence on the inputs P (actual price of the underlying share), S (strike price), i (riskless rate of interest, continuously compounded), T (remaining term of the option), σ^2 (variance per period of the share yield), where Φ is the distribution function of the standardized normal distribution and φ its density: $\varphi(x) = \frac{1}{\sqrt{2\pi}} \cdot \mathrm{e}^{-\frac{x^2}{2}}$.

The change of the call price under a change Δx_i of the i-th input (while keeping the remaining inputs fixed) can be estimated with the help of the *partial differential* $\dfrac{\partial P_{\text{call}}}{\partial x_i} \cdot \Delta x_i$, where e. g.

$\Delta = \dfrac{\partial P_{\text{call}}}{\partial P} = \Phi(d_1) > 0$	– Delta; sensitivity of the call price w.r.t. a change of share price P
$\Lambda = \dfrac{P_{\text{call}}}{\partial \sigma} = P \cdot \varphi(d_1) \cdot \sqrt{T} > 0$	– Lambda; sensitivity of the call price w.r.t. a change of volatility σ

Linear Algebra

Vectors

$\boldsymbol{a}=\begin{pmatrix}a_1\\ \vdots\\ a_n\end{pmatrix}$	–	vector of dimension n with components a_i
$\boldsymbol{e}_1=\begin{pmatrix}1\\0\\ \vdots\\0\end{pmatrix},\quad \boldsymbol{e}_2=\begin{pmatrix}0\\1\\ \vdots\\0\end{pmatrix},\ \dots,\quad \boldsymbol{e}_n=\begin{pmatrix}0\\ \vdots\\0\\1\end{pmatrix}$	–	basic vectors of the co-ordinate system, unit vectors

• The space $\mathbb{R}^n$ is the space of n-dimensional vectors; $\mathbb{R}^1$ – numerical axis, $\mathbb{R}^2$ – plane, $\mathbb{R}^3$ – (three-dimensional) space.

Rules of operation

$\lambda\boldsymbol{a}=\lambda\begin{pmatrix}a_1\\ \vdots\\ a_n\end{pmatrix}=\begin{pmatrix}\lambda a_1\\ \vdots\\ \lambda a_n\end{pmatrix}$	multiplication by a real number λ	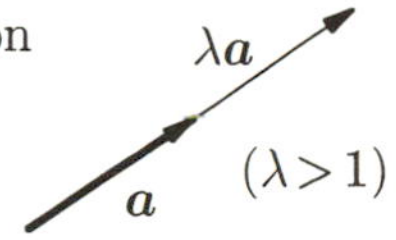
$\boldsymbol{a}\pm\boldsymbol{b}=\begin{pmatrix}a_1\\ \vdots\\ a_n\end{pmatrix}\pm\begin{pmatrix}b_1\\ \vdots\\ b_n\end{pmatrix}=\begin{pmatrix}a_1\pm b_1\\ \vdots\\ a_n\pm b_n\end{pmatrix}$	addition, subtraction	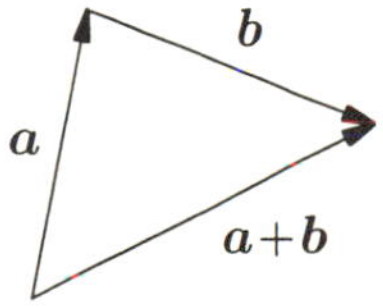
$\boldsymbol{a}\cdot\boldsymbol{b}=\begin{pmatrix}a_1\\ \vdots\\ a_n\end{pmatrix}\cdot\begin{pmatrix}b_1\\ \vdots\\ b_n\end{pmatrix}=\sum\limits_{i=1}^n a_ib_i$	scalar product	
$\boldsymbol{a}\cdot\boldsymbol{b}=\boldsymbol{a}^\top\boldsymbol{b}$ with $\boldsymbol{a}^\top=(a_1,\dots,a_n)$	other notation for the scalar product; $\boldsymbol{a}^\top$ is the vector *transposed* to $\boldsymbol{a}$	
$\boldsymbol{a}\times\boldsymbol{b}=(a_2b_3-a_3b_2)\boldsymbol{e}_1+(a_3b_1-a_1b_3)\boldsymbol{e}_2+(a_1b_2-a_2b_1)\boldsymbol{e}_3$	vector product (or cross product) for $\boldsymbol{a},\boldsymbol{b}\in\mathbb{R}^3$	
$\lvert\boldsymbol{a}\rvert=\sqrt{\boldsymbol{a}^\top\boldsymbol{a}}=\sqrt{\sum\limits_{i=1}^n a_i^2}$	modulus of the vector $\boldsymbol{a}$	

• For any vector $\boldsymbol{a}=(a_1,\dots,a_n)^\top\in\mathbb{R}^n$ the relation $\boldsymbol{a}=a_1\boldsymbol{e}_1+\ldots+a_n\boldsymbol{e}_n$ holds.

Properties of the scalar product and the modulus

$\boldsymbol{a}^\top \boldsymbol{b} = \boldsymbol{b}^\top \boldsymbol{a}$	$\boldsymbol{a}^\top(\lambda \boldsymbol{b}) = \lambda \boldsymbol{a}^\top \boldsymbol{b}, \quad \lambda \in \mathbb{R}$
$\boldsymbol{a}^\top(\boldsymbol{b}+\boldsymbol{c}) = \boldsymbol{a}^\top \boldsymbol{b} + \boldsymbol{a}^\top \boldsymbol{c}$	$\lvert\lambda \boldsymbol{a}\rvert = \lvert\lambda\rvert \cdot \lvert\boldsymbol{a}\rvert$
$\boldsymbol{a}^\top \boldsymbol{b} = \lvert\boldsymbol{a}\rvert \cdot \lvert\boldsymbol{b}\rvert \cdot \cos\varphi$	$(\boldsymbol{a}, \boldsymbol{b} \in \mathbb{R}^2, \mathbb{R}^3;$ see figure)
$\lvert\boldsymbol{a}+\boldsymbol{b}\rvert \le \lvert\boldsymbol{a}\rvert + \lvert\boldsymbol{b}\rvert$	triangular inequality
$\lvert\boldsymbol{a}^\top \boldsymbol{b}\rvert \le \lvert\boldsymbol{a}\rvert \cdot \lvert\boldsymbol{b}\rvert$	Cauchy-Schwarz inequality

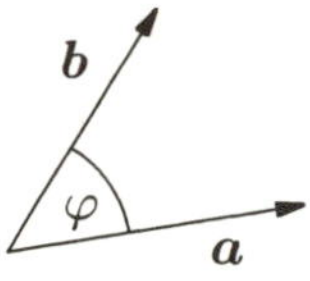

Linear combination of vectors

If the vector $\boldsymbol{b}$ is the sum of the vectors $\boldsymbol{a}_1, \ldots, \boldsymbol{a}_m \in \mathbb{R}^n$ multiplied by scalar coefficients $\lambda_1, \ldots, \lambda_m \in \mathbb{R}$, i. e.

$$\boldsymbol{b} = \lambda_1 \boldsymbol{a}_1 + \ldots + \lambda_m \boldsymbol{a}_m, \qquad (*)$$

then $\boldsymbol{b}$ is called a *linear combination* of the vectors $\boldsymbol{a}_1, \ldots, \boldsymbol{a}_m$.

- If in $(*)$ the relations $\lambda_1 + \lambda_2 + \ldots + \lambda_m = 1$ as well as $\lambda_i \ge 0$, $i = 1, \ldots, m$, hold, then $\boldsymbol{b}$ is called a *convex linear combination* of $\boldsymbol{a}_1, \ldots, \boldsymbol{a}_m$.
- If in $(*)$ the relation $\lambda_1 + \lambda_2 + \ldots + \lambda_m = 1$ holds, but λ_i, $i = 1, \ldots, m$, are arbitrary scalars, then $\boldsymbol{b}$ is called an *affine combination* of $\boldsymbol{a}_1, \ldots, \boldsymbol{a}_m$.
- If in $(*)$ the relations $\lambda_i \ge 0$, $i = 1, \ldots, m$, hold, then $\boldsymbol{b}$ is called a *conical linear combination* of $\boldsymbol{a}_1, \ldots, \boldsymbol{a}_m$.

Linear dependence

The m vectors $\boldsymbol{a}_1, \ldots, \boldsymbol{a}_m \in \mathbb{R}^n$ are said to be *linearly dependent* if there exist numbers $\lambda_1, \ldots, \lambda_m$ not all zero such that

$$\lambda_1 \boldsymbol{a}_1 + \ldots + \lambda_m \boldsymbol{a}_m = \boldsymbol{0}.$$

Otherwise the vectors $\boldsymbol{a}_1, \ldots, \boldsymbol{a}_m$ are *linearly independent.*

- The maximal number of linearly independent vectors in $\mathbb{R}^n$ is n.
- If the vectors $\boldsymbol{a}_1, \ldots, \boldsymbol{a}_n \in \mathbb{R}^n$ are linearly independent, then they form a *basis* of the space $\mathbb{R}^n$, i. e., any vector $\boldsymbol{a} \in \mathbb{R}^n$ can be uniquely represented in the form

$$\boldsymbol{a} = \lambda_1 \boldsymbol{a}_1 + \ldots + \lambda_n \boldsymbol{a}_n.$$

Equations of straight lines and planes

Straight lines in $\mathbb{R}^2$

$Ax + By + C = 0$	–	general form
$y = mx + n, \; m = \tan\alpha$	–	explicit form
$y - y_1 = m(x - x_1)$	–	point-slope form
$\dfrac{y - y_1}{x - x_1} = \dfrac{y_2 - y_1}{x_2 - x_1}$	–	two-point form
$\boldsymbol{x} = \boldsymbol{x}_1 + \lambda(\boldsymbol{x}_2 - \boldsymbol{x}_1)$ $-\infty < \lambda < \infty$	–	two-point form in parametric representation with $\boldsymbol{x}_1 = \begin{pmatrix} x_1 \\ y_1 \end{pmatrix}$, $\boldsymbol{x}_2 = \begin{pmatrix} x_2 \\ y_2 \end{pmatrix}$; cf. the two-point form of a straight line in $\mathbb{R}^3$ on p. 115
$\dfrac{x}{a} + \dfrac{y}{b} = 1$	–	intercept equation
$\tan\varphi = \dfrac{m_2 - m_1}{1 + m_1 m_2}$	–	intersection angle between two lines l_1, l_2
$l_1 \parallel l_2 : m_1 = m_2$	–	parallelism
$l_1 \perp l_2 : m_2 = -\dfrac{1}{m_1}$	–	orthogonality

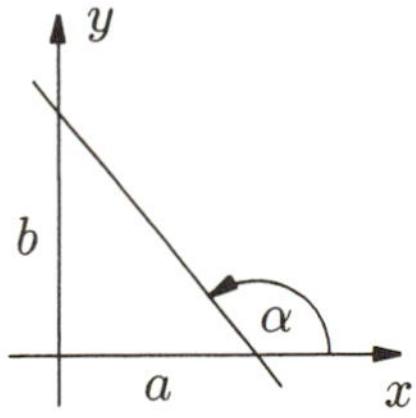

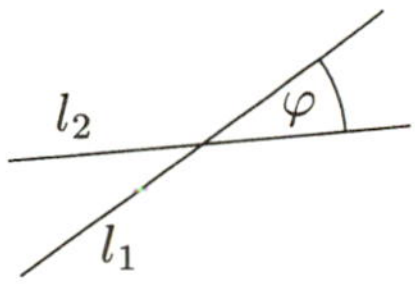

Straight lines in $\mathbb{R}^3$

point-slope (parametric) form: given a point $P_0(x_0, y_0, z_0)$ of the straight line l with fixed vector $\boldsymbol{x}_0$ and a direction vector $\boldsymbol{a} = (a_x, a_y, a_z)^\top$

$$\boldsymbol{x} = \boldsymbol{x}_0 + \lambda\boldsymbol{a}, \quad -\infty < \lambda < \infty$$

componentwise:

$$x = x_0 + \lambda a_x$$
$$y = y_0 + \lambda a_y$$
$$z = z_0 + \lambda a_z$$

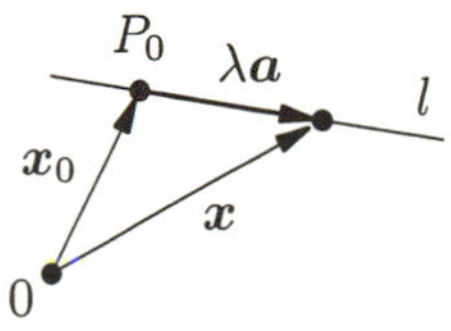

two-point form: given two points $P_1(x_1, y_1, z_1)$ and $P_2(x_2, y_2, z_2)$ of the straight line l with fixed vectors $\boldsymbol{x}_1$ and $\boldsymbol{x}_2$

$$\boldsymbol{x} = \boldsymbol{x}_1 + \lambda(\boldsymbol{x}_2 - \boldsymbol{x}_1), \quad -\infty < \lambda < \infty$$

componentwise:

$$x = x_1 + \lambda(x_2 - x_1)$$
$$y = y_1 + \lambda(y_2 - y_1)$$
$$z = z_1 + \lambda(z_2 - z_1)$$

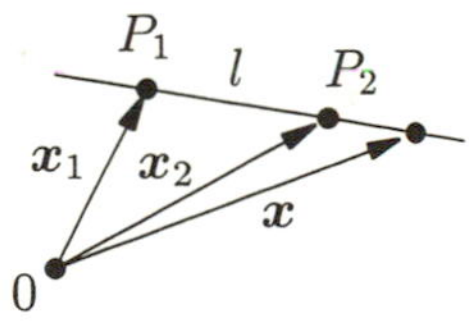

Planes in $\mathbb{R}^3$

parametric form: given a point $P_0(x_0, y_0, z_0)$ of the plane with fixed vector $\boldsymbol{x}_0$ and two direction vectors $\boldsymbol{a} = (a_x, a_y, a_z)^\top$, $\boldsymbol{b} = (b_x, b_y, b_z)^\top$

$\boldsymbol{x} = \boldsymbol{x}_0 + \lambda \boldsymbol{a} + \mu \boldsymbol{b}$	compo-	$x = x_0 + \lambda a_x + \mu b_x$
$-\infty < \lambda < \infty$	nent-	$y = y_0 + \lambda a_y + \mu b_y$
$-\infty < \mu < \infty$	wise:	$z = z_0 + \lambda a_z + \mu b_z$

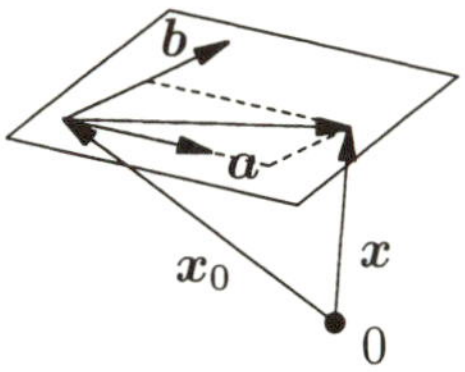

normal (vector) to the plane $\boldsymbol{x} = \boldsymbol{x}_0 + \lambda \boldsymbol{a} + \mu \boldsymbol{b}$:

$$\boldsymbol{n} = \boldsymbol{a} \times \boldsymbol{b}$$

normal form of the equation of the plane (containing the point P_0)

$$\boldsymbol{n} \cdot \boldsymbol{x} = D \quad \text{with} \quad D = \boldsymbol{n} \cdot \boldsymbol{x}_0, \quad \boldsymbol{n} = (A, B, C)^\top$$

componentwise: $Ax + By + Cz = D$

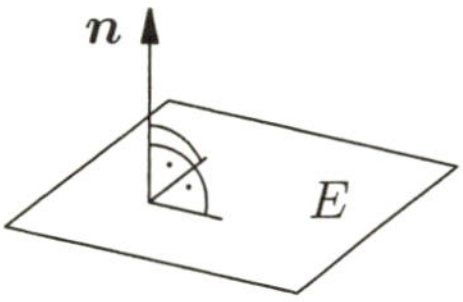

Hesse's normal form

$$\frac{\boldsymbol{n} \cdot \boldsymbol{x} - D}{|\boldsymbol{n}|} = 0$$

componentwise: $$\frac{Ax + By + Cz - D}{\sqrt{A^2 + B^2 + C^2}} = 0$$

distance vector $\boldsymbol{d}$ between the plane $\boldsymbol{n} \cdot \boldsymbol{x} = D$ and the point P with fixed vector $\boldsymbol{p}$

$$\boldsymbol{d} = \frac{\boldsymbol{n} \cdot \boldsymbol{p} - D}{|\boldsymbol{n}|^2} \boldsymbol{n}$$

shortest (signed) distance δ between the plane $\boldsymbol{n} \cdot \boldsymbol{x} = D$ and the point P with fixed vector $\boldsymbol{p}$

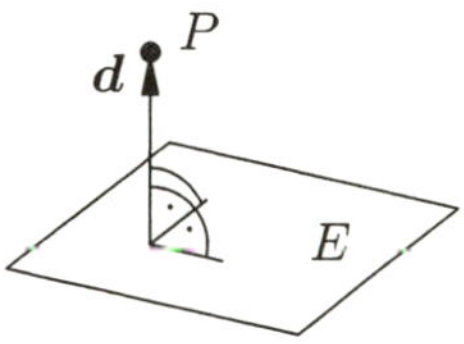

$$\delta = \frac{\boldsymbol{n} \cdot \boldsymbol{p} - D}{|\boldsymbol{n}|}$$

Matrices

A (m,n)-*matrix* $\boldsymbol{A}$ is a rectangular scheme of $m \cdot n$ real numbers (*elements*) a_{ij}, $i = 1, \ldots, m; j = 1, \ldots, n$:

$$\boldsymbol{A} = \begin{pmatrix} a_{11} & \ldots & a_{1n} \\ \vdots & \ddots & \vdots \\ a_{m1} & \ldots & a_{mn} \end{pmatrix} = (a_{ij}) \begin{array}{l} i = 1, \ldots, m \\ j = 1, \ldots, n \end{array}$$

i – row index, j – column index; a $(m,1)$-matrix is called a *column vector* and a $(1,n)$-matrix is called a *row vector*.

- The *row rank* of $\boldsymbol{A}$ is the maximal number of linearly independent row vectors, the *column rank* is the maximal number of linearly independent column vectors.
- The following relation is true: row rank = column rank, i. e. rank $(\boldsymbol{A})$ = row rank = column rank.

Rules of operation

$\boldsymbol{A} = \boldsymbol{B}$	$\iff \quad a_{ij} = b_{ij} \ \forall\, i,j$	–	identity
$\lambda \boldsymbol{A}$:	$(\lambda \boldsymbol{A})_{ij} = \lambda a_{ij}$	–	multiplication by a real number
$\boldsymbol{A} \pm \boldsymbol{B}$:	$(\boldsymbol{A} \pm \boldsymbol{B})_{ij} = a_{ij} \pm b_{ij}$	–	addition, subtraction
$\boldsymbol{A}^\top$:	$(\boldsymbol{A}^\top)_{ij} = a_{ji}$	–	transposition
$\boldsymbol{A} \cdot \boldsymbol{B}$:	$(\boldsymbol{A} \cdot \boldsymbol{B})_{ij} = \sum\limits_{r=1}^{p} a_{ir} b_{rj}$	–	multiplication

Assumption: $\boldsymbol{A}$ and $\boldsymbol{B}$ are *conformable*, i. e., $\boldsymbol{A}$ is an (m,p)-matrix and $\boldsymbol{B}$ is a (p,n)-matrix; the product matrix $\boldsymbol{AB}$ is of the type (m,n).

Falk scheme for multiplication of matrices

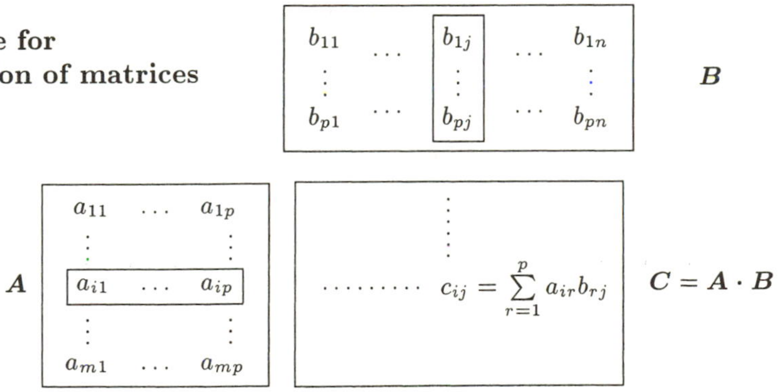

Rules of operation ($\lambda, \mu \in \mathbb{R}$; $\boldsymbol{O} = (a_{ij})$ with $a_{ij} = 0\ \forall\, i, j$ – null matrix)

$\boldsymbol{A}+\boldsymbol{B}=\boldsymbol{B}+\boldsymbol{A}$	$(\boldsymbol{A}+\boldsymbol{B})+\boldsymbol{C}=\boldsymbol{A}+(\boldsymbol{B}+\boldsymbol{C})$
$(\boldsymbol{A}+\boldsymbol{B})\boldsymbol{C}=\boldsymbol{AC}+\boldsymbol{BC}$	$\boldsymbol{A}(\boldsymbol{B}+\boldsymbol{C})=\boldsymbol{AB}+\boldsymbol{AC}$
$(\boldsymbol{A}^\top)^\top=\boldsymbol{A}$	$(\boldsymbol{A}+\boldsymbol{B})^\top=\boldsymbol{A}^\top+\boldsymbol{B}^\top$
$(\lambda+\mu)\boldsymbol{A}=\lambda\boldsymbol{A}+\mu\boldsymbol{A}$	$(\lambda\boldsymbol{A})\boldsymbol{B}=\lambda(\boldsymbol{AB})=\boldsymbol{A}(\lambda\boldsymbol{B})$
$(\boldsymbol{AB})\boldsymbol{C}=\boldsymbol{A}(\boldsymbol{BC})$	$\boldsymbol{AO}=\boldsymbol{O}$
$(\boldsymbol{AB})^\top=\boldsymbol{B}^\top\boldsymbol{A}^\top$	$(\lambda\boldsymbol{A})^\top=\lambda\boldsymbol{A}^\top$

Special matrices

quadratic matrix	– equal numbers of rows and columns
identity matrix $\boldsymbol{I}$	– quadratic matrix with $a_{ii}=1$, $a_{ij}=0$ for $i\neq j$
diagonal matrix $\boldsymbol{D}$	– quadratic matrix with $d_{ij}=0$ for $i\neq j$, notation: $\boldsymbol{D}=\mathrm{diag}\,(d_i)$ with $d_i=d_{ii}$
symmetric matrix	– quadratic matrix with $\boldsymbol{A}^\top=\boldsymbol{A}$
regular matrix	– quadratic matrix with $\det\boldsymbol{A}\neq 0$
singular matrix	– quadratic matrix with $\det\boldsymbol{A}=0$
inverse (matrix) to $\boldsymbol{A}$	– matrix $\boldsymbol{A}^{-1}$ with $\boldsymbol{AA}^{-1}=\boldsymbol{I}$
orthogonal matrix	– regular matrix with $\boldsymbol{AA}^\top=\boldsymbol{I}$
positive definite matrix	– symmetric matrix with $\boldsymbol{x}^\top\boldsymbol{Ax}>0$ $\forall\,\boldsymbol{x}\neq\boldsymbol{0}, \boldsymbol{x}\in\mathbb{R}^n$
positive semidefinite m.	– symmetric matrix with $\boldsymbol{x}^\top\boldsymbol{Ax}\geq 0\ \ \forall\,\boldsymbol{x}\in\mathbb{R}^n$
negative definite matrix	– symmetric matrix with $\boldsymbol{x}^\top\boldsymbol{Ax}<0$ $\forall\,\boldsymbol{x}\neq\boldsymbol{0}, \boldsymbol{x}\in\mathbb{R}^n$
negative semidefinite m.	– symmetric matrix with $\boldsymbol{x}^\top\boldsymbol{Ax}\leq 0\ \ \forall\,\boldsymbol{x}\in\mathbb{R}^n$

Properties of special regular matrices

$\boldsymbol{I}^\top=\boldsymbol{I}$	$\det\boldsymbol{I}=1$	$\boldsymbol{I}^{-1}=\boldsymbol{I}$
$\boldsymbol{AI}=\boldsymbol{IA}=\boldsymbol{A}$	$\boldsymbol{A}^{-1}\boldsymbol{A}=\boldsymbol{I}$	$(\boldsymbol{A}^{-1})^{-1}=\boldsymbol{A}$
$(\boldsymbol{A}^{-1})^\top=(\boldsymbol{A}^\top)^{-1}$	$(\boldsymbol{AB})^{-1}=\boldsymbol{B}^{-1}\boldsymbol{A}^{-1}$	$\det(\boldsymbol{A}^{-1})=\dfrac{1}{\det\boldsymbol{A}}$

Inverse matrix

$$A^{-1} = \frac{1}{\det A} \begin{pmatrix} (-1)^{1+1} \det A_{11} & \ldots & (-1)^{1+n} \det A_{n1} \\ \ldots & \ldots & \ldots \\ (-1)^{n+1} \det A_{1n} & \ldots & (-1)^{n+n} \det A_{nn} \end{pmatrix}$$

A_{ik} is the submatrix obtained from A by removing the i-th row and the k-th column (▶algorithms at p. 124)

Criteria of definiteness

- The real symmetric (n,n)-matrix $A = (a_{ij})$ is positive definite if and only if any of its n minors in principal position is positive:

$$\begin{vmatrix} a_{11} & \ldots & a_{1k} \\ \ldots & \ldots & \ldots \\ a_{k1} & \ldots & a_{kk} \end{vmatrix} > 0 \qquad \text{for } k = 1, \ldots, n.$$

- The real symmetric (n,n)-matrix $A = (a_{ij})$ is negative definite if and only if the sequence of the n minors in principal position has alternating signs starting with minus (or equivalent: if $-A$ is positive definite):

$$(-1)^k \begin{vmatrix} a_{11} & \ldots & a_{1k} \\ \ldots & \ldots & \ldots \\ a_{k1} & \ldots & a_{kk} \end{vmatrix} > 0 \qquad \text{for } k = 1, \ldots, n.$$

- A real symmetric matrix is positive definite (positive semidefinite, negative definite, negative semidefinite) if and only if all its eigenvalues (▶ eigenvalue problems, p. 124) are positive (nonnegative, negative, nonpositive).

Determinants

The *determinant* D of a quadratic (n,n)-matrix A is the recursively defined number

$$D = \det A = \begin{vmatrix} a_{11} & \ldots & a_{1n} \\ \vdots & \ddots & \vdots \\ a_{n1} & \ldots & a_{nn} \end{vmatrix} = a_{i1}(-1)^{i+1} \det A_{i1} + \ldots + a_{in}(-1)^{i+n} \det A_{in} \,,$$

where A_{ik} is the submatrix obtained from A by removing the i-th row and the k-th column. The determinant of a $(1,1)$-matrix is defined as the value of its unique element. The calculation of a determinant according to the above definition is said to be the *Laplace expansion* with respect to the i-th row.

- The same value D is obtained via expansion with respect to an arbitrary row or column, especially to the k-th column:

$$D = \det \boldsymbol{A} = \begin{vmatrix} a_{11} & \dots & a_{1n} \\ \vdots & \ddots & \vdots \\ a_{n1} & \dots & a_{nn} \end{vmatrix} = a_{1j}(-1)^{1+j} \det \boldsymbol{A}_{1j} + \ldots + a_{nj}(-1)^{n+j} \det \boldsymbol{A}_{nj} \,.$$

Special cases (Sarrus' rule)

$n = 2$:

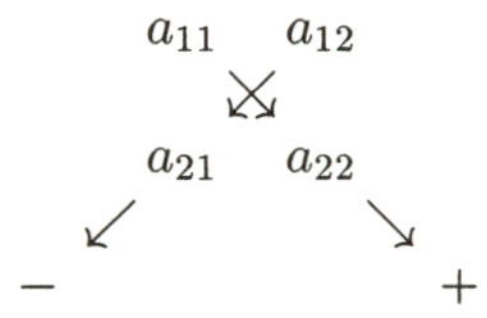

$$\det \boldsymbol{A} = a_{11}a_{22} - a_{12}a_{21}$$

$n = 3$:

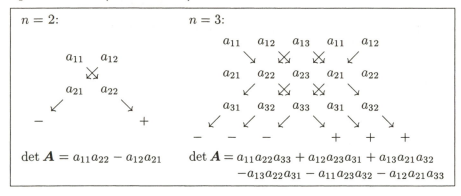

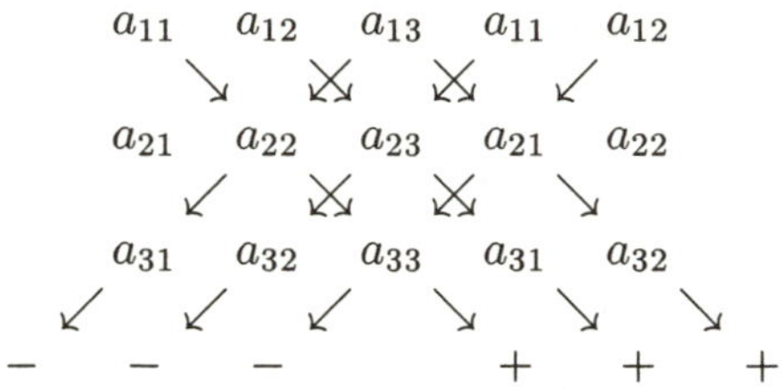

$$\det \boldsymbol{A} = a_{11}a_{22}a_{33} + a_{12}a_{23}a_{31} + a_{13}a_{21}a_{32} - a_{13}a_{22}a_{31} - a_{11}a_{23}a_{32} - a_{12}a_{21}a_{33}$$

Properties of n-th order determinants

- A determinant changes its sign if two rows or two columns of the associated matrix are exchanged.
- If two rows (columns) of a matrix are equal to each other, then the value of its determinant is zero.
- The value of a determinant remains unchanged when adding the multiple of a row (column) of the associated matrix to another row (column) of this matrix.
- If a row (column) of a matrix is multiplied by a number, then the value of its determinant is multiplied by this number.
- The following relations are valid:

$$\det \boldsymbol{A} = \det \boldsymbol{A}^\top, \qquad \det(\boldsymbol{A} \cdot \boldsymbol{B}) = \det \boldsymbol{A} \cdot \det \boldsymbol{B},$$
$$\det(\lambda \boldsymbol{A}) = \lambda^n \det \boldsymbol{A} \qquad (\lambda \text{ – real}).$$

Systems of linear equations

The system of linear equations

$$\boldsymbol{A}\boldsymbol{x} = \boldsymbol{b} \qquad \text{componentwise:} \qquad \begin{array}{l} a_{11}x_1 + \ldots + a_{1n}x_n = b_1 \\ \ldots\ldots\ldots\ldots\ldots\ldots\ldots\ldots \\ a_{m1}x_1 + \ldots + a_{mn}x_m = b_m \end{array} \qquad (*)$$

is called *homogeneous* if $\boldsymbol{b} = \boldsymbol{0}$ (componentwise: $b_i = 0 \;\; \forall\, i = 1, \ldots, m$) and *inhomogeneous* if $\boldsymbol{b} \neq \boldsymbol{0}$ (componentwise: $b_i \neq 0$ for at least one $i \in$

$\{1,\dots,m\}$). If $(*)$ is consistent (i. e., it has a solution), then the set of all solutions is said to be the *general solution.*

- The system $(*)$ is consistent if and only if $\operatorname{rank}(\boldsymbol{A}) = \operatorname{rank}(\boldsymbol{A}, \boldsymbol{b})$.
- In the case $m = n$ the system $(*)$ has a unique solution if and only if $\det \boldsymbol{A} \neq 0$.
- The homogeneous system $\boldsymbol{Ax} = \boldsymbol{0}$ has always the trivial solution $\boldsymbol{x} = \boldsymbol{0}$.
- For $m = n$ the homogeneous system $\boldsymbol{Ax} = \boldsymbol{0}$ has nontrivial solutions if and only if $\det \boldsymbol{A} = 0$.
- If $\boldsymbol{x}_h$ is the general solution of the homogeneous system $\boldsymbol{Ax} = \boldsymbol{0}$ and $\boldsymbol{x}_s$ is a special solution of the inhomogeneous system $(*)$, then for the general solution $\boldsymbol{x}$ of the inhomogeneous system $(*)$ the following representation is valid:

$$\boxed{\boldsymbol{x} = \boldsymbol{x}_h + \boldsymbol{x}_s}$$

Gaussian elimination

Elimination

In this phase, from the system of linear equations $\boldsymbol{Ax} = \boldsymbol{b}$ with $\boldsymbol{A}$ being a (m, n)-matrix at every step a (suitable) variable as well as a (suitable) row is successively eliminated until the method terminates since further suitable variables or further suitable rows cannot be found. In order to calculate the values of the eliminated variables later on, the eliminated row is "marked".

Algorithm (described for the first elimination step)

1. Find a matrix element $a_{pq} \neq 0$. If $a_{ij} = 0$ for all elements of the matrix, then terminate the elimination. The variable x_q is the unknown to be eliminated, the row p is the row to be eliminated, a_{pq} is called the *pivot element.*
2. Generation of zeros in column q:

   Subtract the $\frac{a_{iq}}{a_{pq}}$-fold of row p from all rows i, $i \neq p$:

$$\tilde{a}_{ij} := a_{ij} - \frac{a_{iq}}{a_{pq}} a_{pj}, \quad j = 1, \dots, n; \quad i = 1, \dots, p-1, p+1, \dots, m$$

$$\tilde{b}_i := b_i - \frac{a_{iq}}{a_{pq}} b_p, \qquad i = 1, \dots, p-1, p+1, \dots, m$$

3. Remove the row p from the system of equations and mark it.
4. If the remaining system of equations contains only one row, then the eliminitaion terminates.

Checking consistency

Consider the remaining system $\tilde{\boldsymbol{A}}\boldsymbol{x} = \tilde{\boldsymbol{b}}$.

Case 1 $\tilde{\boldsymbol{A}} = \mathbf{0}, \tilde{\boldsymbol{b}} \neq \mathbf{0} \Longrightarrow$ The system of equations (∗) is inconsistent.

Case 2 $\tilde{\boldsymbol{A}} = \mathbf{0}, \tilde{\boldsymbol{b}} = \mathbf{0} \Longrightarrow$ The system of equations (∗) is consistent. Delete the remaining system.

Case 3 $\tilde{\boldsymbol{A}} \neq \mathbf{0} \Longrightarrow$ The system of equations (∗) is consistent. The remaining system consists of only one row. Add this row to the rows marked in the process of elimination.

Back substitution

The marked equations form a system with triangular matrix (in every equation the variables eliminated in the previous equations fail to occur).

Case 1 $n-1$ elimination steps; then (∗) has a unique solution the components of which are calculated step by step from the last to the first equation of the system by substituting the variables already known and solving the equation under review with respect to the only unknown contained.

Case 2 $k < n-1$ elimination steps; then (∗) has infinitely many solutions. A representation of all solutions is obtained by resolving the last equation with respect to one variable and considering the remaining $n-k$ variables of this equation as parameters. Now the representations for the k eliminated variables depending on these parameters are obtained step by step from the last but one to the first equation analogously to Case 1.

Modifications of the Gaussian elimination

- If the considered system of equations is consistent, then by renumbering of rows and columns it can be achieved that first a_{11} and, after k steps, the element $\tilde{a}_{1,k+1}$ (i. e., the diagonal elements) can be chosen as the pivot elements. In this case, after the process of Gaussian elimination the system of equations has the form

$$\boxed{\boldsymbol{R}\boldsymbol{x}_B + \boldsymbol{S}\boldsymbol{x}_N = \boldsymbol{c},}$$

where $\boldsymbol{R}$ is a right upper triangle matrix ($\boldsymbol{x}_B$ – basic variables, $\boldsymbol{x}_N$ – nonbasic variables). The term $\boldsymbol{S}\boldsymbol{x}_N$ may fail to occur (in this case, there is a unique solution). By an additional generation of zeros above the diagonal it can be achieved that $\boldsymbol{R} = \boldsymbol{D}$ (diagonal matrix) or $\boldsymbol{R} = \boldsymbol{I}$. In this case, back substitution is not necessary.

- The ▶ exchange method (p. 123) is another variant of the Gaussian elimination.

Cramer's rule

If $\boldsymbol{A}$ is a regular matrix, then the solution $\boldsymbol{x} = (x_1, \ldots, x_n)^\top$ of $\boldsymbol{Ax} = \boldsymbol{b}$ is:

$$x_k = \frac{\det \boldsymbol{A}_k}{\det \boldsymbol{A}} \quad \text{with } \boldsymbol{A}_k = \begin{pmatrix} a_{11} & \ldots & a_{1,k-1} & b_1 & a_{1,k+1} & \ldots & a_{1n} \\ \ldots & \ldots & \ldots & \ldots & \ldots & \ldots & \ldots \\ a_{n1} & \ldots & a_{n,k-1} & b_n & a_{n,k+1} & \ldots & a_{nn} \end{pmatrix}, \; k=1,\ldots,n.$$

Exchange method

system of affine linear functions

$$\begin{aligned} y_1 &= a_{11}x_1 + \ldots + a_{1n}x_n + a_1 \\ &\ldots\ldots\ldots\ldots\ldots\ldots \\ y_m &= a_{m1}x_1 + \ldots + a_{mn}x_n + a_m \end{aligned}$$

vector representation

$$\boldsymbol{y} = \boldsymbol{Ax} + \boldsymbol{a}$$

y_i	–	dependent variable, basic variable ($i = 1, \ldots, m$)
x_k	–	independent variable, nonbasic variable ($k = 1, \ldots, n$)
$a_i = 0$	–	function y_i is a linear function
$\boldsymbol{a} = \boldsymbol{0}$	–	the system of functions is called homogeneous

Exchange of a basic variable by a nonbasic variable

The basic variable y_p is exchanged by the nonbasic variable x_q.

Assumption: $a_{pq} \neq 0$. The element a_{pq} is called the *pivot*.

old scheme

$\boldsymbol{x}_B = \boldsymbol{A}\boldsymbol{x}_N + \boldsymbol{a}$ with

$\boldsymbol{x}_B = (y_1, \ldots, y_m)^\top$

$\boldsymbol{x}_N = (x_1, \ldots, x_n)^\top$

new scheme

$\boldsymbol{x}_B = \boldsymbol{B}\boldsymbol{x}_N + \boldsymbol{b}$ with

$\boldsymbol{x}_B = (y_1, \ldots, y_{p-1}, x_q, y_{p+1}, \ldots, y_m)^\top$

$\boldsymbol{x}_N = (x_1, \ldots, x_{q-1}, y_p, x_{q+1}, \ldots, x_n)^\top$

Old scheme:

	...	x_k	...	↓ x_q	...	1
⋮		⋮		⋮		⋮
$y_i =$	...	a_{ik}	...	a_{iq}	...	a_i
⋮		⋮		⋮		⋮
→ $y_p =$	...	a_{pk}	...	a_{pq}	...	a_p
⋮		⋮		⋮		⋮
auxil. row	...	b_{pk}	...	*	...	b_p

New scheme:

	...	x_k	...	↓ y_p	...	1
⋮		⋮		⋮		⋮
$y_i =$	...	b_{ik}	...	b_{iq}	...	b_i
⋮		⋮		⋮		⋮
→ $x_q =$	...	b_{pk}	...	b_{pq}	...	b_p
⋮		⋮		⋮		⋮

Rules of exchange

(A1)	$b_{pq} := \dfrac{1}{a_{pq}}$		
(A2)	$b_{pk} := -\dfrac{a_{pk}}{a_{pq}}$	for $k=1,\ldots,q-1,q+1,\ldots,n$	$b_p := -\dfrac{a_p}{a_{pq}}$
(A3)	$b_{iq} := \dfrac{a_{iq}}{a_{pq}}$	for $i=1,\ldots,p-1,p+1,\ldots,m$	
(A4)	$b_{ik} := a_{ik} + b_{pk} \cdot a_{iq}$	for $i=1,\ldots,p-1,p+1,\ldots,m$; $k=1,\ldots,q-1,q+1,\ldots,n$	
	$b_i := a_i + b_p \cdot a_{iq}$	for $i=1,\ldots,p-1,p+1,\ldots,m$	

- The auxiliary row serves for simplification when using rule (A4).

Inverse matrix

If $\boldsymbol{A}$ is a regular matrix, then the complete exchange $\boldsymbol{y} \leftrightarrow \boldsymbol{x}$ in the homogeneous system of functions $\boldsymbol{y} = \boldsymbol{A}\boldsymbol{x}$ is always possible. The result is $\boldsymbol{x} = \boldsymbol{B}\boldsymbol{y}$ with $\boldsymbol{B} = \boldsymbol{A}^{-1}$:

$$\begin{array}{r|c} & \boldsymbol{x} \\ \hline \boldsymbol{y} = & \boldsymbol{A} \end{array} \qquad \Longrightarrow \qquad \begin{array}{r|c} & \boldsymbol{y} \\ \hline \boldsymbol{x} = & \boldsymbol{A}^{-1} \end{array}$$

With the help of the Gaussian elimination the matrix $\boldsymbol{A}^{-1}$ can be calulated according to the following scheme:

$$(\boldsymbol{A} \mid \boldsymbol{I}) \qquad \Longrightarrow \qquad (\boldsymbol{I} \mid \boldsymbol{A}^{-1})$$

- This means: Write down the original matrix $\boldsymbol{A}$ and the identity matrix $\boldsymbol{I}$ and apply the Gaussian elimination in such a way that $\boldsymbol{A}$ turns into $\boldsymbol{I}$. Then at the ride-hand side there arises the inverse matrix $\boldsymbol{A}^{-1}$.

Eigenvalue problems for matrices

A number $\lambda \in \mathbb{C}$ is called an *eigenvalue* of the quadratic (n, n)-matrix $\boldsymbol{A}$ if there exists a vector $\boldsymbol{r} \neq \boldsymbol{0}$ such that:

$$\boldsymbol{A}\boldsymbol{r} = \lambda \boldsymbol{r} \qquad \text{componentwise:} \qquad \begin{array}{ccccccc} a_{11}r_1 & + & \ldots & + & a_{1n}r_n & = & \lambda r_1 \\ \ldots & & & & & & \ldots \\ a_{n1}r_1 & + & \ldots & + & a_{nn}r_n & = & \lambda r_n \end{array}$$

A vector $\boldsymbol{r}$ belonging to the eigenvalue λ and satisfying the above equation is called an *eigenvector* of $\boldsymbol{A}$. It is a solution of the homogeneous system of linear equations $(\boldsymbol{A} - \lambda \boldsymbol{I})\boldsymbol{x} = \boldsymbol{0}$.

Properties of eigenvalues

• If $\boldsymbol{r}_1, \ldots, \boldsymbol{r}_k$ are eigenvectors belonging to the eigenvalue λ, then

$$\boldsymbol{r} = \alpha_1 \boldsymbol{r}_1 + \ldots + \alpha_k \boldsymbol{r}_k$$

is also an eigenvector belonging to λ provided that not all α_i are equal to zero.

• A number λ is an eigenvalue of the matrix $\boldsymbol{A}$ if and only if

$$p_n(\lambda) := \det(\boldsymbol{A} - \lambda \boldsymbol{I}) = 0\,.$$

The polynomial $p_n(\lambda)$ of n-th order is called the *characteristic polynomial* of the matrix $\boldsymbol{A}$. The multiplicity of the zero λ of the characteristic polynomial is denoted as the *algebraic multiplicity* of the eigenvalue λ.

• The number of linearly independent eigenvectors belonging to the eigenvalue λ is

$$n - \operatorname{rank}(\boldsymbol{A} - \lambda \boldsymbol{I})$$

and is called the *geometric multiplicity* of the eigenvalue λ. It is not greater than the algebraic multiplicity of the eigenvalue λ.

• If λ_j, $j = 1, \ldots, k$, are pairwise different eigenvalues and $\boldsymbol{r}_j$, $j = 1, \ldots, k$, are the eigenvectors belonging to them, then the latter are linearly independent.

• A (n, n) diagonal matrix $\boldsymbol{D} = \operatorname{diag}(d_j)$ has the eigenvalues $\lambda_j = d_j$, $j = 1, \ldots, n$.

• The eigenvalues of a real symmetric matrix are always real numbers. Every of its eigenvectors can be represented in real form. Eigenvectors belonging to different eigenvalues are orthogonal to each other.

Matrix models

Input-output analysis

$\boldsymbol{r} = (r_i)$	r_i	– total expense of raw material i
$\boldsymbol{e} = (e_k)$	e_k	– produced quantity of product k
$\boldsymbol{A} = (a_{ik})$	a_{ik}	– expense of raw material i for one unit of quantity of product k
$\boldsymbol{r} = \boldsymbol{A} \cdot \boldsymbol{e}$		*direct input-output analysis*
$\boldsymbol{e} = \boldsymbol{A}^{-1} \cdot \boldsymbol{r}$		*inverse input-output analysis* (assumption: $\boldsymbol{A}$ regular)

Composite input-output analysis

$\boldsymbol{r} = (r_i)$	r_i	– total expense of raw material i
$\boldsymbol{e} = (e_k)$	e_k	– produced quantity of final product k
$\boldsymbol{Z} = (z_{jk})$	z_{jk}	– expense of intermediate product j for one unit of quantity of final product k
$\boldsymbol{A} = (a_{ij})$	a_{ij}	– expense of raw material i for one unit of quantity of intermediate product j
$\boldsymbol{r} = \boldsymbol{A} \cdot \boldsymbol{Z} \cdot \boldsymbol{e}$		

Leontief's model

$\boldsymbol{x} = (x_i)$	x_i	– gross output of product i
$\boldsymbol{y} = (y_i)$	y_i	– net output of product i
$\boldsymbol{A} = (a_{ij})$	a_{ij}	– consumption of product i for the production of one unit of quantity of product j
$\boldsymbol{y} = \boldsymbol{x} - \boldsymbol{A}\boldsymbol{x}$		
$\boldsymbol{x} = (\boldsymbol{I} - \boldsymbol{A})^{-1}\boldsymbol{y}$		Assumption: $\boldsymbol{I} - \boldsymbol{A}$ regular matrix

Transition model of market research

$\boldsymbol{m} = (m_i)$	m_i	– market share of product i at moment T, $0 \le m_i \le 1,\ m_1 + \ldots + m_n = 1$
$\boldsymbol{z} = (z_i)$	z_i	– market share of product i at moment $T + k \cdot \Delta T$, $k = 1, 2, \ldots,\ \ 0 \le z_i \le 1,\ \ z_1 + \ldots + z_n = 1$
$\boldsymbol{s} = (s_i)$	s_i	– market share of product i in stationary (time invariant) market distribution; $0 \le s_i \le 1$, $s_1 + \ldots + s_n = 1$
$\boldsymbol{A} = (a_{ij})$	a_{ij}	– part of buyers of product i at moment T who will buy the product j at moment $T + \Delta T$ $0 \le a_{ij} \le 1$, $i, j = 1, \ldots, n,\ \ \sum\limits_{j=1}^{n} a_{ij} = 1 \ \text{ for } \ i = 1, \ldots, n$
$\boldsymbol{z} = (\boldsymbol{A}^k)^\top \boldsymbol{m}$		

$\boldsymbol{A}$ is the matrix of buyers' fluctuation and $\boldsymbol{s}$ a nontrivial solution of the linear homogeneous system $(\boldsymbol{A}^\top - \boldsymbol{I})\boldsymbol{s} = \boldsymbol{0}$ with $s_1 + \ldots + s_n = 1$.

Linear Programming and Transportation Problem

Normal form of a linear programming problem

The problem to find a vector $\boldsymbol{x}^* = (x_1^*, x_2^*, \dots, x_n^*)^\top$ such that its components satisfy the conditions

$$\begin{array}{ccccccccc}
\alpha_{11}x_1 & + & \alpha_{12}x_2 & + & \dots & + & \alpha_{1n}x_n & \le & \alpha_1 \\
\dots & \dots & \dots & \dots & \dots & \dots & \dots & \dots & \dots \\
\alpha_{r1}x_1 & + & \alpha_{r2}x_2 & + & \dots & + & \alpha_{rn}x_n & \le & \alpha_r \\
\beta_{11}x_1 & + & \beta_{12}x_2 & + & \dots & + & \beta_{1n}x_n & \ge & \beta_1 \\
\dots & \dots & \dots & \dots & \dots & \dots & \dots & \dots & \dots \\
\beta_{s1}x_1 & + & \beta_{s2}x_2 & + & \dots & + & \beta_{sn}x_n & \ge & \beta_s \\
\gamma_{11}x_1 & + & \gamma_{12}x_2 & + & \dots & + & \gamma_{1n}x_n & = & \gamma_1 \\
\dots & \dots & \dots & \dots & \dots & \dots & \dots & \dots & \dots \\
\gamma_{t1}x_1 & + & \gamma_{t2}x_2 & + & \dots & + & \gamma_{tn}x_n & = & \gamma_t
\end{array}$$

and a given objective function $z(\boldsymbol{x}) = \boldsymbol{c}^\top \boldsymbol{x} + c_0 = c_1x_1 + c_2x_2 + \dots + c_nx_n + c_0$ attains its smallest value (*minimum problem*) or its greatest value (*maximum problem*) under all vectors $\boldsymbol{x} = (x_1, x_2, \dots, x_n)^\top$ fulfilling these conditions is called a *linear programming* (or *optimization) problem.* The conditions posed above are called the *constraints* or the *restrictions* of the problem. A vector $\boldsymbol{x} = (x_1, \dots, x_n)^\top$ satisfying all constraints is said to be *feasible.* A variable x_i for which the relation $x_i \ge 0$ (*non-negativity requirement*) fails to occur among the constraints is referred to as a *free* or *unrestricted variable.*

• A linear programming problem is in *normal form* if it is a maximum or a minimum problem and, except for the inequalities $x_i \ge 0$, $i = 1, \dots, n$, there are no further inequalities to be fulfilled:

$$z = \boldsymbol{c}^\top \boldsymbol{x} + c_0 \longrightarrow \min / \max; \qquad \boldsymbol{A}\boldsymbol{x} = \boldsymbol{a}, \quad \boldsymbol{x} \ge 0$$ **normal form**

Transformation into normal form

Transform inequalities into equalities by slack variables s_i:

$$\alpha_{i1}x_1 + \alpha_{i2}x_2 + \dots + \alpha_{in}x_n \le \alpha_i \quad \Longrightarrow$$
$$\alpha_{i1}x_1 + \dots + \alpha_{in}x_n + s_i = \alpha_i, \qquad s_i \ge 0$$

$$\beta_{i1}x_1 + \beta_{i2}x_2 + \dots + \beta_{in}x_n \ge \beta_i \quad \Longrightarrow$$
$$\beta_{i1}x_1 + \dots + \beta_{in}x_n - s_i = \beta_i, \qquad s_i \ge 0$$

Remove unrestricted variables by substitution:

$$x_i \quad \text{free} \quad \Longrightarrow \quad x_i := u_i - v_i, \quad u_i \ge 0, \quad v_i \ge 0$$

Transform a maximum problem into a minimum problem or vice versa:

$$z = \boldsymbol{c}^\top \boldsymbol{x} + c_0 \longrightarrow \max \quad \Longrightarrow \quad \overline{z} := -z = (-\boldsymbol{c})^\top \boldsymbol{x} - c_0 \longrightarrow \min$$
$$z = \boldsymbol{c}^\top \boldsymbol{x} + c_0 \longrightarrow \min \quad \Longrightarrow \quad \overline{z} := -z = (-\boldsymbol{c})^\top \boldsymbol{x} - c_0 \longrightarrow \max$$

Simplex method

In order to perform the necessary transformations of the system of equations one can either use the ▶ Gaussian elimination (p. 121 or the ▶ exchange method (p. 123).

Basic representation

In the system of equations $\boldsymbol{Ax} = \boldsymbol{a}$, $z - \boldsymbol{c}^\top \boldsymbol{x} = c_0$ (where $\boldsymbol{A}$ is a (m,n)-matrix, $\boldsymbol{x}, \boldsymbol{c} \in \mathbb{R}^n$, $\boldsymbol{a} \in \mathbb{R}^m$, $c_0 \in \mathbb{R}$) from each row a variable x_i is eliminated. From the normal form one gets the following relations when combining the eliminated variables (*basic variables*) to the vector $\boldsymbol{x}_B$ and the remaining variables (*nonbasic variables*) to the vector $\boldsymbol{x}_N$:

Gaussian elimination

$$\begin{aligned} z &\to \max \\ \boldsymbol{Ix}_B + \boldsymbol{Bx}_N &= \boldsymbol{b} \\ z + \boldsymbol{d}^\top \boldsymbol{x}_N &= d_0 \\ \boldsymbol{x}_B \geq \boldsymbol{0}, \quad \boldsymbol{x}_N &\geq \boldsymbol{0} \end{aligned}$$

table:

x_{B_1}	$\ldots$	x_{B_m}	z	x_{N_1}	$\ldots$	$x_{N_{n-m}}$	$=$
1			0	b_{11}	$\ldots$	$b_{1,n-m}$	b_1
	$\ddots$		$\vdots$	$\vdots$		$\vdots$	$\vdots$
		1	0	b_{m1}	$\ldots$	$b_{m,n-m}$	b_m
0	$\ldots$	0	1	d_1	$\ldots$	d_{n-m}	d_0

Exchange method

$$\begin{aligned} z &\to \min \\ \boldsymbol{x}_B &= \tilde{\boldsymbol{B}}\boldsymbol{x}_N + \tilde{\boldsymbol{b}} \\ z &= \tilde{\boldsymbol{d}}^\top \boldsymbol{x}_N + \tilde{d}_0 \\ \boldsymbol{x}_B \geq \boldsymbol{0}, \quad \boldsymbol{x}_N &\geq \boldsymbol{0} \end{aligned}$$

table:

	x_{N_1}	$\ldots$	$x_{N_{n-m}}$	1
$x_{B_1} =$	$\tilde{b}_{11}$	$\ldots$	$\tilde{b}_{1,n-m}$	$\tilde{b}_1$
$\vdots$	$\vdots$		$\vdots$	$\vdots$
$x_{B_m} =$	$\tilde{b}_{m1}$	$\ldots$	$\tilde{b}_{m,n-m}$	$\tilde{b}_m$
$z =$	$\tilde{d}_1$	$\ldots$	$\tilde{d}_{n-m}$	$\tilde{d}_0$

The z-column is usually omitted.

- If $\boldsymbol{Ax} = \boldsymbol{a}$ has already the form $\boldsymbol{Ix}_B + \boldsymbol{Bx}_N = \boldsymbol{a}$, then the following relations hold: $\boldsymbol{b} = \tilde{\boldsymbol{b}} = \boldsymbol{a}$, $d_0 = \tilde{d}_0 = \boldsymbol{c}_B^\top \boldsymbol{a} + c_0$, $\tilde{\boldsymbol{B}} = -\boldsymbol{B}$, $\boldsymbol{d}^\top = -\tilde{\boldsymbol{d}}^\top = \boldsymbol{c}_B^\top \boldsymbol{B} - \boldsymbol{c}_N^\top$, where $\boldsymbol{c}^\top = (\boldsymbol{c}_B^\top, \boldsymbol{c}_N^\top)$.

- A basic representation with $b_i \geq 0$ and $\tilde{b}_i \geq 0$, $i = 1, \ldots, m$, respectively, is called a *feasible basic representation* or a *simplex table*.

Optimality criterion (simplex criterion)

From a simplex table satisfying the conditions $d_i \geq 0$ and $\tilde{d}_i \geq 0$, $i = 1, \ldots, n-m$, resp. (such a simplex table is called an *optimal simplex table*), one can read off the optimal solution of the linear programming problem:

$$\boldsymbol{x}_B^* = \boldsymbol{b}, \quad \boldsymbol{x}_N^* = \boldsymbol{0}, \quad z^* = d_0 \qquad \text{resp.} \qquad \boldsymbol{x}_B^* = \tilde{\boldsymbol{b}}, \quad \boldsymbol{x}_N^* = \boldsymbol{0}, \quad z^* = \tilde{d}_0.$$

Simplex method

Starting from a simplex table by means of the following algorithm one either gets an optimal simplex table or one recognizes that the programming problem is unsolvable.

Gaussian elimination	Exchange method
1. Choose an element d_q, $q=1,\dots,n{-}m$, such that $d_q<0$. The q-th column is the *pivot column*. The variable x_{N_q} will be the new basic variable. If there does not exist such an element ▶ optimality criterion.	**1.** Choose an element $\tilde{d}_q$, $q=1,\dots,n-m$, such that $\tilde{d}_q<0$. The q-th column is the *pivot column*. If there does not exist such an element ▶ optimality criterion.
2. Consider all positive column elements $b_{iq}>0$. Choose among them an element b_{pq} satisfying $$\frac{b_p}{b_{pq}}=\min_{b_{iq}>0}\frac{b_i}{b_{iq}}.$$ The p-th row is the *pivot row*. The variable x_{B_p} is excluded from the basis, the element b_{pq} is the *pivot*. If there does not exist a positive column element b_{iq}, then the problem is unsolvable since $z\to\infty$.	**2.** Find all negative elements $\tilde{b}_{iq}<0$ of the pivot column. Choose among them an element $\tilde{b}_{pq}$ satisfying $$\frac{\tilde{b}_p}{-\tilde{b}_{pq}}=\min_{\tilde{b}_{iq}<0}\frac{\tilde{b}_i}{-\tilde{b}_{iq}}.$$ The p-th row is the *pivot row*, the element $\tilde{b}_{pq}$ is the *pivot*. If there does not exist a negative element $\tilde{b}_{iq}$, then the programming problem is unsolvable since $z\to-\infty$.
3. Divide row p by b_{pq} and generate zeros in column x_{N_q} (except for position p) by means of ▶ Gaussian elimination. This leads to a new simplex table. Go to Step 1.	**3.** Make an exchange of variables $x_{B_p}\Longleftrightarrow x_{N_q}$ by means of the ▶ exchange method. This leads to a new simplex table. Go to Step 1.

- If at every iteration $b_p>0$ resp. $\tilde{b}_p>0$, then the simplex method is finite.
- If in the optimal simplex table there is an element d_q with $d_q=0$ resp. $\tilde{d}_q$ with $\tilde{d}_q=0$, then continuing the algorithm by Steps 2 and 3, one again gets an optimal simplex table. The corresponding optimal solution can be different from the former one.
- If the vectors $\boldsymbol{x}^{(1)},\dots,\boldsymbol{x}^{(k)}$ are optimal solutions, then the *convex linear combination* $\boldsymbol{x}^*=\lambda_1\boldsymbol{x}^{(1)}+\ldots+\lambda_k\boldsymbol{x}^{(k)}$ with $\sum\limits_{i=1}^{k}\lambda_i=1$ and $\lambda_i\ge 0$, $i=1,\dots,k$, is also an optimal solution.

Dual simplex method

Dual simplex table

A basic representation with $d_j \geq 0$ resp. $\tilde{d}_j \geq 0$, $j = 1, \ldots, n-m$, is called a *dual simplex table.*

• Starting from a dual simplex table by means of the following algorithm one either obtains an optimal simplex table or one recognizes that the underlying programming problem is unsolvable.

Gaussian elimination	**Exchange method**
1. Find an element b_p, $p = 1, \ldots, m$, such that $b_p < 0$. Row p is the *pivot row.* The variable x_{B_p} is excluded from the basis. If such an element does not exist ▶ optimality criterion.	**1.** Find an element $\tilde{b}_p$, $p = 1, \ldots, m$, such that $\tilde{b}_p < 0$. The p-th row is the *pivot row.* If there does not exist such an element ▶ optimality criterion.
2. Choose among all negative row elements $b_{pj} < 0$ an element b_{pq} with $$\frac{d_q}{-b_{pq}} = \min_{b_{pj}<0} \frac{d_j}{-b_{pj}}.$$ The variable x_{N_q} will be the new basic variable, the element b_{pq} is the *pivot.* If in the p-th row there does not exist a negative element b_{pj}, then the programming problem is unsolvable since feasible vectors fail to exist.	**2.** Choose among all positive elements $\tilde{b}_{pj} > 0$ of the pivot row a $\tilde{b}_{pq}$ with $$\frac{\tilde{d}_q}{\tilde{b}_{pq}} = \min_{\tilde{b}_{pj}>0} \frac{\tilde{d}_j}{\tilde{b}_{pj}}.$$ The q-th column is the *pivot column*, the element $\tilde{b}_{pq}$ is the *pivot.* If there does not exist a positive element $\tilde{b}_{pj}$, then the programming problem fails to have feasible vectors.
3. Dividing row p by b_{pq} and generating zeros in column x_{N_q} (except for position p) by means of the ▶ Gaussian elimination a new dual simplex table is obtained. Go to Step 1.	**3.** Exchanging the variables $x_{B_p} \Longleftrightarrow x_{N_q}$ by means of the ▶ exchange method a new dual simplex table is obtained. Go to Step 1.

Generation of an initial simplex table

Starting from the ▶ normal form of a linear programming problem with the property $\boldsymbol{a} \geq 0$ the following algorithm leads either to a simplex table or shows the unsolvability of the linear programming problem. If necessary, the assumption $\boldsymbol{a} \geq 0$ can be ensured via multiplying the corresponding rows of the system of equations $\boldsymbol{Ax} = \boldsymbol{a}$ by the factor -1.

Gaussian elimination

1. Add an *artificial variable* y_i to the left-hand side in all equations i. In doing so, the following equations arise:

$$\boldsymbol{Iy}+\boldsymbol{Ax} = \boldsymbol{a}, \quad \text{where} \quad \boldsymbol{y} = (y_i)$$

2. Complete the table by the objective function $z - \boldsymbol{c}^\top \boldsymbol{x} = c_0$ and by the *auxiliary function* $h = \sum\limits_{i=1}^{m}(-y_i)$:

$$h + \sum_{k=1}^{n} \delta_k x_k = \delta_0 \quad \text{with}$$

$$\delta_k = \sum_{i=1}^{m}(-a_{ik}), \quad \delta_0 = \sum_{i=1}^{m}(-a_i)$$

The table obtained

$\boldsymbol{y}$	z	h	$\boldsymbol{x}$	$=$
$\boldsymbol{I}$	0	0	$\boldsymbol{A}$	$\boldsymbol{a}$
$\boldsymbol{0}^\top$	1	0	$-c_1 \ \ldots \ -c_n$	c_0
$\boldsymbol{0}^\top$	0	1	$\delta_1 \ \ldots \ \delta_n$	δ_0

is a simplex table of the *auxiliary problem*

$$h = \sum_{i=1}^{m}(-y_i) \to \max$$

$$\boldsymbol{y} + \boldsymbol{Ax} = \boldsymbol{a}, \quad \boldsymbol{x} \geq \boldsymbol{0}, \quad \boldsymbol{y} \geq \boldsymbol{0}\,.$$

Exchange method

1. Rewrite the constraints in the form $\boldsymbol{0} = -\boldsymbol{Ax}+\boldsymbol{a}$ and replace the zeros on the left-hand side by *artificial variables* y_i. Then one gets

$$\boldsymbol{y} = -\boldsymbol{Ax}+\boldsymbol{a}, \quad \text{where} \quad \boldsymbol{y} = (y_i)$$

2. Complete the table by the objective function $z = \boldsymbol{c}^\top \boldsymbol{x} + c_0$ and by the *auxiliary function* $\tilde{h} = \sum\limits_{i=1}^{m} y_i$:

$$\tilde{h} = \sum_{k=1}^{n} \tilde{\delta}_k x_k = \tilde{\delta}_0 \quad \text{with}$$

$$\tilde{\delta}_k = \sum_{i=1}^{m}(-a_{ik}), \quad \tilde{\delta}_0 = \sum_{i=1}^{m} a_i$$

The table obtained

	$\boldsymbol{x}$	1
$\boldsymbol{y}=$	$-\boldsymbol{A}$	$\boldsymbol{a}$
$z=$	$\boldsymbol{c}^\top$	c_0
$\tilde{h}=$	$\tilde{\delta}_1 \ \ldots \ \tilde{\delta}_n$	$\tilde{\delta}_0$

is a simplex table of the *auxiliary problem*

$$\tilde{h} = \sum_{i=1}^{m} y_i \to \min$$

$$\boldsymbol{y} = -\boldsymbol{Ax} + \boldsymbol{a}, \quad \boldsymbol{x} \geq \boldsymbol{0}, \quad \boldsymbol{y} \geq \boldsymbol{0}\,.$$

Gaussian elimination

3. Solve the auxiliary problem by the simplex method. The optimal table of the auxiliary problem has the form

$\boldsymbol{x}_B$	$\boldsymbol{y}_B$	z	h	$\boldsymbol{x}_N$ $\boldsymbol{y}_N$	$=$
1 ⋱ 1					
	1 ⋱ 1				
		1			
			1		h_0

The z- and the h-column are usually omitted.

Exchange method

3. Solve the auxiliary problem by the simplex method. The optimal table of the auxiliary problem has the form

	$\boldsymbol{x}_N$ $\boldsymbol{y}_N$	1
$\boldsymbol{x}_B=$		
$\boldsymbol{y}_B=$		
$z=$		
$\tilde{h}=$		$\tilde{h}_0$

Case 1 In the case $h_0 < 0$ resp. $\tilde{h}_0 > 0$ the original problem is unsolvable, since it fails to have feasible vectors.

Case 2 If $h_0 = 0$ and $\tilde{h}_0 = 0$, respectively, and if not any artificial variable is a basic variable, then after deleting the $\boldsymbol{y}_N$-columns and the auxiliary objective function one obtains a simplex table of the original problem.

Case 3 If $h_0 = 0$ and $\tilde{h}_0 = 0$, respectively, but there are still artificial variables in the basis, these variables can be made to basic ones by an exchange $\boldsymbol{y}_B \Longleftrightarrow \boldsymbol{x}_N$. If, in doing so, a table occurs in which the exchange cannot be continued, then in this table one can remove the rows $\boldsymbol{y}_B=$ as well as the $\boldsymbol{y}_N$-columns and the auxiliary objective function. After that one has a simplex table of the original problem.

- Remark to Step 1: In rows i with $a_i \geq 0$ already possessing a basic variable x_k, artificial variables need not be introduced. In this case the quantities δ_k and $\tilde{\delta}_k$, resp., are to be replaced by $\sum(-a_{ik})$, δ_0 has to be replaced by $\sum(-a_i)$ and $\tilde{\delta}_0$ by $\sum a_i$, resp. (summation only over those rows i in which artificial variables occur).
- Remark to Step 3: The $\boldsymbol{y}_N$-columns can be removed immediately.
- The combination of *Phase 1* (generation of an initial simplex table) and *Phase 2* (simplex method) is usually denoted as the *two-phase method*.

Duality

Basic version of a linear programming problem

$$\begin{array}{c} z(\boldsymbol{x}) = \boldsymbol{c}^\top \boldsymbol{x} \to \max \\ \boldsymbol{A}\boldsymbol{x} \le \boldsymbol{a} \\ \boldsymbol{x} \ge \boldsymbol{0} \end{array} \quad \Longleftrightarrow \quad \begin{array}{c} w(\boldsymbol{u}) = \boldsymbol{a}^\top \boldsymbol{u} \to \min \\ \boldsymbol{A}^\top \boldsymbol{u} \ge \boldsymbol{c} \\ \boldsymbol{u} \ge \boldsymbol{0} \end{array}$$

Generalized version of a linear programming problem

$$\begin{array}{c} z(\boldsymbol{x},\boldsymbol{y}) = \boldsymbol{c}^\top \boldsymbol{x} + \boldsymbol{d}^\top \boldsymbol{y} \to \max \\ \boldsymbol{A}\boldsymbol{x} + \boldsymbol{B}\boldsymbol{y} \le \boldsymbol{a} \\ \boldsymbol{C}\boldsymbol{x} + \boldsymbol{D}\boldsymbol{y} = \boldsymbol{b} \\ \boldsymbol{x} \ge \boldsymbol{0},\ \boldsymbol{y} \text{ frei} \end{array} \quad \Longleftrightarrow \quad \begin{array}{c} w(\boldsymbol{u},\boldsymbol{v}) = \boldsymbol{a}^\top \boldsymbol{u} + \boldsymbol{b}^\top \boldsymbol{v} \to \min \\ \boldsymbol{A}^\top \boldsymbol{u} + \boldsymbol{C}^\top \boldsymbol{v} \ge \boldsymbol{c} \\ \boldsymbol{B}^\top \boldsymbol{u} + \boldsymbol{D}^\top \boldsymbol{v} = \boldsymbol{d} \\ \boldsymbol{u} \ge \boldsymbol{0},\ \boldsymbol{v} \text{ frei} \end{array}$$

primal problem **dual problem**

Properties

- The dual to the dual problem is the primal problem.
- *Weak duality theorem.* If the vectors $\boldsymbol{x}$ and $(\boldsymbol{x},\boldsymbol{y})^\top$, resp., are primal feasible and $\boldsymbol{u}$ resp. $(\boldsymbol{u},\boldsymbol{v})^\top$ are dual feasible, then $z(\boldsymbol{x}) \le w(\boldsymbol{u})$ and $z(\boldsymbol{x},\boldsymbol{y}) \le w(\boldsymbol{u},\boldsymbol{v})$, respectively.
- *Strong duality theorem.* If the vectors $\boldsymbol{x}^*$ resp. $(\boldsymbol{x}^*,\boldsymbol{y}^*)^\top$ are primal feasible and $\boldsymbol{u}^*$ resp. $(\boldsymbol{u}^*,\boldsymbol{v}^*)^\top$ are dual feasible, and if $z(\boldsymbol{x}^*) = w(\boldsymbol{u}^*)$ resp. $z(\boldsymbol{x}^*,\boldsymbol{y}^*) = w(\boldsymbol{u}^*,\boldsymbol{v}^*)$, then $\boldsymbol{x}^*$ resp. $(\boldsymbol{x}^*,\boldsymbol{y}^*)^\top$ is an optimal solution of the primal problem and $\boldsymbol{u}^*$ resp. $(\boldsymbol{u}^*,\boldsymbol{v}^*)^\top$ is a dual optimal solution.
- A primal feasible solution $\boldsymbol{x}^*$ resp. $(\boldsymbol{x}^*,\boldsymbol{y}^*)^\top$ is an optimal solution of the primal problem if and only if there exists a dual feasible solution $\boldsymbol{u}^*$ resp. $(\boldsymbol{u}^*,\boldsymbol{v}^*)^\top$ such that $z(\boldsymbol{x}^*) = w(\boldsymbol{u}^*)$ resp. $z(\boldsymbol{x}^*,\boldsymbol{y}^*) = w(\boldsymbol{u}^*,\boldsymbol{v}^*)$.
- If both the primal and the dual problem have feasible solutions, then both problems have also optimal solutions, where $z^* = w^*$.
- If the primal (dual) problem has feasible solutions and if the dual (primal) problem is unsolvable, since it fails to have feasible solutions, then the primal (dual) problem is unsolvable due to $z \to +\infty$ ($w \to -\infty$).
- *Complementarity theorem* (for the basic version). A primal feasible solution $\boldsymbol{x}^*$ is an optimal solution of the primal problem if and only if there exists a dual feasible solution $\boldsymbol{u}^*$ such that for all components of the vectors $\boldsymbol{x}^*$, $\boldsymbol{A}\boldsymbol{x}^* - \boldsymbol{a}$, $\boldsymbol{u}^*$ and $\boldsymbol{A}^\top\boldsymbol{u}^* - \boldsymbol{c}$ the following relations (*complementary slackness conditions*) are fulfilled:

$$\begin{array}{llll} x_i^* = 0 \quad \text{if} \quad (\boldsymbol{A}^\top\boldsymbol{u}^* - \boldsymbol{c})_i > 0 & \qquad (\boldsymbol{A}\boldsymbol{x}^* - \boldsymbol{a})_i = 0 \quad \text{if} \quad u_i^* > 0 \\ u_i^* = 0 \quad \text{if} \quad (\boldsymbol{A}\boldsymbol{x}^* - \boldsymbol{a})_i > 0 & \qquad (\boldsymbol{A}^\top\boldsymbol{u}^* - \boldsymbol{c})_i = 0 \quad \text{if} \quad x_i^* > 0 \end{array}$$

Shadow prices

If the primal problem (basic version) represents a production planning model with profit vector $\boldsymbol{c}$ and resource vector $\boldsymbol{a}$, and if $\boldsymbol{u}^* = (u_1^*, \dots, u_m^*)^\top$ is the optimal solution of the corresponding dual problem, then under certain assumptions the following assertion is true: an increase of the resource a_i by one unit implies the growth of the maximal profit by u_i units (*shadow prices*).

Transportation problem

Statement of the problem

From m stockhouses A_i with stocks $a_i \geq 0$, $i=1, \dots, m$, n consumers B_j with demand $b_j \geq 0$, $j=1, \dots, n$, are to be supplied. Knowing the transportation costs which are linear with respect to the quantities of delivery having the price coefficients c_{ij}, the total transportation costs are to be minimized.

Mathematical model (transportation problem)

$$
\begin{aligned}
& z = \sum_{i=1}^{m} \sum_{j=1}^{n} c_{ij} x_{ij} \to \min; \\
\text{subject to} \quad & \sum_{j=1}^{n} x_{ij} = a_i, \quad i = 1, \dots, m \\
& \sum_{i=1}^{m} x_{ij} = b_j, \quad j = 1, \dots, n \\
& x_{ij} \geq 0 \quad \forall\, i, j
\end{aligned}
$$

- The (m,n)-matrix $\boldsymbol{X} = (x_{ij})$ of quantities of a good to be delivered from A_i to B_j is called a *feasible solution (transportation plan)* if it satisfies the constraints.
- The transportation problem is solvable if and only if

$$
\sum_{i=1}^{m} a_i = \sum_{j=1}^{n} b_j \qquad \textbf{saturation condition}
$$

- An ordered set $\{(i_k, j_k)\}_{k=1}^{2l}$ of double indices is said to be a *cycle* if

$$
\begin{aligned}
i_{k+1} &= i_k \quad \text{for} \quad k = 1, 3, \dots, 2l-1, \\
j_{k+1} &= j_k \quad \text{for} \quad k = 2, 4, \dots, 2l-2, \qquad j_{2l} = j_1
\end{aligned}
$$

- If, by adding further double indices, the index set $J_+(\boldsymbol{X}) = \{(i,j) \mid x_{ij} > 0\}$ can be extended to a set $J_S(\boldsymbol{X})$ not containing a cycle and consisting of exactly $m+n-1$ elements, then the feasible solution $\boldsymbol{X}$ is called a *basic solution*.

Transportation algorithm

Starting point: basic solution $\boldsymbol{X}$

1. Find numbers u_i, $i = 1, \ldots, m$, and v_j, $j = 1, \ldots, n$, such that $u_i + v_j = c_{ij} \quad \forall (i,j) \in J_S(\boldsymbol{X})$. If $w_{ij} := c_{ij} - u_i - v_j \geq 0$ for $i = 1, \ldots, m$ and $j = 1, \ldots, n$, then $\boldsymbol{X}$ is optimal.

2. Choose (p, q) with $w_{pq} < 0$ and find, starting from $(i_1, j_1) := (p, q)$, a cycle Z in the set $J_S(\boldsymbol{X}) \cup \{(p,q)\}$.

3. Determine a new solution $\boldsymbol{X}$ by setting $x_{ij} := x_{ij} + (-1)^{k+1} x_{rs}$ for $(i,j) \in Z$, where $x_{rs} := \min\{x_{i_k j_k} \mid (i_k, j_k) \in Z, k = 2, 4, \ldots, 2l\}$. The new solution $\boldsymbol{X}$ is a basic solution associated with the double index set $J_S(\boldsymbol{X}) := J_S(\boldsymbol{X}) \cup \{(p,q)\} \setminus \{(r,s)\}$. Go to Step 1.

Tabular representation of the transportation algorithm

The iterations of the transportation algorithm can be represented in the following tabular form by placing only the variables $x_{ij} \in \boldsymbol{X}$ (boxed) with $(i,j) \in J_S(\boldsymbol{X})$ and only the variables w_{ij} with $(i,j) \notin J_S(\boldsymbol{X})$. The remaining variables x_{ij}, $(i,j) \notin J_S(\boldsymbol{X})$, and w_{ij}, $(i,j) \in J_S(\boldsymbol{X})$, not occurring in the table are automatically equal to zero. The cycle for the considered example is indicated by an rectangle.

	v_1	v_2	$\cdots$	v_q	$\cdots$	v_m
u_1	$w_{1,1}$	x_{12}	$\cdots$	x_{1q}	$\cdots$	w_{1m}
u_2	$w_{2,1}$	w_{22}	$\cdots$	x_{2q}	$\cdots$	x_{2m}
$\vdots$	$\vdots$	$\vdots$		$\vdots$		$\vdots$
u_p	x_{p1}	x_{p2}	$\cdots$	$w_{pq} < 0$	$\cdots$	w_{pm}
$\vdots$	$\vdots$	$\vdots$		$\vdots$		$\vdots$
u_m	x_{m1}	w_{m2}	$\cdots$	w_{mq}	$\cdots$	w_{mn}

A cycle with four elements

The values of u_i, v_j, w_{ij} can be found starting with $u_1 = 0$ and proceeding by following the boxes (cf. the table):
$v_2 = c_{12}$ (due to $w_{12} = 0$), $v_q = c_{1q}$ (due to $w_{1q} = 0$), $u_2 = c_{2q} - v_q$ (due to $w_{2q} = 0$), $v_m = c_{2m} - u_2$ (due to $w_{2m} = 0$), $u_p = \ldots$, $v_1 = \ldots$, $u_m = \ldots$ etc.

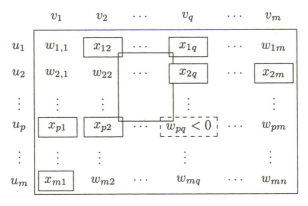

Suppose that in the table at p. 135 $w_{pq} < 0$ and $x_{p2} \leq x_{1q}$ (so that in this example $x_{rs} = x_{p2}$). Then the next table will be computed as follows:

	$\bar{v}_1$	$\bar{v}_2$	$\cdots$	$\bar{v}_q$	$\cdots$	$\bar{v}_m$
$\bar{u}_1$	$\bar{w}_{1,1}$	$\bar{x}_{12}$	$\cdots$	$\bar{x}_{1q}$	$\cdots$	$\bar{w}_{1m}$
$\bar{u}_2$	$\bar{w}_{2,1}$	$\bar{w}_{22}$	$\cdots$	x_{2q}	$\cdots$	x_{2m}
$\vdots$	$\vdots$	$\vdots$		$\vdots$		$\vdots$
$\bar{u}_p$	x_{p1}	$\bar{w}_{p2}$	$\cdots$	$\bar{x}_{pq}$	$\cdots$	$\bar{w}_{pm}$
$\vdots$	$\vdots$	$\vdots$		$\vdots$		$\vdots$
$\bar{u}_m$	x_{m1}	$\bar{w}_{m2}$	$\cdots$	$\bar{w}_{mq}$	$\cdots$	$\bar{w}_{mn}$

The values are $\bar{x}_{p2} = 0, \quad \bar{x}_{pq} = x_{p2}, \quad \bar{x}_{12} = x_{12} + x_{p2}, \quad \bar{x}_{1q} = x_{1q} - x_{p2}$.

The quantities $\bar{u}_i, \bar{v}_j, \bar{w}_{ij}$ can be calculated in the same way as above, beginning with $\bar{u}_1 = 0$.

Rules for finding an initial basic solution

North-West corner rule

Assign to the nord west corner the maximal possible quantity of the good. Remove the empty stockhouse or the consumer saturated and repeat the step. Only in the last step both the stockhouse **and** the consumer are removed.

Rule of minimal costs

Assign to the cheapest transportation route the maximal possible quantity of the good. Remove the empty stockhouse or the consumer saturated and repeat the step. Only in the last step both the stockhouse **and** the consumer are removed.

Vogel's rule

For each row and column, find the difference between the maximal and minimal cost price coefficient. In that row or column, which is determined by the greatest of these differences, assign to the cheapest transportation route the maximal possible quantity of the good. Remove the empty stockhouse or the consumer saturated and repeat the step, beginning with correcting the differences. Only in the last step both the stockhouse **and** the consumer are removed.

Descriptive Statistics

Basic notions

Basis of a statistical analysis is a set (*statistical mass*) of objects (*statistical unit*), for which one (in the univariate case) or several (in the multivariate case) *characters* are tested. The results which can occur in observing a character are called the *character values*.

A character is said to be *discrete* if it has finite or countably many character values. It is referred to as *continuous* if the character values can take any value from an interval. The character values $x_1, \ldots, x_n$ concretely observed are called the *sample values*, and $(x_1, \ldots, x_n)$ is a *sample of size* n. When ordering the sample values, the *ordered sample* $x_{(1)} \le x_{(2)} \le \ldots \le x_{(n)}$ is obtained, where $x_{\min} = x_{(1)}$, $x_{\max} = x_{(n)}$.

Univariate data analysis

Discrete character

Given: k character values $a_1, \ldots, a_k$ such that $a_1 < \ldots < a_k$ and a sample $(x_1, \ldots, x_n)$ of size n

$H_n(a_j)$	–	absolute frequency of a_j; number of sample values with character value a_j, $j = 1, \ldots, k$
$h_n(a_j) = \frac{1}{n} H_n(a_j)$	–	relative frequency of a_j; $0 \le h_n(a_j) \le 1,\ j = 1, \ldots, k,\ \sum\limits_{j=1}^{k} h_n(a_j) = 1$
$\sum\limits_{i=1}^{j} H_n(a_i)$	–	absolute cumulative frequency, $j = 1, \ldots, k$
$\sum\limits_{i=1}^{j} h_n(a_i)$	–	relative cumulative frequency, $j = 1, \ldots, k$
$F_n(x) = \sum\limits_{j: a_j \le x} h_n(a_j)$	–	empirical distribution function $(-\infty < x < \infty)$

Continuous character

Given: sample $(x_1, \ldots, x_n)$ of size n and a grouping in classes $K_j = [x_{j,l}; x_{j,u})$, $j = 1, \ldots, m$

$x_{j,l}$	–	lower class bound of the j-th class
$x_{j,u}$	–	upper class bound of the j-th class
$u_j = \frac{1}{2}(x_{j,l} + x_{j,u})$	–	class mark of the j-th class
H_j	–	j-th absolute class frequency; number of sample values belonging to the class K_j
$h_j = \frac{1}{n} H_j$	–	j-th relative class frequency
$F_n(x) = \sum\limits_{j: x_{j,u} \le x} h_j$	–	empirical distribution function $(-\infty < x < \infty)$

Statistical parameters

Means

$\overline{x}_n = \frac{1}{n}\sum_{i=1}^{n} x_i$	– arithmetic mean (average) for non-classified data
$\overline{x}_{(n)} = \frac{1}{n}\sum_{j=1}^{m} u_j H_j$	– arithmetic mean for classified data
$\tilde{x}_{(n)} = \begin{cases} x_{(\frac{n+1}{2})} & n \text{ odd} \\ \frac{1}{2}[x_{(\frac{n}{2})} + x_{(\frac{n}{2}+1)}] & n \text{ even} \end{cases}$	– empirical median
$\dot{x} = \sqrt[n]{x_1 \cdot x_2 \cdot \ldots \cdot x_n} \quad (x_j > 0)$	– geometric mean

Measures of dispersion

$R = x_{\max} - x_{\min}$	– range of variation
$s^2 = \frac{1}{n-1}\sum_{i=1}^{n}(x_i - \overline{x}_n)^2$	– empirical variance for non-classified data
$s^2 = \frac{1}{n-1}\sum_{j=1}^{m}(u_j - \overline{x}_{(n)})^2 H_j$	– empirical variance for classified data
$s = \sqrt{s^2}$	– empirical standard deviation
$s_*^2 = s^2 - \frac{b^2}{12}$	– Sheppard's correction (for constant class length b)
$\nu = \frac{s}{\overline{x}_n}$	– coefficient of variation $(\overline{x}_n \neq 0)$
$\tilde{d} = \frac{1}{n}\sum_{i=1}^{n} \lvert x_i - \tilde{x}_{(n)} \rvert$	– mean absolute deviation from the median $\tilde{x}_{(n)}$
$\bar{d} = \frac{1}{n}\sum_{i=1}^{n} \lvert x_i - \overline{x}_n \rvert$	– mean absolute deviation from the mean $\overline{x}_n$

q-quantiles

$$\tilde{x}_q = \begin{cases} \frac{1}{2}[x_{(nq)} + x_{(nq+1)}] & nq \in \mathbb{N} \\ x_{(\lfloor nq \rfloor + 1)} & \text{otherwise} \end{cases}$$

– q-quantile $(0 < q < 1)$

In particular:

$\tilde{x}_{0.5} = \tilde{x}_{(n)}$; $\tilde{x}_{0.25}$ – lower quartile; $\tilde{x}_{0.75}$ – upper quartile

Empirical skewness

$$g_1 = \frac{\frac{1}{n}\sum_{i=1}^{n}(x_i - \overline{x}_n)^3}{\sqrt{\left(\frac{1}{n}\sum_{i=1}^{n}(x_i - \overline{x}_n)^2\right)^3}} \qquad g_1 = \frac{\frac{1}{n}\sum_{j=1}^{m}(u_j - \overline{x}_{(n)})^3 H_j}{\sqrt{\left(\frac{1}{n}\sum_{j=1}^{m}(u_j - \overline{x}_{(n)})^2 H_j\right)^3}}$$

(non-classified data) (classified data)

Empirical kurtosis

$$g_2 = \frac{\frac{1}{n}\sum_{i=1}^{n}(x_i - \overline{x}_n)^4}{\left(\frac{1}{n}\sum_{i=1}^{n}(x_i - \overline{x}_n)^2\right)^2} - 3 \qquad g_2 = \frac{\frac{1}{n}\sum_{j=1}^{m}(u_j - \overline{x}_{(n)})^4 H_j}{\left(\frac{1}{n}\sum_{j=1}^{m}(u_j - \overline{x}_{(n)})^2 H_j\right)^2} - 3$$

(non-classified data) (classified data)

Moments of order r (for non-classified data)

$$\hat{m}_r = \frac{1}{n}\sum_{i=1}^{n} x_i^r$$ – empirical initial moment

$$\hat{\mu}_r = \frac{1}{n}\sum_{i=1}^{n}(x_i - \overline{x}_n)^r$$ – empirical central moment

- In particular, one has $\hat{m}_1 = \overline{x}_n$, $\hat{\mu}_2 = \frac{n-1}{n} s^2$.

Bivariate data analysis

Given: sample $(x_1, y_1), \dots, (x_n, y_n)$ with respect to two characters x und y

Empirical values

$$\overline{x}_n = \frac{1}{n}\sum_{i=1}^{n} x_i$$ – mean with respect to character x

$$\overline{y}_n = \frac{1}{n}\sum_{i=1}^{n} y_i$$ – mean with respect to character y

Empirical values

$$s_x^2 = \frac{1}{n-1}\sum_{i=1}^{n}(x_i - \overline{x}_n)^2 = \frac{1}{n-1}\left(\sum_{i=1}^{n} x_i^2 - n\overline{x}_n^2\right)$$

– empirical variance with respect to character x

$$s_y^2 = \frac{1}{n-1}\sum_{i=1}^{n}(y_i - \overline{y}_n)^2 = \frac{1}{n-1}\left(\sum_{i=1}^{n} y_i^2 - n\overline{y}_n^2\right)$$

– empirical variance with respect to character y

$$s_{xy} = \frac{1}{n-1}\sum_{i=1}^{n}(x_i - \overline{x}_n)(y_i - \overline{y}_n)$$

– empirical covariance

$$= \frac{1}{n-1}\left(\sum_{i=1}^{n} x_i y_i - n\overline{x}_n\overline{y}_n\right)$$

$$r_{xy} = \frac{s_{xy}}{\sqrt{s_x^2 \cdot s_y^2}} \qquad (-1 \le r_{xy} \le 1)$$

– empirical coefficient of correlation

$$B_{xy} = r_{xy}^2$$

– empirical coefficient of determination

Linear regression

The coefficients $\hat{a}$ and $\hat{b}$ are referred to as *empirical* (linear) *regression coefficients* if the condition $\sum\limits_{i=1}^{n}[y_i - (\hat{a} + \hat{b}x_i)]^2 = \min\limits_{a,b} \sum\limits_{i=1}^{n}[y_i - (a + bx_i)]^2$ is satisfied.

$y = \hat{a} + \hat{b}x$ – empirical regression line (linear regression function)

$$\hat{a} = \overline{y}_n - \hat{b}\overline{x}_n, \qquad \hat{b} = \frac{s_{xy}}{s_x^2} = r_{xy}\sqrt{\frac{s_y^2}{s_x^2}}$$

$$\hat{s}^2 = \frac{1}{n-2}\sum_{i=1}^{n}\left[y_i - (\hat{a} + \hat{b}x_i)\right]^2 = \frac{n-1}{n-2} \cdot s_y^2\,(1 - r_{xy}^2)$$

– empirical residual variance

Quadratic regression

The coefficients $\hat{a}$, $\hat{b}$ and $\hat{c}$ are called *empirical* (quadratic) *regression coefficients* if they satisfy the condition $\sum_{i=1}^{n}(y_i - (\hat{a} + \hat{b}x_i + \hat{c}x_i^2))^2 = \min_{a,b,c} \sum_{i=1}^{n}(y_i - (a + bx_i + cx_i^2))^2$ They are the solution of the following system of equations:

$$
\begin{aligned}
\hat{a} \cdot n &+ \hat{b}\sum_{i=1}^{n} x_i &+ \hat{c}\sum_{i=1}^{n} x_i^2 &= \sum_{i=1}^{n} y_i \\
\hat{a}\sum_{i=1}^{n} x_i &+ \hat{b}\sum_{i=1}^{n} x_i^2 &+ \hat{c}\sum_{i=1}^{n} x_i^3 &= \sum_{i=1}^{n} x_i y_i \\
\hat{a}\sum_{i=1}^{n} x_i^2 &+ \hat{b}\sum_{i=1}^{n} x_i^3 &+ \hat{c}\sum_{i=1}^{n} x_i^4 &= \sum_{i=1}^{n} x_i^2 y_i
\end{aligned}
$$

$y = \hat{a} + \hat{b}x + \hat{c}x^2$ – empirical (quadratic) regression function

$\hat{s}^2 = \frac{1}{n-3}\sum_{i=1}^{n}\left[y_i - (\hat{a} + \hat{b}x_i + \hat{c}x_i^2)\right]^2$ – empirical residual variance

Exponential regression

The coefficients $\hat{a}$ and $\hat{b}$ satisfying the condition $\sum_{i=1}^{n}(\ln y_i - (\ln \hat{a} + \hat{b}x_i))^2 = \min_{a,b} \sum_{i=1}^{n}(\ln y_i - (\ln a + bx_i))^2$ are called *empirical* (exponential) *regression coefficients* (where it is assumed that $y_i > 0$, $i = 1, \ldots, n$).

$y = \hat{a}e^{\hat{b}x}$ – *empirical* (exponential) *regression function*

$$\hat{a} = e^{\frac{1}{n}\sum_{i=1}^{n}\ln y_i - \hat{b}\overline{x}_n}, \qquad \hat{b} = \frac{\sum_{i=1}^{n}(x_i - \overline{x}_n)(\ln y_i - \frac{1}{n}\sum_{i=1}^{n}\ln y_i)}{\sum_{i=1}^{n}(x_i - \overline{x}_n)^2}$$

Ratios

Given a basket of goods W consisting of n goods. Let the good i have the price p_i and the amount q_i, $i = 1, \ldots, n$.

Notations

$W_i = p_i \cdot q_i$	–	value of good i
$\sum\limits_{i=1}^{n} W_i = \sum\limits_{i=1}^{n} p_i q_i$	–	total value of the basket of goods W
$p_{i\tau}$, p_{it}	–	price of good i in the basic period and in the given period, resp. (= basic and actual price, resp.)
$q_{i\tau}$ bzw. q_{it}	–	amount of good i in the basic and in the given period, resp. (= basic and actual quantity, resp.)

Indices

$m_i^W = \dfrac{W_{it}}{W_{i\tau}} = \dfrac{p_{it} \cdot q_{it}}{p_{i\tau} \cdot q_{i\tau}}$	–	(dynamical) measure of value of good i
$I_{\tau,t}^{W} = \dfrac{\sum\limits_{i=1}^{n} W_{it}}{\sum\limits_{i=1}^{n} W_{i\tau}} = \dfrac{\sum\limits_{i=1}^{n} p_{it} q_{it}}{\sum\limits_{i=1}^{n} p_{i\tau} q_{i\tau}}$	–	value index of the basket of goods W; sales index (sale oriented) or consumer expenditure index (consumer oriented)
$I_{\tau,t}^{\mathrm{Paa},p} = \dfrac{\sum\limits_{i=1}^{n} p_{it} q_{it}}{\sum\limits_{i=1}^{n} p_{i\tau} q_{it}}$	–	Paasche's price index
$I_{\tau,t}^{\mathrm{Paa},q} = \dfrac{\sum\limits_{i=1}^{n} p_{it} q_{it}}{\sum\limits_{i=1}^{n} p_{it} q_{i\tau}}$	–	Paasche's quantum index
$I_{\tau,t}^{\mathrm{Las},p} = \dfrac{\sum\limits_{i=1}^{n} p_{it} q_{i\tau}}{\sum\limits_{i=1}^{n} p_{i\tau} q_{i\tau}}$	–	Laspeyres' price index
$I_{\tau,t}^{\mathrm{Las},q} = \dfrac{\sum\limits_{i=1}^{n} p_{i\tau} q_{it}}{\sum\limits_{i=1}^{n} p_{i\tau} q_{i\tau}}$		Laspeyres' quantum index

• Paasche's indices describe the average relative change of a component (price or quantity) by means of weights (quantities or prices) of the given period.

• Laspeyres' indices describe the average relative change of a component (price or quantity) by means of weights (quantities or prices) of the basic period.

Drobisch's indices

The goods from a basket of goods are called *commensurable* with respect to quantities if they are measured by the same sizes. For such goods the following indices are defined.

$I_{\tau,t}^{\mathrm{Dro},p} = \dfrac{\sum\limits_{i=1}^{n} p_{it}\cdot q_{it}}{\sum\limits_{i=1}^{n} q_{it}} \Big/ \dfrac{\sum\limits_{i=1}^{n} p_{i\tau}\cdot q_{i\tau}}{\sum\limits_{i=1}^{n} q_{i\tau}} = \dfrac{\overline{p}_t}{\overline{p}_\tau}$	– Drobisch's price index ($\overline{p}_\tau > 0$); it describes the change of average prices
$I_{\tau,t}^{\mathrm{Dro,str},\tau} = \dfrac{\sum\limits_{i=1}^{n} p_{i\tau}\cdot q_{it}}{\sum\limits_{i=1}^{n} q_{it}} \Big/ \dfrac{\sum\limits_{i=1}^{n} p_{i\tau}\cdot q_{i\tau}}{\sum\limits_{i=1}^{n} q_{i\tau}}$	– Drobisch's structure index related to basic prices
$I_{\tau,t}^{\mathrm{Dro,str},t} = \dfrac{\sum\limits_{i=1}^{n} p_{it}\cdot q_{it}}{\sum\limits_{i=1}^{n} q_{it}} \Big/ \dfrac{\sum\limits_{i=1}^{n} p_{it}\cdot q_{i\tau}}{\sum\limits_{i=1}^{n} q_{i\tau}}$	– Drobisch's structure index related to actual prices

• Drobisch's structure indices are statistical parameters formed from fictitious and nominal average prices.

Inventory analysis

A statistical mass considered within the period (t_A, t_E) under review is called a *population of period data* (stock). It is said to be *closed* if the stock before t_A and after t_E is equal to zero, otherwise it is said to be *open*. A statistical mass occurring only at certain moments is called a *period-based population* (e. g. accession mass, replacement mass).

Notations

B_j	–	stock (in units of quantity) at moment t_j, $t_A \le t_j \le t_E$
B_A or B_E	–	initial and final stock at moment t_A and t_E, resp.
Z_i	–	accession mass (in units) in the time interval $(t_{i-1}, t_i]$
A_i	–	replacement mass (in units) in the time interval $(t_{i-1}, t_i]$

Stocktaking

$B_j = B_A + Z_{(j)} - A_{(j)}$	– stock mass at moment t_j with:
$Z_{(j)} = \sum\limits_{i=1}^{j} Z_i$	– sum of accession masses
$A_{(j)} = \sum\limits_{i=1}^{j} A_i$	– sum of replacement masses

Average stocks

$\overline{Z} = \frac{1}{m} \sum\limits_{i=1}^{m} Z_i$	– average accession rate (with respect to m time intervals)
$\overline{A} = \frac{1}{m} \sum\limits_{i=1}^{m} A_i$	– average replacement rate (with respect to m time intervals)
$\overline{B} = \frac{1}{t_m - t_0} \sum\limits_{j=1}^{m} B_{j-1}(t_j - t_{j-1})$	– average stock for m time intervals (if the measurement of the stock is possible at all moments of changes)

$$\overline{B} = \frac{1}{t_m - t_0} \left(\frac{B_0(t_1 - t_0)}{2} + \sum_{j=1}^{m-1} \frac{B_j \cdot (t_{j+1} - t_{j-1})}{2} + \frac{B_m(t_m - t_{m-1})}{2} \right)$$

– average stock for m time intervals (if the measurement of B_j is possible at **all** moments t_j)

In the case $t_j - t_{j-1} = \text{const} \ \forall j$ one has:

$$\overline{B} = \frac{1}{m} \sum_{j=0}^{m-1} B_j \qquad \text{or} \qquad \overline{B} = \frac{1}{m} \left(\frac{B_0}{2} + \sum_{j=1}^{m-1} B_j + \frac{B_m}{2} \right)$$

Average length of stay

$$\overline{\nu} = \frac{\overline{B}(t_m - t_0)}{A_{(m)}} = \frac{\overline{B}(t_m - t_0)}{Z_{(m)}}$$

– closed stock

$$\overline{\nu} = \frac{2\overline{B}(t_m - t_0)}{A_{(m)} + Z_{(m)}} \qquad \text{or} \qquad \overline{\nu} = \frac{2\overline{B}(t_m - t_0)}{A_{(m-1)} + Z_{(m-1)}}$$

– open stock

the second formula holds if accession and replacement occur at the moment t_m

Time series analysis

By a time series $y_t = y(t)$, $t = t_1, t_2, \ldots$, an ordered in time sequence of values of a quantitatively observable character is understood.

Additive and multiplicative model

$y(t) = T(t) + Z(t) + S(t) + R(t)$ resp. $y(t) = T(t) \cdot Z(t) \cdot S(t) \cdot R(t)$					
$T(t)$	–	trend component	$Z(t)$	–	cyclic component
$S(t)$	–	seasonal component	$R(t)$	–	stochastic component

Trend behaviour

$T(t) = a + bt$	–	linear trend
$T(t) = a + bt + ct^2$	–	quadratic trend
$T(t) = a \cdot b^t$	–	exponential trend

- The exponential trend $T(t) = a \cdot b^t$ can be reduced by the transformations

$$T^*(t) = \ln T(t),$$
$$a^* = \ln a,$$
$$b^* = \ln b$$

to the linear case $T^*(t) = a^* + b^*t$.

Least squares method

This method serves for the estimation of the linear trend $T(t) = a + bt$ and the quadratic trend $T(t) = a + bt + ct^2$, respectively (see p. 110).

Moving average methods

These methods serve for the estimation of the trend component by means of n observation values $y_1, \ldots, y_n$.

m odd

$$\hat{T}_{\frac{m+1}{2}} = \frac{1}{m}(y_1 + y_2 + \ldots + y_m)$$
$$\hat{T}_{\frac{m+3}{2}} = \frac{1}{m}(y_2 + y_3 + \ldots + y_{m+1})$$
$$\vdots$$
$$\hat{T}_{n-\frac{m-1}{2}} = \frac{1}{m}(y_{n-m+1} + \ldots + y_n)$$

m even

$$\begin{aligned}
\hat{T}_{\frac{m}{2}+1} &= \tfrac{1}{m}\left(\tfrac{1}{2}y_1 + y_2 + \ldots + y_m + \tfrac{1}{2}y_{m+1}\right) \\
\hat{T}_{\frac{m}{2}+2} &= \tfrac{1}{m}\left(\tfrac{1}{2}y_2 + y_3 + \ldots + y_{m+1} + \tfrac{1}{2}y_{m+2}\right) \\
&\vdots \\
\hat{T}_{n-\frac{m}{2}} &= \tfrac{1}{m}\left(\tfrac{1}{2}y_{n-m} + \ldots + y_{n-1} + \tfrac{1}{2}y_n\right)
\end{aligned}$$

Seasonal adjustment

For trend adjusted time series (without cyclic components) with given period p and k observations per period the equations

$$y^*_{ij} = s_j + r_{ij} \qquad (i = 1, \ldots, k;\ j = 1, \ldots, p)$$

provide an additive time series model with seasonal components s_j the estimations of which are denoted by $\hat{s}_j$.

$$\overline{y}^*_{\cdot j} = \frac{1}{k}\sum_{i=1}^{k} y^*_{ij}, \quad j = 1, \ldots, p$$ – period mean

$$\overline{\overline{y}}^* = \frac{1}{p}\sum_{j=1}^{p} \overline{y}^*_{\cdot j}$$ – total mean

$$\hat{s}_j = y^*_{\cdot j} - \overline{\overline{y}}^*$$ – seasonal indices

$$\begin{array}{cccc}
y^*_{11} - \hat{s}_1, & y^*_{12} - \hat{s}_2, & \ldots, & y^*_{1p} - \hat{s}_p \\
\cdots & \cdots & \cdots & \cdots \\
y^*_{k1} - \hat{s}_1, & y^*_{k2} - \hat{s}_2, & \ldots, & y^*_{kp} - \hat{s}_p
\end{array}$$ – seasonally adjusted time series

Exponential smoothing

For a time series $y_1, \ldots, y_t$ (in general, without trend) one obtains the forecasting $\hat{y}_{t+1} = \alpha y_t + \alpha(1-\alpha)y_{t-1} + \alpha(1-\alpha)^2 y_{t-2} + \ldots$ for the moment $t+1$ in a recursive way via $\hat{y}_{t+1} = \alpha y_t + (1-\alpha)\hat{y}_t$ with $\hat{y}_1 = y_1$ and a *smoothing factor* α $(0 < \alpha < 1)$.

Impact of the smoothing factor α	α large	α small
consideration of "older" values	little	strong
consideration of "newer" values	strong	little
smoothing of the time series	little	strong

Calculus of Probability

Random events and their probabilities

A *trial* is an attempt (observation, experiment) the result of which is uncertain within the scope of some possibilities and which is, at least in ideas, arbitrarily often reproducible when remaining unchanged the external conditions characterizing the attempt.

The set Ω of possible results ω of a trial is called the *sample space* (space of events, basic space). A *random event* A is a subset of Ω ("A happens" $\Longleftrightarrow$ $\omega \in A$) is the result of the trial).

Basic notions

$\{\omega\},\ \ \omega \in \Omega$	–	simple events
Ω	–	sure event = event that always happens
$\emptyset$	–	impossible event = event that never happens
$A \subseteq B$	–	event A implies event B
$A = B \Longleftrightarrow A \subseteq B \wedge B \subseteq A$	–	identity of two events
$A \cup B$	–	event that happens if A or B (or both) happen (union)
$A \cap B$	–	event that happens if A and B happen simultaneously (intersection)
$A \setminus B$	–	event that happens if A happens but B does not happen (difference)
$\overline{A} := \Omega \setminus A$	–	event complementary to A
$A \cap B = \emptyset$	–	A and B are disjoint (non-intersecting, incompatible)

Properties of events

$A \cup \Omega = \Omega$	$A \cap \Omega = A$
$A \cup \emptyset = A$	$A \cap \emptyset = \emptyset$
$A \cup (B \cup C) = (A \cup B) \cup C$	$A \cap (B \cap C) = (A \cap B) \cap C$
$A \cup B = B \cup A$	$A \cap B = B \cap A$
$\overline{A \cup B} = \overline{A} \cap \overline{B}$	$\overline{A \cap B} = \overline{A} \cup \overline{B}$
$A \cup \overline{A} = \Omega$	$A \cap \overline{A} = \emptyset$
$A \subseteq A \cup B$	$A \cap B \subseteq A$
$A \cap (B \cup C) = (A \cap B) \cup (A \cap C)$	$A \cup (B \cap C) = (A \cup B) \cap (A \cup C)$

Field of events

$\bigcup_{n=1}^{\infty} A_n$ – the event that at least one of the events A_n happens	
$\bigcap_{n=1}^{\infty} A_n$ – the event that any of the events A_n happens (simultaneously)	
$\overline{\bigcap_{n=1}^{\infty} A_n} = \bigcup_{n=1}^{\infty} \overline{A_n}$, $\overline{\bigcup_{n=1}^{\infty} A_n} = \bigcap_{n=1}^{\infty} \overline{A_n}$	– De Morgan's laws

• A *field of events* is a set $\mathfrak{E}$ of events occurring in the result of a trial satisfying the following conditions:

(1) $\Omega \in \mathfrak{E}$, $\emptyset \in \mathfrak{E}$

(2) $A \in \mathfrak{E} \implies \overline{A} \in \mathfrak{E}$

(3) $A_1, A_2, \ldots \in \mathfrak{E} \implies \bigcup_{n=1}^{\infty} A_n \in \mathfrak{E}$.

• A subset $\{A_1, A_2, \ldots, A_n\}$ of a field of events is called a *complete system* of events if $\bigcup_{i=1}^{n} A_i = \Omega$ and $A_i \cap A_j = \emptyset$ $(i \neq j)$ (i. e., in the result of a trial there always happens exactly one of the events A_i).

Relative frequency

If an event $A \in \mathfrak{E}$ happens m times under n independent repetitions of a trial, then $h_n(A) = \frac{m}{n}$ is called the *relative frequency* of A.

Properties of the relative frequency

$0 \le h_n(A) \le 1$,	$h_n(\Omega) = 1$,	$h_n(\emptyset) = 0$,	$h_n(\overline{A}) = 1 - h_n(A)$
$h_n(A \cup B) = h_n(A) + h_n(B) - h_n(A \cap B)$			
$h_n(A \cup B) = h_n(A) + h_n(B)$ if $A \cap B = \emptyset$			
$A \subseteq B \implies h_n(A) \le h_n(B)$			

Classical definition of the probability

If the sample space $\Omega = \{\omega_1, \omega_2, \ldots, \omega_k\}$ is finite, then for an event A the quantity

$$\mathrm{P}(A) = \frac{\text{number of } \omega_i \text{ with } \omega_i \in A}{k} = \frac{\text{number of cases favourable for } A}{\text{number of all possible cases}}$$

is the *classical probability* of A.

The simple events $\{\omega_i\}$ are equally probable (equally possible), i. e. $\mathrm{P}(\{\omega_i\}) = \frac{1}{k}$, $i = 1, \ldots, k$ (*"Laplace's field of events"*).

Properties of the classical probability

$$0 \le \mathrm{P}(A) \le 1, \qquad \mathrm{P}(\Omega) = 1, \qquad \mathrm{P}(\emptyset) = 0, \qquad \mathrm{P}(\overline{A}) = 1 - \mathrm{P}(A)$$

$$\mathrm{P}(A \cup B) = \mathrm{P}(A) + \mathrm{P}(B) - \mathrm{P}(A \cap B), \qquad A \subseteq B \implies \mathrm{P}(A) \le \mathrm{P}(B)$$

$$\mathrm{P}(A \cup B) = \mathrm{P}(A) + \mathrm{P}(B) \quad \text{if} \quad A \cap B = \emptyset$$

Axiomatic definition of the probability

Axiom 1: Any random event $A \in \mathfrak{E}$ has a probability $\mathrm{P}(A)$ satisfying the relation $0 \le \mathrm{P}(A) \le 1$.

Axiom 2: The probability of the certain event is equal to one: $\mathrm{P}(\Omega) = 1$.

Axiom 3: The probability of the event that there happens exactly one of two mutually disjoint events $A \in \mathfrak{E}$ and $B \in \mathfrak{E}$ is equal to the sum of the probabilities of A and B, i. e. $P(A \cup B) = \mathrm{P}(A) + \mathrm{P}(B)$ provided that $A \cap B = \emptyset$.

Axiom 3': The probability of the event that there happens exactly one of the pairwise disjoint events $A_1, A_2, \ldots$ is equal to the sum of the probabilities of A_i, $i = 1, 2, \ldots$, i. e. $\mathrm{P}(\bigcup\limits_{i=1}^{\infty} A_i) = \sum\limits_{i=1}^{\infty} \mathrm{P}(A_i)$ if $A_i \cap A_j = \emptyset$, $i \neq j$ (*σ-additivity*).

Rules of operation for probabilities

$$\mathrm{P}(\emptyset) = 0, \qquad \mathrm{P}(A \cup B) = \mathrm{P}(A) + \mathrm{P}(B) - \mathrm{P}(A \cap B)$$

$$\mathrm{P}(\overline{A}) = 1 - \mathrm{P}(A), \qquad \mathrm{P}(A \setminus B) = \mathrm{P}(A) - \mathrm{P}(A \cap B)$$

$$A \subseteq B \Longrightarrow \mathrm{P}(A) \le \mathrm{P}(B)$$

$$\mathrm{P}(A_1 \cup A_2 \cup \ldots \cup A_n) = \sum_{i=1}^{n} \mathrm{P}(A_i) - \sum_{1 \le i_1 < i_2 \le n} \mathrm{P}(A_{i_1} \cap A_{i_2})$$
$$+ \sum_{1 \le i_1 < i_2 < i_3 \le n} \mathrm{P}(A_{i_1} \cap A_{i_2} \cap A_{i_3}) - \ldots + (-1)^{n+1} \mathrm{P}(A_1 \cap A_2 \cap \ldots \cap A_n)$$

Conditional probabilities

For two events A and B with $\mathrm{P}(B) \neq 0$, the expression $\mathrm{P}(A \mid B) = \dfrac{\mathrm{P}(A \cap B)}{\mathrm{P}(B)}$ denotes the *conditional probability* of A with respect to B.

Properties

$$P(A \mid B) = 1 \text{ if } B \subset A \qquad P(A \mid B) = 0 \text{ if } A \cap B = \emptyset$$

$$P(A \mid B) = \frac{P(A)}{P(B)} \text{ if } A \subset B \qquad P(\overline{A} \mid B) = 1 - P(A \mid B)$$

$$P(A_1 \cup A_2 \mid B) = P(A_1 \mid B) + P(A_2 \mid B) \text{ if } A_1 \cap A_2 = \emptyset$$

Multiplication theorem:

$$P(A \cap B) = P(B) \cdot P(A \mid B) = P(A) \cdot P(B \mid A)$$

General multiplication theorem:

$$P(A_1 \cap \ldots \cap A_n) = P(A_1) \cdot P(A_2 \mid A_1) \cdot P(A_3 \mid A_1 \cap A_2) \cdot \ldots \cdot P(A_n \mid A_1 \cap \ldots \cap A_{n-1})$$

- If $\{A_1, \ldots, A_n\}$ is a complete system of events, then the following two formulas hold true.

Total probability formula

$$P(B) = \sum_{i=1}^{n} P(A_i)P(B \mid A_i)$$

Bayes' formula

$$P(A_j \mid B) = \frac{P(A_j)P(B \mid A_j)}{\sum_{i=1}^{n} P(A_i)P(B \mid A_i)}, \qquad j = 1, \ldots, n$$

Here $P(A_1), \ldots, P(A_n)$ are called the *priori probabilities*, while the quantities $P(A_1 \mid B), \ldots, P(A_n \mid B)$ are the *posteriori probabilities.*

Independence

Two events A, B are called *independent* if $P(A \cap B) = P(A) \cdot P(B)$ (multiplication theorem for independent events). As a corollary one gets

$$P(A \cap B) = P(A) \cdot P(B) \iff P(A \mid B) = P(A) \quad \text{for} \quad P(B) > 0$$

The n events $A_1, \ldots, A_n$ are said to be *pairwise independent* if every two of these events are independent, i. e. $P(A_i \cap A_j) = P(A_i) \cdot P(A_j)$ for $i \neq j$, and *completely independent* if for any $k \in \{2, \ldots, n\}$ and an arbitrary selection of k events $A_{i_1}, \ldots, A_{i_k}$, $1 \leq i_1 < i_2 < \ldots < i_k \leq n$, one has: $P(A_{i_1} \cap \ldots \cap A_{i_k}) = P(A_{i_1}) \cdot \ldots \cdot P(A_{i_k})$.

Random variables and their distributions

A *random variable* is a real-valued mapping $X : \Omega \to \mathbb{R}$ defined on the sample space Ω such that for all $x \in \mathbb{R}$ one has $\{\omega \in \Omega : X(\omega) \le x\} \in \mathfrak{E}$, i. e., $\{X \le x\}$ is an event. The function $F_X : x \to F_X(x) \in [0,1]$ defined by $F_X(x) := \mathrm{P}(X \le x)$, $-\infty < x < \infty$, is called the *distribution function* (*distribution*) of X.

Properties of the distribution function

$\lim\limits_{x\to-\infty} F_X(x) = 0$	$\lim\limits_{x\to\infty} F_X(x) = 1$
$F_X(x_0) \le F_X(x_1)$ if $x_0 < x_1$	(F_X is monotonously non-decreasing)
$\lim\limits_{h\downarrow 0} F_X(x+h) = F_X(x)$	(F_X is continuous on the right)
$\mathrm{P}(X = x_0) = F_X(x_0) - \lim\limits_{h\uparrow 0} F_X(x_0+h)$	
$\mathrm{P}(x_0 < X \le x_1) = F_X(x_1) - F_X(x_0)$	
$\mathrm{P}(x_0 \le X < x_1) = \lim\limits_{h\uparrow 0} F_X(x_1+h) - \lim\limits_{h\uparrow 0} F_X(x_0+h)$	
$\mathrm{P}(x_0 \le X \le x_1) = F_X(x_1) - \lim\limits_{h\uparrow 0} F_X(x_0+h)$	
$\mathrm{P}(X > x_0) = 1 - F_X(x_0)$	

A random variable X is called *discrete* (*discretely distributed*; see below) if its distribution function F_X is a step function (i. e. piecewise constant); it is called *continuous (continuously distributed)* if F_X is differentiable (i. e. $\dfrac{\mathrm{d}F_X(x)}{\mathrm{d}x}$ exists) ► p. 153.

Discrete distributions

If a discrete random variable X takes the values $x_1, x_2, \ldots, x_n$ ($x_1 < \ldots < x_n$) resp. $x_1, x_2, \ldots$ ($x_1 < x_2 < \ldots$), i. e. if $\lim\limits_{h\uparrow 0} F_X(x_k+h) \ne F_X(x_k)$ for $k = 1, 2, \ldots$, then

x_k	x_1	x_2	$\ldots$
$\mathrm{P}(X = x_k)$	p_1	p_2	$\ldots$

with $\sum\limits_k p_k = 1$

is called the *distribution table* of X; $p_k = \mathrm{P}(X = x_k)$ are the *individual probabilities* of X, and $x_1, x_2, \ldots$ are the jump points of F_X.

Notations

$\mathrm{E}X = \sum_k x_k p_k$	–	expected value (assumption: $\sum_k \lvert x_k \rvert p_k < \infty$)
$\mathrm{Var}\,(X) = \sum_k (x_k - \mathrm{E}X)^2 p_k = \sum_k x_k^2 p_k - (\mathrm{E}X)^2$	–	variance (dispersion) (assumption: $\sum_k x_k^2 p_k < \infty$)
$\sigma_X = \sqrt{\mathrm{Var}\,(X)}$	–	standard deviation
$\dfrac{\sigma_X}{\mathrm{E}X} \quad (\mathrm{E}X \neq 0)$	–	coefficient of variation
$\mu_r = \mathrm{E}(X - \mathrm{E}X)^r = \sum_k (x_k - \mathrm{E}X)^r p_k$	–	r-th central moment ($r = 2, 3, \ldots$)
$\gamma_1 = \dfrac{\mu_3}{(\mu_2)^{3/2}}$	–	skewness
$\gamma_2 = \dfrac{\mu_4}{(\mu_2)^2} - 3$	–	excess

Special discrete distributions

	individual probabilities p_k	$\mathrm{E}X$	$\mathrm{Var}\,(X)$
discrete uniform distribution	$p_k = \mathrm{P}(X = x_k) = \frac{1}{n}$ $(k = 1, \ldots, n)$	$\frac{1}{n} \sum_{k=1}^{n} x_k$	$\frac{1}{n} \sum_{k=1}^{n} x_k^2 - (\mathrm{E}X)^2$
binomial distribution * $(0 \leq p \leq 1, n \in \mathbb{N})$	$p_k = \binom{n}{k} p^k (1-p)^{n-k}$ $(k = 0, \ldots, n)$	np	$np(1-p)$
hypergeometric distribution * $(M \leq N, n \leq N)$	$p_k = \dfrac{\binom{M}{k}\binom{N-M}{n-k}}{\binom{N}{n}}$ **	$n \cdot \dfrac{M}{N}$	$n\frac{M}{N}\left(1-\frac{M}{N}\right) \times \left(1-\frac{n-1}{N-1}\right)$
geometric distribution * $(0<p<1)$	$p_k = (1-p)^{k-1} p$ $(k = 1, 2, \ldots)$	$\dfrac{1}{p}$	$\dfrac{1-p}{p^2}$
Poisson distribution * $(\lambda > 0)$	$p_k = \dfrac{\lambda^k}{k!} \mathrm{e}^{-\lambda}$ $(k = 0, 1, 2, \ldots)$	λ	λ

* $\mathrm{P}(X = k) = p_k$; ** $\max\{0, n - (N - M)\} \leq k \leq \min\{M, n\}$.

Recursion formulas $(p_{k+1} = f(p_k))$

binomial distribution:	$\frac{n-k}{k+1} \cdot \frac{p}{1-p} \cdot p_k$
geometric distribution:	$(1-p) \cdot p_k$
hypergeometric distribution:	$\frac{n-k}{k+1} \cdot \frac{M-k}{N-M-n+k+1} \cdot p_k$
Poisson distribution:	$\frac{\lambda}{k+1} \cdot p_k$

Binomial approximation (of the hypergeometric distribution)

$$\lim_{N\to\infty} \frac{\binom{M}{k}\binom{N-M}{n-k}}{\binom{N}{n}} = \binom{n}{k} p^k (1-p)^{n-k} \quad \text{with}$$

$$M = M(N), \qquad \lim_{N\to\infty} \frac{M(N)}{N} = p$$

- Consequently, for "large" N one has $\frac{\binom{M}{k}\binom{N-M}{n-k}}{\binom{N}{n}} \approx \binom{n}{k} p^k (1-p)^{n-k}$,

where $p = \frac{M}{N}$.

Poisson approximation (of the binomial distribution)

$$\lim_{n\to\infty} \binom{n}{k} p^k (1-p)^{n-k} = \frac{\lambda^k}{k!} e^{-\lambda}, \quad k = 0, 1, \ldots, \quad \text{with}$$

$$p = p(n), \quad \lim_{n\to\infty} n \cdot p(n) = \lambda = \text{const}$$

- For "large" n one thus has $\binom{n}{k} p^k (1-p)^{n-k} \approx \frac{\lambda^k}{k!} e^{-\lambda}$, where $\lambda = n \cdot p$.

Continuous distributions

The first derivative $f_X(x) = \frac{dF_X(x)}{dx} = F'_X(x)$ of the distribution function F_X of a continuous random variable X is called the *density* (*probability density function*) of X, i. e.

$$F_X(x) = \int_{-\infty}^{x} f_X(t)\, dt.$$

Notations

$$\mathrm{E}X = \int_{-\infty}^{\infty} x f_X(x)\,\mathrm{d}x$$ – expected value of X (ass.: $\int_{-\infty}^{\infty} |x| f_X(x)\,\mathrm{d}x < \infty$)

$$\mathrm{Var}\,(X) = \int_{-\infty}^{\infty} (x-\mathrm{E}X)^2 f_X(x)\,\mathrm{d}x = \int_{-\infty}^{\infty} x^2 f_X(x)\,\mathrm{d}x - (\mathrm{E}X)^2$$

– variance (dispersion; ass.: $\int_{-\infty}^{\infty} x^2 f_X(x)\,\mathrm{d}x < \infty$)

$\sigma_X = \sqrt{\mathrm{Var}\,(X)}$ – standard deviation

$\dfrac{\sigma_X}{\mathrm{E}X}$ $(\mathrm{E}X \neq 0)$ – coefficient of variation

$$\mu_r = \mathrm{E}(X-\mathrm{E}X)^r = \int_{-\infty}^{\infty} (x-\mathrm{E}X)^r f_X(x)\,\mathrm{d}x$$

– r-th central moment $(r = 2, 3, \ldots)$

$\gamma_1 = \dfrac{\mu_3}{(\mu_2)^{3/2}}$ – skewness $\qquad \gamma_2 = \dfrac{\mu_4}{(\mu_2)^2} - 3$ – excess

Special continuous distributions

Uniform distribution

$$f(x) = \begin{cases} \dfrac{1}{b-a} & \text{if } a<x<b \\ 0 & \text{otherwise} \end{cases}$$

$$\mathrm{E}X = \frac{a+b}{2}$$

$$\mathrm{Var}\,(X) = \frac{(b-a)^2}{12}$$

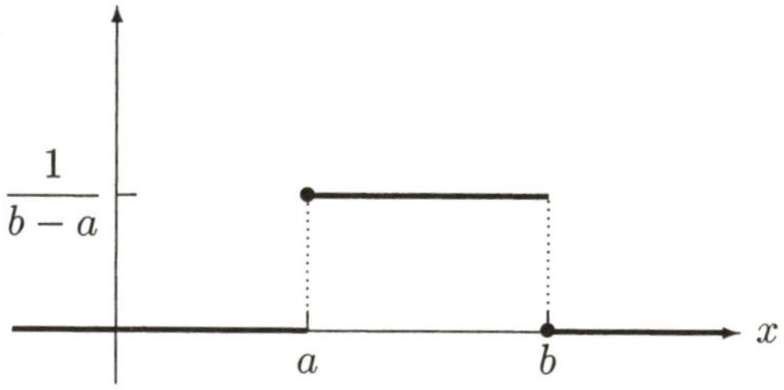

Exponential distribution

$$f(x) = \begin{cases} 0 & \text{if } x \le 0 \\ \lambda \mathrm{e}^{-\lambda x} & \text{if } x > 0 \end{cases}$$

$$\mathrm{E}X = \frac{1}{\lambda}$$

$$\mathrm{Var}\,(X) = \frac{1}{\lambda^2}$$

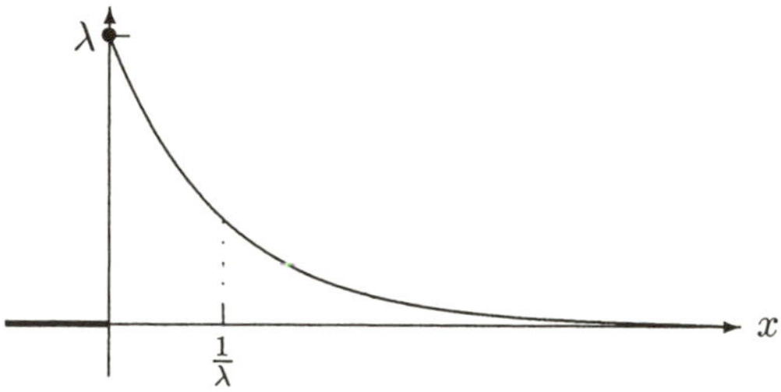

Normal distribution, $N(\mu, \sigma^2)$-distribution $(-\infty < \mu < \infty, \sigma > 0)$

$f(x) = \frac{1}{\sqrt{2\pi\sigma^2}} \cdot e^{-\frac{(x-\mu)^2}{2\sigma^2}}$

$(-\infty < x < \infty)$

$EX = \mu$

$\text{Var}(X) = \sigma^2$

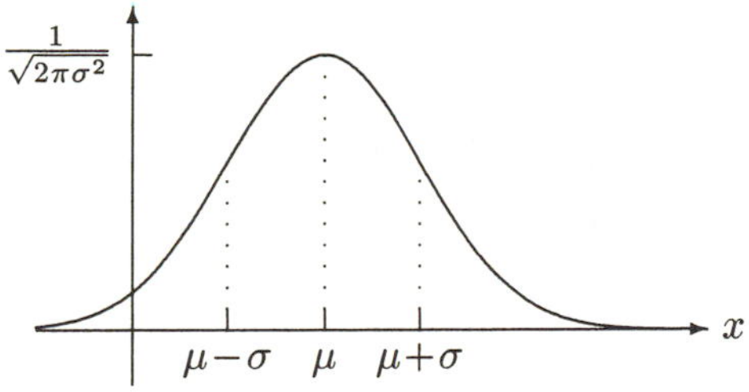

Standardized normal distribution

$$f(x) = \frac{1}{\sqrt{2\pi}} \cdot e^{-\frac{x^2}{2}}, \qquad EX = 0, \qquad \text{Var}(X) = 1$$

Logarithmic normal distribution

$$f(x) = \begin{cases} 0 & \text{if} \quad x \le 0 \\ \frac{1}{\sqrt{2\pi\sigma^2 x}} e^{-\frac{\ln x-\mu)^2}{2\sigma^2}} & \text{if} \quad x > 0 \end{cases}$$

$EX = e^{\mu+\frac{\sigma^2}{2}}$

$\text{Var}(X) = e^{2\mu+\sigma^2}\left(e^{\sigma^2}-1\right)$

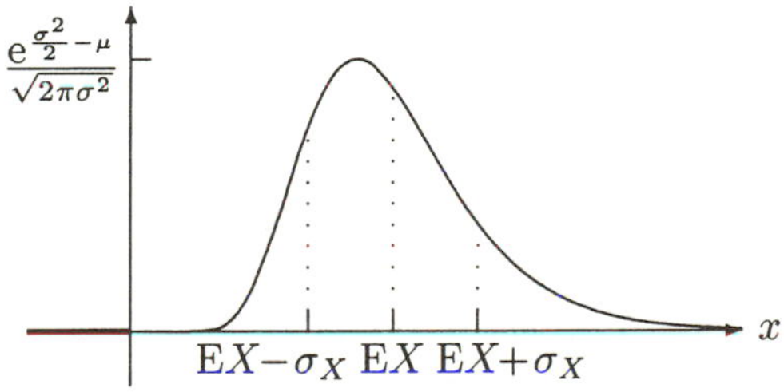

Weibull distribution $(a > 0,\ b > 0,\ -\infty < c < \infty)$

$$f(x) = \begin{cases} 0 & \text{if } x \le c \\ \frac{b}{a}\left(\frac{x-c}{a}\right)^{b-1} e^{-\left(\frac{x-c}{a}\right)^b} & \text{if } x > c \end{cases}$$

$EX = c + a \cdot \Gamma\left(\frac{b+1}{b}\right)$

$\text{Var}(X) = a^2\left[\Gamma\left(\frac{b+2}{b}\right) - \Gamma^2\left(\frac{b+1}{b}\right)\right]$

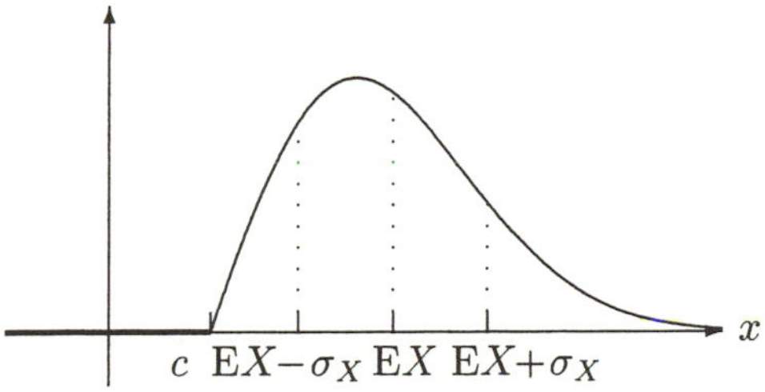

Beta distribution $(p > 0,\ q > 0)$

$$f(x) = \begin{cases} \dfrac{x^{p-1}(1-x)^{q-1}}{B(p,q)} & \text{if } 0 < x < 1 \\ 0 & \text{otherwise} \end{cases}$$

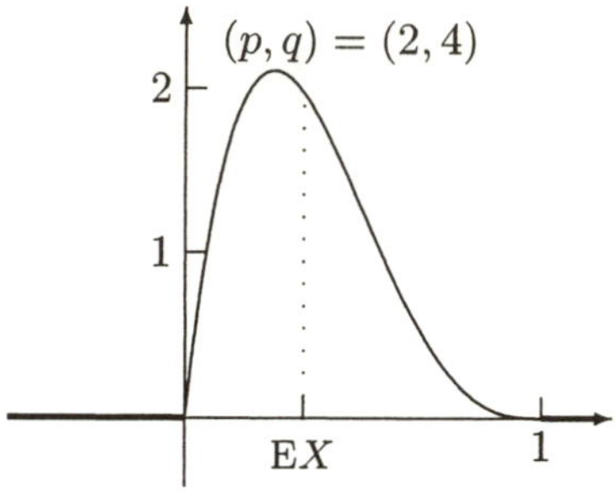

$$\mathrm{E}X = \frac{p}{p+q}$$

$$\mathrm{Var}\,(X) = \frac{pq}{(p+q)^2(p+q+1)}$$

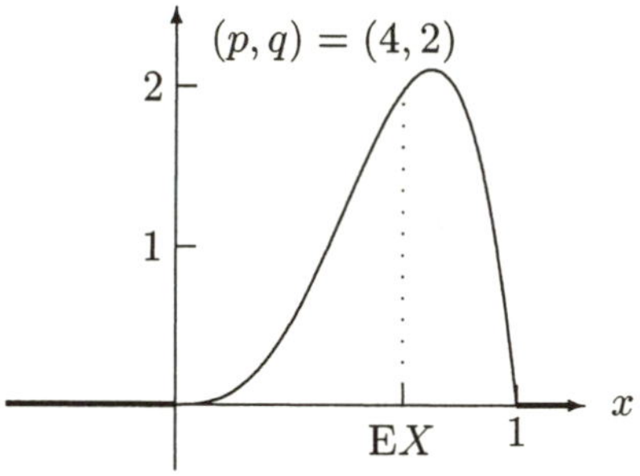

t-distribution with m degrees of freedom $(m \geq 3)$

$$f(x) = \frac{\Gamma\left(\frac{m+1}{2}\right)}{\sqrt{\pi m}\,\Gamma\left(\frac{m}{2}\right)}\left(1+\frac{x^2}{m}\right)^{-\frac{m+1}{2}},$$

$$\mathrm{E}X = 0, \qquad \mathrm{Var}\,(X) = \frac{m}{m-2}$$

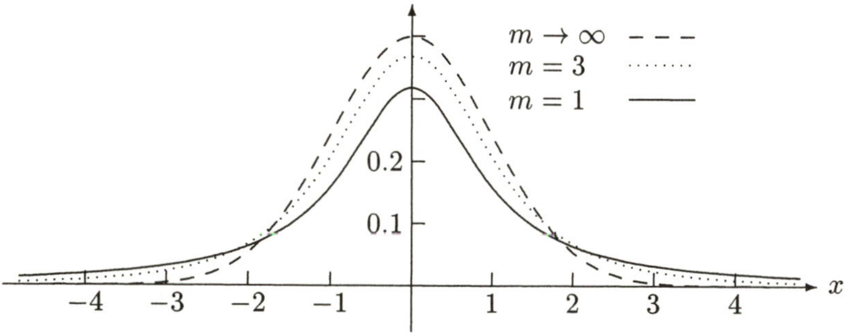

F-distribution with (m,n) degrees of freedom $(m \geq 1,\ n \geq 1)$

$$f(x) = \begin{cases} 0 & \text{if} \quad x \leq 0 \\ \dfrac{\Gamma\left(\frac{m+n}{2}\right) m^{\frac{m}{2}} n^{\frac{n}{2}} x^{\frac{m}{2}-1}}{\Gamma\left(\frac{m}{2}\right)\Gamma\left(\frac{n}{2}\right)(n+mx)^{\frac{m+n}{2}}} & \text{if} \quad x > 0, \end{cases}$$

$$\mathrm{E}X = \frac{n}{n-2} \quad (n \geq 3),$$

$$\mathrm{Var}\,(X) = \frac{2n^2}{n-4} \cdot \frac{m+n-2}{m(n-2)^2}$$

$$(n \geq 5)$$

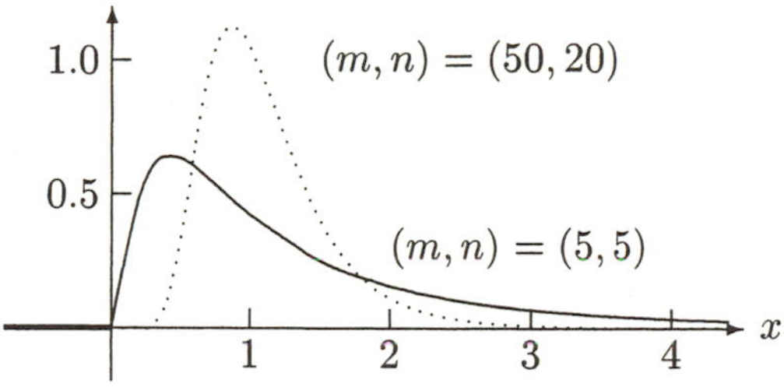

χ^2-distribution with m degrees of freedom $(m \geq 1)$

$$f(x) = \begin{cases} 0 & \text{if} \quad x \leq 0 \\ \dfrac{x^{\frac{m}{2}-1} \mathrm{e}^{-\frac{x}{2}}}{2^{\frac{m}{2}} \Gamma\left(\frac{m}{2}\right)} & \text{if} \quad x \geq 0 \end{cases}$$

$$\mathrm{E}X = m$$

$$\mathrm{Var}\,(X) = 2m$$

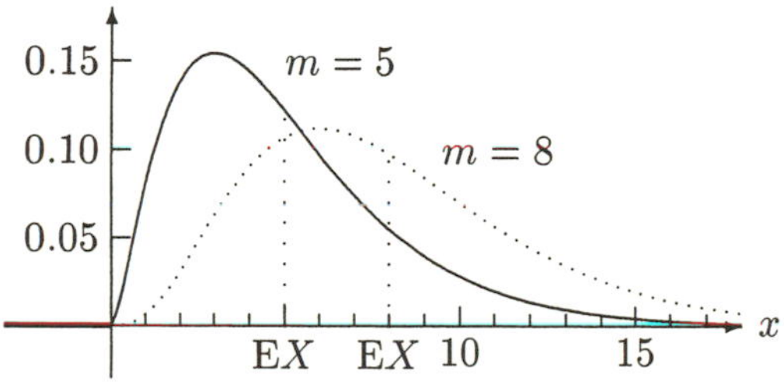

Random vectors

If $X_1, X_2, \ldots, X_n$ are random variables (over one and the same sample space Ω), then $\boldsymbol{X} = (X_1, \ldots, X_n)$ is called a *random vector*, and $X_1, \ldots, X_n$ are its *components*. The function $F_{\boldsymbol{X}} : F_{\boldsymbol{X}}(x_1, \ldots, x_n) = \mathrm{P}(X_1 \leq x_1, \ldots, X_n \leq x_n)$ with $(x_1, \ldots, x_n) \in \mathbb{R}^n$ is said to be the *distribution function* of $\boldsymbol{X}$.

Properties

$$\lim_{x_i \to -\infty} F_{\boldsymbol{X}}(x_1, \ldots, x_i, \ldots, x_n) = 0, \quad i = 1, \ldots, n,$$

$$\lim_{\substack{x_1 \to \infty \\ \vdots \\ x_n \to \infty}} F_{\boldsymbol{X}}(x_1, \ldots, x_n) = 1$$

$$\lim_{h \downarrow 0} F_{\boldsymbol{X}}(x_1, \ldots, x_i + h, \ldots, x_n) = F_{\boldsymbol{X}}(x_1, \ldots, x_i, \ldots, x_n), \quad i = 1, \ldots, n$$

$$F_{X_i}(x) = \lim_{\substack{x_j \to \infty \\ j \neq i}} F_{\boldsymbol{X}}(x_1, \ldots, x_{i-1}, x, x_{i+1}, \ldots, x_n), \quad i = 1, \ldots, n$$

(marginal distribution functions)

Independence

$X_1, \ldots, X_n$ are called *independent* if for any $(x_1, \ldots, x_n) \in \mathbb{R}^n$ one has

$$F_{\boldsymbol{X}}(x_1, \ldots, x_n) = F_{X_1}(x_1) \cdot F_{X_2}(x_2) \cdot \ldots \cdot F_{X_n}(x_n)$$

Two-dimensional random vectors

• The vector $\boldsymbol{X} = (X_1, X_2)$ is called *continuous (continuously distributed)* if there exists a *density (function)* $f_{\boldsymbol{X}}$ such that the representation $F_{\boldsymbol{X}}(x_1, x_2) = \int\limits_{-\infty}^{x_1} \int\limits_{-\infty}^{x_2} f_{\boldsymbol{X}}(t_1, t_2)\, \mathrm{d}t_1 \mathrm{d}t_2$, $(x_1, x_2) \in \mathbb{R}^2$ holds, i. e. $\dfrac{\partial^2 F_{\boldsymbol{X}}(x_1, x_2)}{\partial x_1 \partial x_2} = f_{\boldsymbol{X}}(x_1, x_2)$.

The random variables X_1 (with density f_{X_1}) and X_2 (with density f_{X_2}) are *independent* if $f_{\boldsymbol{X}}(x_1, x_2) = f_{X_1}(x_1) \cdot f_{X_2}(x_2)$ for all $(x_1, x_2) \in \mathbb{R}^2$.

• $\boldsymbol{X} = (X_1, X_2)$ is called *discrete (discretely distributed)* with individual probabilities $p_{ij} = \mathrm{P}(X_1 = x_1^{(i)}, X_2 = x_2^{(j)})$ if X_1 and X_2 are discretely distributed with individual probabilities $p_i = \mathrm{P}(X_1 = x_1^{(i)})$, $i = 1, 2, \ldots$ and $q_j = \mathrm{P}(X_2 = x_2^{(j)})$, $j = 1, 2, \ldots$, respectively. The random variables X_1 and X_2 are independent if $p_{ij} = p_i \cdot q_j$ for all $i, j = 1, 2, \ldots$

First moments of two-dimensional random vectors

expected value	discrete	continuous
$\mathrm{E}X_1$	$\sum\limits_i \sum\limits_j x_1^{(i)} p_{ij}$	$\int\limits_{-\infty}^{\infty} \int\limits_{-\infty}^{\infty} x_1 f_{\boldsymbol{X}}(x_1, x_2)\, \mathrm{d}x_1 \mathrm{d}x_2$
$\mathrm{E}X_2$	$\sum\limits_i \sum\limits_j x_2^{(j)} p_{ij}$	$\int\limits_{-\infty}^{\infty} \int\limits_{-\infty}^{\infty} x_2 f_{\boldsymbol{X}}(x_1, x_2)\, \mathrm{d}x_1 \mathrm{d}x_2$

Second moments of two-dimensional random vectors

variances	discrete	continuous
$\mathrm{Var}\,(X_1) = \sigma_{X_1}^2$ $= \mathrm{E}(X_1 - \mathrm{E}X_1)^2$	$\sum\limits_i \sum\limits_j (x_1^{(i)} - \mathrm{E}X_1)^2 p_{ij}$	$\int\limits_{-\infty}^{\infty} \int\limits_{-\infty}^{\infty} (x_1 - \mathrm{E}X_1)^2 f_{\boldsymbol{X}}(x_1, x_2)\, \mathrm{d}x_1 \mathrm{d}x_2$
$\mathrm{Var}\,(X_2) = \sigma_{X_2}^2$ $= \mathrm{E}(X_2 - \mathrm{E}X_2)^2$	$\sum\limits_i \sum\limits_j (x_2^{(j)} - \mathrm{E}X_2)^2 p_{ij}$	$\int\limits_{-\infty}^{\infty} \int\limits_{-\infty}^{\infty} (x_2 - \mathrm{E}X_2)^2 f_{\boldsymbol{X}}(x_1, x_2)\, \mathrm{d}x_1 \mathrm{d}x_2$

covariance:

$$\operatorname{cov}(X_1, X_2) = \mathrm{E}(X_1 - \mathrm{E}X_1)(X_2 - \mathrm{E}X_2) = \mathrm{E}(X_1 X_2) - \mathrm{E}X_1 \cdot \mathrm{E}X_2$$

$$\sum_i \sum_j (x_1^{(i)} - \mathrm{E}X_1)(x_2^{(j)} - \mathrm{E}X_2) p_{ij} \qquad \text{– discrete distribution}$$

$$\int_{-\infty}^{\infty} \int_{-\infty}^{\infty} (x_1 - \mathrm{E}X_1)(x_2 - \mathrm{E}X_2) f_{\boldsymbol{X}}(x_1, x_2)\, \mathrm{d}x_1 \mathrm{d}x_2 \qquad \text{– continuous distribution}$$

Correlation

$$\rho_{X_1 X_2} = \frac{\operatorname{cov}(X_1, X_2)}{\sqrt{\operatorname{Var}(X_1)\operatorname{Var}(X_2)}} = \frac{\operatorname{cov}(X_1, X_2)}{\sigma_{X_1}\sigma_{X_2}}$$

correlation coefficient

- The correlation coefficient describes the (linear) interdependence between the components X_1 and X_2 of a random vector $\boldsymbol{X} = (X_1, X_2)$.
- $-1 \le \rho_{X_1 X_2} \le 1$
- If $\rho_{X_1 X_2} = 0$, then X_1, X_2 are called *uncorrelated.*
- If X_1, X_2 are independent, then they are uncorrelated.

Two-dimensional normal distribution

$$f_{\boldsymbol{X}}(x_1, x_2) = \frac{1}{2\pi\sigma_1\sigma_2\sqrt{1-\rho^2}} \times$$
$$\times \; \mathrm{e}^{-\frac{1}{2(1-\rho^2)}\left[\frac{(x_1-\mu_1)^2}{\sigma_1^2} - 2\rho\frac{(x_1-\mu_1)(x_2-\mu_2)}{\sigma_1\sigma_2} + \frac{(x_2-\mu_2)^2}{\sigma_2^2}\right]}$$

density of the two-dimensional normal distribution with $-\infty < \mu_1, \mu_2 < \infty$; $\sigma_1 > 0$, $\sigma_2 > 0$, $-1 < \rho < 1$; $-\infty < x_1, x_2 < \infty$

Moments:

$\mathrm{E}X_1 = \mu_1$, $\mathrm{E}X_2 = \mu_2$,
$\operatorname{Var}(X_1) = \sigma_1^2$,
$\operatorname{Var}(X_2) = \sigma_2^2$,
$\operatorname{cov}(X_1, X_2) = \rho\sigma_1\sigma_2$

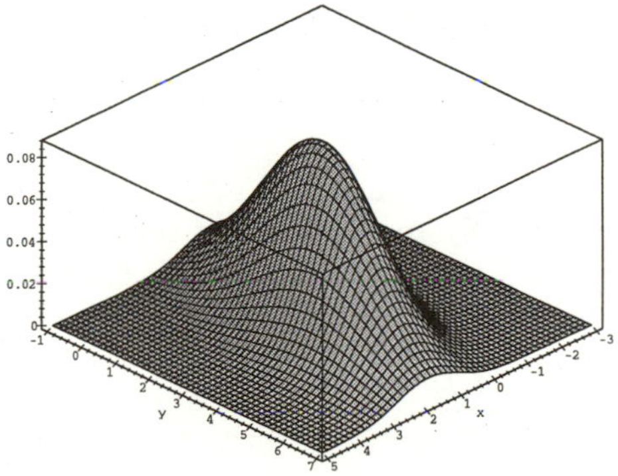

Sums of two independent random variables

• If X_1 and X_2 are independent discrete random variables with probabilities $p_i = \mathrm{P}(X_1 = x_1^{(i)})$, $i = 1, 2, \ldots$, and $q_j = \mathrm{P}(X_2 = x_2^{(j)})$, $j = 1, 2, \ldots$, then

$$\mathrm{P}(X_1 + X_2 = y) = \sum_{i,j:\, x_1^{(i)} + x_2^{(j)} = y} p_i\, q_j\,.$$

If, in particular, $x_1^{(i)} = i$, $i = 1, 2, \ldots$ and $x_2^{(j)} = j$, $j = 1, 2, \ldots$, then

$$\mathrm{P}(X_1 + X_2 = k) = \sum_{i=1}^{k} \mathrm{P}(X_1 = i)\, \mathrm{P}(X_2 = k - i), \quad k = 1, 2, \ldots$$

• If X_1, X_2 are independent continuous random variables with densities f_{X_1} and f_{X_2}, then $Y = X_1 + X_2$ is a continuous random variable with density

$$f_Y(y) = \int_{-\infty}^{\infty} f_{X_1}(x) f_{X_2}(y - x)\, \mathrm{d}x\,.$$

• In general, the relation $\mathrm{E}(X_1 + X_2) = \mathrm{E}X_1 + \mathrm{E}X_2$ is true. Moreover, under independence one has $\mathrm{Var}\,(X_1 + X_2) = \mathrm{Var}\,(X_1) + \mathrm{Var}\,(X_2)$.

Examples of sums of independent random variables

• If X_1 and X_2 are binomially distributed with (n_1, p) and (n_2, p), resp., then the sum $X_1 + X_2$ is binomially distributed with $(n_1 + n_2, p)$.

• If X_1 and X_2 are Poisson distributed with λ_1 and λ_2, resp., then the sum $X_1 + X_2$ is Poisson distributed with $\lambda_1 + \lambda_2$.

• If X_1 and X_2 are normally distributed with (μ_1, σ_1^2) and (μ_2, σ_2^2), resp., then the linear combination $\alpha_1 X_1 + \alpha_2 X_2$ is normally distributed with $(\alpha_1 \mu_1 + \alpha_2 \mu_2,\ \alpha_1^2 \sigma_1^2 + \alpha_2^2 \sigma_2^2)$, where $\alpha_1, \alpha_2 \in \mathbb{R}$.

• If X_1 and X_2 are χ^2-distributed with m and n degrees of freedom, resp., then the sum $X_1 + X_2$ is χ^2-distributed with $m + n$ degrees of freedom.

Products of two independent random variables

• If X_1, X_2 are independent discrete random variables with probabilities $p_i = \mathrm{P}(X_1 = x_1^{(i)})$, $i = 1, 2, \ldots$, and $q_j = \mathrm{P}(X_2 = x_2^{(j)})$, $j = 1, 2, \ldots$, then

$$\mathrm{P}(X_1 \cdot X_2 = y) = \sum_{i,j:\, x_1^{(i)} \cdot x_2^{(j)} = y} p_i\, q_j\,.$$

• If X_1, X_2 are independent continuous random variables with densities f_{X_1} and f_{X_2}, resp., then $Y = X_1 \cdot X_2$ is a continuous random variable with density

$$f_Y(y) = \int_{-\infty}^{\infty} f_{X_1}(x) f_{X_2}\left(\frac{y}{x}\right) \frac{\mathrm{d}x}{|x|}\,.$$

Inductive Statistics

Sample

By a *mathematical sample* of size n chosen from a parent population M_X one understands a n-dimensional random vector $\boldsymbol{X} = (X_1, \ldots, X_n)$ the components of which are independent and distributed like X. Every realization $\boldsymbol{x} = (x_1, \ldots, x_n)$ of $\boldsymbol{X}$ is called a *concrete sample.*

Point estimates

Task: To obtain suitable approximation values for unknown parameters θ of a distribution or for functions $g : \theta \to g(\theta)$ one uses estimates.

A *sample function* $t_n = T_n(\boldsymbol{x})$ depending on a concrete sample $\boldsymbol{x} = (x_1, \ldots, x_n)$ and used for the estimation of θ is called an *estimating value (estimator)* for θ; notation: $t_n = \hat{\theta}(\boldsymbol{x}) = \tilde{\theta}$. The sample function $T_n = T_n(\boldsymbol{X}) = \hat{\theta}(\boldsymbol{X})$ of the corresponding mathematical sample $\boldsymbol{X}$ is called a *point estimate* or *estimating function.*

Properties of point estimates

- T_n is called *unbiased* for $g(\theta)$ if $\mathrm{E}T_n = g(\theta)$.
- $(T_n)_{n=1,2,\ldots}$ is called *asymptotically unbiased* for $g(\theta)$ if $\lim\limits_{n\to\infty} \mathrm{E}T_n = g(\theta)$.
- $(T_n)_{n=1,2,\ldots}$ is called (weakly) *consistent* for $g(\theta)$ if the relation $\lim\limits_{n\to\infty} \mathrm{P}(|T_n - g(\theta)| < \varepsilon) = 1$ holds ($\varepsilon > 0$ arbitrary).

Estimators for expected value and variance

parameter to be estimated	estimator	remarks
expected value $\mu = \mathrm{E}X$	$\tilde{\mu} = \overline{x}_n = \frac{1}{n}\sum_{i=1}^{n} x_i$	(arithmetic) mean
variance $\sigma^2 = \mathrm{Var}\,(X)$	$\tilde{\sigma}^2 = s^{*2} = \frac{1}{n}\sum_{i=1}^{n}(x_i - \mathrm{E}X)^2$	application only if $\mathrm{E}X$ is known
	$\tilde{\sigma}^2 = s_X^2 = \frac{1}{n-1}\sum_{i=1}^{n}(x_i - \overline{x}_n)^2$	empirical variance

Further estimators

probabilities of an event $p = \mathrm{P}(A)$	$\tilde{p} = h_n(A)$	$h_n(A)$ is the relative frequency of A
covariance $\sigma_{XY} = \operatorname{cov}(X,Y)$	$\tilde{\sigma}_{XY} = \frac{1}{n-1}\sum\limits_{i=1}^{n}(x_i - \overline{x}_n)(y_i - \overline{y}_n)$	empirical covariance
correlation coefficient ρ_{XY}	$\tilde{\rho}_{XY} = \dfrac{\tilde{\sigma}_{XY}}{\sqrt{s_X^2 s_Y^2}}$	empirical correlation coefficient

Maximum likelihood method for the construction of point estimates

Assumption: A distribution function F is known except for the parameter $\boldsymbol{\theta} = (\theta_1, \ldots, \theta_p) \in \Theta \subset \mathbb{R}^p$

- The function $\boldsymbol{\theta} \to L(\boldsymbol{\theta}; \boldsymbol{x}) = p(\boldsymbol{\theta}; x_1) \cdot \ldots \cdot p(\boldsymbol{\theta}; x_n) = \prod\limits_{i=1}^{n} p(\boldsymbol{\theta}; x_i)$ is called the *likelihood function* belonging to the sample $\boldsymbol{x} = (x_1, \ldots, x_n)$, where

$$p(\boldsymbol{\theta}; x_i) = \begin{cases} \text{density } f_X(x_i), & \text{if } X \text{ is continuous} \\ \text{individual probability } \mathrm{P}(X = x_i) & \text{if } X \text{ is discrete.} \end{cases}$$

- The quantity $\tilde{\boldsymbol{\theta}} = \tilde{\boldsymbol{\theta}}(\boldsymbol{x}) = (\tilde{\theta}_1, \ldots, \tilde{\theta}_p)$ such that $L(\tilde{\boldsymbol{\theta}}; \boldsymbol{x}) \geq L(\boldsymbol{\theta}; \boldsymbol{x})$ for all $\boldsymbol{\theta} \in \Theta$ is said to be a maximum likelihood estimator for $\boldsymbol{\theta}$.

- If L is differentiable with respect to $\boldsymbol{\theta}$, then $\tilde{\boldsymbol{\theta}}(\boldsymbol{x})$ is a solution of
$$\frac{\partial \ln L(\boldsymbol{\theta}; x)}{\partial \theta_j} = 0, \quad j = 1, \ldots, p \qquad \textit{(maximum likelihood equations).}$$

Method of moments

Assumption: A distribution function F is known except for the parameter $\boldsymbol{\theta} = (\theta_1, \ldots, \theta_p) \in \Theta \subset \mathbb{R}^p$

This method for construction of point estimates is based on the relations between the parameters $\theta_1, \ldots, \theta_p$ and the central moments μ_r $(r = 2, 3, \ldots)$ as well as the expected value μ of the distribution function F. By replacing μ by $\hat{\mu} = \frac{1}{n}\sum\limits_{i=1}^{n} x_i$ and μ_r by $\hat{\mu}_r = \frac{1}{n}\sum\limits_{i=1}^{n}(x_i - \hat{\mu})$ resp. in these relations and solving the related equations, one obtains the moment-estimates $\hat{\theta}_j = T_j^*(\hat{m}_1, \hat{m}_2, \ldots, \hat{m}_p)$ for θ_j, $j = 1, \ldots, p$.

Confidence interval estimates

Task: To assess the accuracy of the estimate of an unknown parameter θ of a distribution one has to construct intervals, so-called *confidence intervals*, which cover θ by a large probability.

- A random interval $I(\boldsymbol{X}) = [g_u(\boldsymbol{X}); g_o(\boldsymbol{X})]$ with $g_u(\boldsymbol{X}) < g_o(\boldsymbol{X})$ for the parameter θ depending on the mathematical sample $\boldsymbol{X} = (X_1, \ldots, X_n)$ such that

$$\mathrm{P}(g_u(\boldsymbol{X}) \leq \theta \leq g_o(\boldsymbol{X})) \geq \varepsilon = 1 - \alpha$$

is called a *two-sided confidence interval* for θ to the *confidence level* ε $(0 < \varepsilon < 1)$.

- For a realization $\boldsymbol{x}$ of $\boldsymbol{X}$ the interval $I(\boldsymbol{x}) = [g_u(\boldsymbol{x}); g_0(\boldsymbol{x})]$ is called a *concrete confidence interval* for θ.
- If $g_u \equiv -\infty$ or $g_o \equiv +\infty$, then $[-\infty; g_o(\boldsymbol{X})]$ and $[g_u(\boldsymbol{X}); \infty]$, resp., are said to be *one-sided confidence intervals* with

$$\mathrm{P}(\theta \leq g_o(\boldsymbol{X})) \geq \varepsilon \quad \text{and} \quad \mathrm{P}(\theta \geq g_u(\boldsymbol{X})) \geq \varepsilon.$$

One-sided confidence intervals for parameters of the normal distribution

for the expected value μ :

σ^2 known: $\left(-\infty; \overline{x}_n + z_{1-\alpha}\frac{\sigma}{\sqrt{n}}\right]$ or $\left[\overline{x}_n - z_{1-\alpha}\frac{\sigma}{\sqrt{n}}; +\infty\right)$

σ^2 unknown: $\left(-\infty; \overline{x}_n + t_{n-1;1-\alpha}\frac{s}{\sqrt{n}}\right]$ or $\left[\overline{x}_n - t_{n-1;1-\alpha}\frac{s}{\sqrt{n}}; +\infty\right)$

for the variance σ^2 :

μ known: $\left[0; \dfrac{n \cdot s^{*2}}{\chi^2_{n;\alpha}}\right]$ or $\left[\dfrac{n \cdot s^{*2}}{\chi^2_{n;1-\alpha}}; +\infty\right)$

μ unknown: $\left[0; \dfrac{(n-1) \cdot s^2}{\chi^2_{n-1;\alpha}}\right]$ or $\left[\dfrac{(n-1) \cdot s^2}{\chi^2_{n-1;1-\alpha}}; +\infty\right)$

Here $\overline{x}_n = \frac{1}{n}\sum\limits_{i=1}^{n} x_i$, $s^{*2} = \frac{1}{n}\sum\limits_{i=1}^{n}(x_i - \mu)^2$, $s^2 = \frac{1}{n-1}\sum\limits_{i=1}^{n}(x_i - \overline{x}_n)^2$; for the quantiles z_q, $t_{m;q}$, $\chi^2_{m;q}$ see tables I b, II, III on p. 170 ff.

Two-sided confidence intervals for parameters of the normal distribution

for expected value μ :

σ^2 known: $$\left[\overline{x}_n - z_{1-\frac{\alpha}{2}} \frac{\sigma}{\sqrt{n}};\ \overline{x}_n + z_{1-\frac{\alpha}{2}} \frac{\sigma}{\sqrt{n}}\right]$$

σ^2 unknown: $$\left[\overline{x}_n - t_{n-1;1-\frac{\alpha}{2}} \frac{s}{\sqrt{n}};\ \overline{x}_n + t_{n-1;1-\frac{\alpha}{2}} \frac{s}{\sqrt{n}}\right]$$

for variance σ^2 :

μ known: $$\left[\frac{n \cdot s^{*2}}{\chi^2_{n;1-\frac{\alpha}{2}}};\ \frac{n \cdot s^{*2}}{\chi^2_{n;\frac{\alpha}{2}}}\right]$$

μ unknown: $$\left[\frac{(n-1) \cdot s^2}{\chi^2_{n-1;1-\frac{\alpha}{2}}};\ \frac{(n-1) \cdot s^2}{\chi^2_{n-1;\frac{\alpha}{2}}}\right]$$

Here $\overline{x}_n = \frac{1}{n}\sum_{i=1}^{n} x_i$, $s^{*2} = \frac{1}{n}\sum_{i=1}^{n}(x_i - \mu)^2$, $s^2 = \frac{1}{n-1}\sum_{i=1}^{n}(x_i - \overline{x}_n)^2$. For the quantiles z_q, $t_{m;q}$, $\chi^2_{m,q}$ see tables Ib, II, III on p. 170ff.

Asymptotic confidence interval for probability $p = \mathrm{P}(A)$

to the confidence level $\varepsilon = 1 - \alpha$

$$[g_u; g_o] = \left[\frac{1}{n+z_q^2}\left(x + \frac{z_q^2}{2} - z_q\sqrt{\frac{x(n-x)}{n} + \frac{z_q^2}{4}}\right);\right.$$
$$\left.\frac{1}{n+z_q^2}\left(x + \frac{z_q^2}{2} + z_q\sqrt{\frac{x(n-x)}{n} + \frac{z_q^2}{4}}\right)\right]$$

Here $q = 1 - \frac{\alpha}{2}$, while x describes how often the random event A occurs in n trials.

Statistical tests

Task: Statistical tests serve for the verification of so-called statistical hypotheses concerning the (completely of partially) unknown distributions F by means of corresponding samples.

Assumption: $F = F_\theta, \ \theta \in \Theta$

- *Null hypothesis* $H_0 : \theta \in \Theta_0 \, (\subset \Theta)$;
- *Alternative hypothesis* $H_1 : \theta \in \Theta_1 \, (\subset \Theta \setminus \Theta_0)$
- A hypothesis is called *simple* if $H_0 : \theta = \theta_0$, i. e. $\Theta_0 = \{\theta_0\}$, otherwise it is called *composite.*
- A *two-sided statement of the problem* or *two-sided test (problem)* is dealt with if $H_0 : \theta = \theta_0$ and $H_1 : \theta \neq \theta_0$ (i. e. $\theta > \theta_0$ and $\theta < \theta_0$). A *one-sided statement of the problem* is considered if either $H_0 : \theta \leq \theta_0$ and $H_1 : \theta > \theta_0$ or $H_0 : \theta \geq \theta_0$ and $H_1 : \theta < \theta_0$.

Significance test

1. Formulation of a *null hypothesis* H_0 (and an alternative hypothesis H_1 if necessary).

2. Construction of a *test statistic* $T = T(X_1, \ldots, X_n)$ for a mathematical sample. (In this case the distribution of T must be known if H_0 is true.)

3. Choice of a *critical region* K^* (part of the range of the test statistic T being as large as possible so that the probability p^* for the case that T takes values from K^* is not greater than the *significance level* α ($0 < \alpha < 1$) if H_0 is true; usually: $\alpha = 0.05; 0.01; 0.001$).

4. *Decision rule:* If for some concrete sample $(x_1, \ldots, x_n)$ the value t of the test statistic T (i. e. $t = T(x_1, \ldots, x_n)$) is in K^* (i. e. $t \in K^*$), then H_0 is rejected in favour of H_1. In the other case there is no objection to H_0.

Decision structure

decision	real (unknown) situation	
	H_0 is true	H_0 is not true
H_0 is rejected	error of first kind	right decision
H_0 is not rejected	right decision	error of second kind

with P(error of first kind) $\leq \alpha$.

Significance tests under normal distribution

One-sample problems: Let $\boldsymbol{x} = (x_1, \ldots, x_n)$ be a sample of size n chosen from a normally distributed parent population with expected value μ and variance σ^2.

hypotheses H_0 H_1	assumptions	realization t of the test variable T	distribution of T	critical region
Gauss test				
a) $\mu = \mu_0,\ \mu \neq \mu_0$				$\lvert t\rvert \geq z_{1-\frac{\alpha}{2}}$
b) $\mu \leq \mu_0,\ \mu > \mu_0$	σ^2 known	$\dfrac{\overline{x}_n - \mu_0}{\sigma}\sqrt{n}$	$\mathrm{N}(0;1)$	$t \geq z_{1-\alpha}$
c) $\mu \geq \mu_0,\ \mu < \mu_0$				$t \leq -z_{1-\alpha}$
simple t-test				
a) $\mu = \mu_0,\ \mu \neq \mu_0$				$\lvert t\rvert \geq t_{n-1;1-\frac{\alpha}{2}}$
b) $\mu \leq \mu_0,\ \mu > \mu_0$	σ^2 unknown	$\dfrac{\overline{x}_n - \mu_0}{s}\sqrt{n}$	t_m $(m=n-1)$	$t \geq t_{n-1;1-\alpha}$
c) $\mu \geq \mu_0,\ \mu < \mu_0$				$t \leq -t_{n-1;1-\alpha}$
a) $\sigma^2=\sigma_0^2,\ \sigma^2\neq\sigma_0^2$				$t \geq \chi^2_{n;1-\frac{\alpha}{2}}$ $\vee$ $t \leq \chi^2_{n;\frac{\alpha}{2}}$
b) $\sigma^2\leq\sigma_0^2,\ \sigma^2>\sigma_0^2$	μ known	$\dfrac{n \cdot s^{*2}}{\sigma_0^2}$	χ^2_n	$t \geq \chi^2_{n;1-\alpha}$
c) $\sigma^2\geq\sigma_0^2,\ \sigma^2<\sigma_0^2$				$t \leq \chi^2_{n;\alpha}$
chi-squared test of variances				
a) $\sigma^2=\sigma_0^2,\ \sigma^2\neq\sigma_0^2$				$t \geq \chi^2_{n-1;1-\frac{\alpha}{2}}$ $\vee$ $t \leq \chi^2_{n-1;\frac{\alpha}{2}}$
b) $\sigma^2\leq\sigma_0^2,\ \sigma^2>\sigma_0^2$	μ unknown	$\dfrac{(n-1) \cdot s^2}{\sigma_0^2}$	χ^2_m $(m=n-1)$	$t \geq \chi^2_{n-1;1-\alpha}$
c) $\sigma^2\geq\sigma_0^2,\ \sigma^2<\sigma_0^2$				$t \leq \chi^2_{n-1;\alpha}$

a) two-sided, b) and c) one-sided problems

Two-sample problems: $\boldsymbol{x} = (x_1, \ldots, x_{n_1})$ and $\boldsymbol{x}' = (x'_1, \ldots, x'_{n_2})$ are samples of size n_1 and n_2, resp., chosen from two normally distributed parent populations with expected values μ_1 and μ_2 and variances σ_1^2 and σ_2^2, resp. (T – test statistic):

hypotheses H_0 H_1	realization of T	distribution of T	critical region
Difference method (assumptions: $\boldsymbol{x}$, $\boldsymbol{x}'$ dependent samples, $n_1 = n_2 = n$, $D = X - X' \in \mathrm{N}(\mu_D, \sigma_D^2)$, $\mu_D = \mu_1 - \mu_2$, σ_D^2 unknown)			
a) $\mu_D = 0, \mu_D \neq 0$ b) $\mu_D \leq 0, \mu_D > 0$ c) $\mu_D \geq 0, \mu_D < 0$	$\frac{\overline{d}}{s_D}\sqrt{n}$	t_m-distribution $m = n - 1$	$\|t\| \geq t_{n-1;1-\frac{\alpha}{2}}$ $t \geq t_{n-1;1-\alpha}$ $t \leq -t_{n-1;1-\alpha}$
Double t-test (assumptions: $\boldsymbol{x}$, $\boldsymbol{x}'$ independent samples, $X \in \mathrm{N}(\mu_1, \sigma_1^2)$, $X' \in \mathrm{N}(\mu_2, \sigma_2^2)$, $\sigma_1^2 = \sigma_2^2$)			
a) $\mu_1 = \mu_2, \mu_1 \neq \mu_2$ b) $\mu_1 \leq \mu_2, \mu_1 > \mu_2$ c) $\mu_1 \geq \mu_2, \mu_1 < \mu_2$	$\frac{\overline{x}_{(1)} - \overline{x}_{(2)}}{s_g} \times$ $\times \sqrt{\frac{n_1 n_2}{n_1 + n_2}}$ (s_g s. below)	t_m-distribution $m = n_1 + n_2 - 2$	$\|t\| \geq t_{m;1-\frac{\alpha}{2}}$ $t \geq t_{m;1-\alpha}$ $t \leq -t_{m;1-\alpha}$ $(m = n_1 + n_2 - 2)$
Welch-Test (assumptions: $\boldsymbol{x}$, $\boldsymbol{x}'$ independent samples, $X \in \mathrm{N}(\mu_1, \sigma_1^2)$, $X' \in \mathrm{N}(\mu_2, \sigma_2^2)$, $\sigma_1^2 \neq \sigma_2^2$)			
a) $\mu_1 = \mu_2, \mu_1 \neq \mu_2$ b) $\mu_1 \leq \mu_2, \mu_1 > \mu_2$ c) $\mu_1 \geq \mu_2, \mu_1 < \mu_2$	$\frac{\overline{x}_{(1)} - \overline{x}_{(2)}}{\sqrt{\frac{s_1^2}{n_1} + \frac{s_2^2}{n_2}}}$	approximately t_m-distribution $m \approx \left[\frac{c^2}{n_1 - 1} + \frac{(1-c)^2}{n_2 - 1}\right]^{-1}$ $c = \frac{s_1^2/n_1}{s_1^2/n_1 + s_2^2/n_2}$	$\|t\| \geq t_{m;1-\frac{\alpha}{2}}$ $t \geq t_{m;1-\alpha}$ $t \leq -t_{m;1-\alpha}$
F-Test ($\boldsymbol{x}$, $\boldsymbol{x}'$ independent samples, $X \in \mathrm{N}(\mu_1, \sigma_1^2)$, $X' \in \mathrm{N}(\mu_2, \sigma_2^2)$, μ_1, μ_2 unknown)			
a) $\sigma_1^2 = \sigma_2^2, \sigma_1^2 \neq \sigma_2^2$ b) $\sigma_1^2 \leq \sigma_2^2, \sigma_1^2 > \sigma_2^2$	s_1^2/s_2^2	F_{m_1,m_2}-distrib. $(m_1 = n_1 - 1)$ $(m_2 = n_2 - 1)$	$t \geq F_{m_1,m_2;1-\frac{\alpha}{2}}$ or $t \leq F_{m_1,m_2;1-\frac{\alpha}{2}}$ $t \geq F_{m_1,m_2;1-\alpha}$
c) $\sigma_1^2 \geq \sigma_2^2, \sigma_1^2 < \sigma_2^2$	s_2^2/s_1^2	F_{m_2,m_1}-distrib.	$t \geq F_{m_2,m_1;1-\alpha}$

a) two-sided, b) and c) one-sided problems; here $n_k, \overline{x}_k$ and s_k^2 denote sample size, arithmetic mean and empirical variance, resp., of the k-th sample, $k = 1, 2$, while $\overline{d}$ and s_D^2 are the arithmetic mean and the empirical variance of the difference series $d_i = x_i - x'_i$, $i = 1, 2, \ldots, n$ formed from the values of the dependent samples. Furthermore $s_g = \sqrt{[(n_1 - 1)s_1^2 + (n_2 - 1)s_2^2](n_1 + n_2 - 2)^{-1}}$.

Table 1 a Distribution function $\Phi(x)$ of the standardized normal distribution

x	0.00	0.01	0.02	0.03	0.04
0.0	.500000	.503989	.507978	.511966	.515953
0.1	.539828	.543795	.547758	.551717	.555670
0.2	.579260	.583166	.587064	.590954	.594835
0.3	.617911	.621720	.625516	.629300	.633072
0.4	.655422	.659097	.662757	.666402	.670031
0.5	.691462	.694974	.698468	.701944	.705401
0.6	.725747	.729069	.732371	.735653	.738914
0.7	.758036	.761148	.764238	.767305	.770350
0.8	.788145	.791030	.793892	.796731	.799546
0.9	.815940	.818589	.821214	.823814	.826391
1.0	.841345	.843752	.846136	.848495	.850830
1.1	.864334	.866500	.868643	.870762	.872857
1.2	.884930	.886861	.888768	.890651	.892512
1.3	.903200	.904902	.906582	.908241	.909877
1.4	.919243	.920730	.922196	.923641	.925066
1.5	.933193	.934478	.935745	.936992	.938220
1.6	.945201	.946301	.947384	.948449	.949497
1.7	.955435	.956367	.957284	.958185	.959070
1.8	.964070	.964852	.965620	.966375	.967116
1.9	.971283	.971933	.972571	.973197	.973810
2.0	.977250	.977784	.978308	.978822	.979325
2.1	.982136	.982571	.982997	.983414	.983823
2.2	.986097	.986447	.986791	.987126	.987455
2.3	.989276	.989556	.989830	.990097	.990358
2.4	.991802	.992024	.992240	.992451	.992656
2.5	.993790	.993963	.994132	.994297	.994457
2.6	.995339	.995473	.995604	.995731	.995855
2.7	.996533	.996636	.996736	.996833	.996928
2.8	.997445	.997523	.997599	.997673	.997744
2.9	.998134	.998193	.998250	.998305	.998359
3.0	.998650	.999032	.999313	.999517	.999663
x	0.0	0.1	0.2	0.3	0.4

Table 1 a Distribution function $\Phi(x)$ of the standardized normal distribution

x	0.05	0.06	0.07	0.08	0.09
0.0	.519938	.523922	.527903	.531881	.535856
0.1	.559618	.563559	.567495	.571424	.575345
0.2	.598706	.602568	.606420	.610261	.614092
0.3	.636831	.640576	.644309	.648027	.651732
0.4	.673645	.677242	.680822	.684386	.687933
0.5	.708840	.712260	.715661	.719043	.722405
0.6	.742154	.745373	.748571	.751748	.754903
0.7	.773373	.776373	.779350	.782305	.785236
0.8	.802338	.805105	.807850	.810570	.813267
0.9	.828944	.831472	.833977	.836457	.838913
1.0	.853141	.855428	.857690	.859929	.862143
1.1	.874928	.876976	.879000	.881000	.882977
1.2	.894350	.896165	.897958	.899727	.901475
1.3	.911492	.913085	.914657	.916207	.917736
1.4	.926471	.927855	.929219	.930563	.931888
1.5	.939429	.940620	.941792	.942947	.944083
1.6	.950529	.951543	.952540	.953521	.954486
1.7	.959941	.960796	.961636	.962462	.963273
1.8	.967843	.968557	.969258	.969946	.970621
1.9	.974412	.975002	.975581	.976148	.976705
2.0	.979818	.980301	.980774	.981237	.981691
2.1	.984222	.984614	.984997	.985371	.985738
2.2	.987776	.988089	.988396	.988696	.988989
2.3	.990613	.990863	.991106	.991344	.991576
2.4	.992857	.993053	.993244	.993431	.993613
2.5	.994614	.994766	.994915	.995060	.995201
2.6	.995975	.996093	.996207	.996319	.996427
2.7	.997020	.997110	.997197	.997282	.997365
2.8	.997814	.997882	.997948	.998012	.998074
2.9	.998411	.998462	.998511	.998559	.998605
3.0	.999767	.999841	.999892	.999928	.999952
x	0.5	0.6	0.7	0.8	0.9

Table 1 b Quantiles z_q of the standardized normal distribution

q	z_q	q	z_q	q	z_q
0.5	0	0.91	1.34076	**0.975**	**1.95996**
0.55	0.12566	0.92	1.40507	0.98	2.05375
0.6	0.25335	0.93	1.47579	0.985	2.17009
0.65	0.38532	0.94	1.55478	**0.99**	**2.32635**
0.7	0.52440	**0.95**	**1.64485**	**0.995**	**2.57583**
0.75	0.67449	0.955	1.69540	0.99865	3.00000
0.8	0.84162	0.96	1.75069	**0.999**	**3.09023**
0.85	1.03644	0.965	1.81191	**0.9995**	**3.29053**
0.9	**1.28155**	0.97	1.88080	0.999767	3.50000

Table 2 Quantiles $t_{m;q}$ of the t–distribution

m \ q	0.9	0.95	0.975	0.99	0.995	0.999	0.9995
1	3.08	6.31	12.71	31.82	63.7	318.3	636.6
2	1.89	2.92	4.30	6.96	9.92	22.33	31.6
3	1.64	2.35	3.18	4.54	5.84	10.21	12.9
4	1.53	2.13	2.78	3.75	4.60	7.17	8.61
5	1.48	2.02	2.57	3.36	4.03	5.89	6.87
6	1.44	1.94	2.45	3.14	3.71	5.21	5.96
7	1.41	1.89	2.36	3.00	3.50	4.79	5.41
8	1.40	1.86	2.31	2.90	3.36	4.50	5.04
9	1.38	1.83	2.26	2.82	3.25	4.30	4.78
10	1.37	1.81	2.23	2.76	3.17	4.14	4.59
11	1.36	1.80	2.20	2.72	3.11	4.02	4.44
12	1.36	1.78	2.18	2.68	3.05	3.93	4.32
13	1.35	1.77	2.16	2.65	3.01	3.85	4.22
14	1.35	1.76	2.14	2.62	2.98	3.79	4.14
15	1.34	1.75	2.13	2.60	2.95	3.73	4.07
16	1.34	1.75	2.12	2.58	2.92	3.69	4.01
17	1.33	1.74	2.11	2.57	2.90	3.65	3.97
18	1.33	1.73	2.10	2.55	2.88	3.61	3.92
19	1.33	1.73	2.09	2.54	2.86	3.58	3.88
20	1.33	1.72	2.09	2.53	2.85	3.55	3.85
21	1.32	1.72	2.08	2.52	2.83	3.53	3.82
22	1.32	1.72	2.07	2.51	2.82	3.50	3.79
23	1.32	1.71	2.07	2.50	2.81	3.48	3.77
24	1.32	1.71	2.06	2.49	2.80	3.47	3.75
25	1.32	1.71	2.06	2.49	2.79	3.45	3.73
26	1.31	1.71	2.06	2.48	2.78	3.43	3.71
27	1.31	1.70	2.05	2.47	2.77	3.42	3.69
28	1.31	1.70	2.05	2.46	2.76	3.41	3.67
29	1.31	1.70	2.05	2.46	2.76	3.40	3.66
30	1.31	1.70	2.04	2.46	2.75	3.39	3.65
40	1.30	1.68	2.02	2.42	2.70	3.31	3.55
60	1.30	1.67	2.00	2.39	2.66	3.23	3.46
120	1.29	1.66	1.98	2.36	2.62	3.16	3.37
∞	1.28	1.64	1.96	2.33	2.58	3.09	3.29

Table 3 Probability density $\varphi(x)$ of the standardized normal distribution

x	0	1	2	3	4	5	6	7	8	9
0,0	0,3989	3989	3989	3988	3986	3984	3982	3980	3977	3973
0,1	3970	3965	3961	3956	3951	3945	3939	3932	3925	3918
0,2	3910	3902	3894	3885	3876	3867	3857	3847	3836	3825
0,3	3814	3802	3790	3778	3765	3752	3739	3725	3712	3697
0,4	3683	3668	3653	3637	3621	3605	3589	3572	3555	3538
0,5	3521	3503	3485	3467	3448	3429	3410	3391	3372	3352
0,6	3332	3312	3292	3271	3251	3230	3209	3187	3166	3144
0,7	3123	3101	3079	3056	3034	3011	2989	2966	2943	2920
0,8	2897	2874	2850	2827	2803	2780	2756	2732	2709	2685
0,9	2661	2637	2613	2589	2565	2541	2516	2492	2468	2444
1,0	0,2420	2396	2371	2347	2323	2299	2275	2251	2227	2203
1,1	2179	2155	2131	2107	2083	2059	2036	2012	1989	1965
1,2	1942	1919	1895	1872	1849	1826	1804	1781	1758	1736
1,3	1714	1691	1669	1647	1626	1604	1582	1561	1539	1518
1,4	1497	1476	1456	1435	1415	1394	1374	1354	1334	1315
1,5	1295	1276	1257	1238	1219	1200	1182	1163	1145	1127
1,6	1109	1092	1074	1057	1040	1023	1006	0989	0973	0957
1,7	0940	0925	0909	0893	0878	0863	0848	0833	0818	0804
1,8	0790	0775	0761	0748	0734	0721	0707	0694	0681	0669
1,9	0656	0644	0632	0620	0608	0596	0584	0573	0562	0551
2,0	0,0540	0529	0519	0508	0498	0488	0478	0468	0459	0449
2,1	0440	0431	0422	0413	0404	0396	0387	0379	0371	0363
2,2	0355	0347	0339	0332	0325	0317	0310	0303	0297	0290
2,3	0283	0277	0270	0264	0258	0252	0246	0241	0235	0229
2,4	0224	0219	0213	0208	0203	0198	0194	0189	0184	0180
2,5	0175	0171	0167	0163	0158	0154	0151	0147	0143	0139
2,6	0136	0132	0129	0126	0122	0119	0116	0113	0110	0107
2,7	0104	0101	0099	0096	0093	0091	0088	0086	0084	0081
2,8	0079	0077	0075	0073	0071	0069	0067	0065	0063	0061
2,9	0060	0058	0056	0055	0053	0051	0050	0048	0047	0046
3,0	0,0044	0043	0042	0040	0039	0038	0037	0036	0035	0034
3,1	0033	0032	0031	0030	0029	0028	0027	0026	0025	0025
3,2	0024	0023	0022	0022	0021	0020	0020	0019	0018	0018
3,3	0017	0017	0016	0016	0015	0015	0014	0014	0013	0013
3,4	0012	0012	0012	0011	0011	0010	0010	0010	0009	0009
3,5	0009	0008	0008	0008	0008	0007	0007	0007	0007	0006
3,6	0006	0006	0006	0005	0005	0005	0005	0005	0005	0004
3,7	0004	0004	0004	0004	0004	0004	0003	0003	0003	0003
3,8	0003	0003	0003	0003	0003	0002	0002	0002	0002	0002
3,9	0002	0002	0002	0002	0002	0002	0002	0002	0001	0001

Table 4a Quantiles $F_{m_1,m_2;\,q}$ of the F–distribution for $q = 0.95$

m_2 \ m_1	1	2	3	4	5	6	7	8	9	10
1	161	200	216	225	230	234	37	239	41	242
2	18.5	19.0	19.2	19.2	19.3	19.3	19.4	19.4	19.4	19.4
3	10.1	9.55	9.28	9.12	9.01	8.94	8.89	8.85	8.81	8.79
4	7.71	6.94	6.59	6.39	6.26	6.16	6.09	6.04	6.00	5.96
5	4.68	4.64	4.60	4.56	4.50	4.44	4.42	4.41	4.37	4.36
6	5.99	5.14	4.76	4.53	4.39	4.28	4.21	4.15	4.10	4.06
7	5.59	4.74	4.35	4.12	3.97	3.87	3.79	3.73	3.68	3.64
8	5.32	4.46	4.07	3.84	3.69	3.58	3.50	3.44	3.39	3.35
9	5.12	4.26	3.86	3.63	3.48	3.37	3.29	3.23	3.18	3.14
10	4.96	4.10	3.71	3.48	3.33	3.22	3.14	3.07	3.02	2.98
11	4.84	3.98	3.59	3.36	3.20	3.09	3.01	2.95	2.90	2.85
12	4.75	3.89	3.49	3.26	3.11	3.00	2.91	2.85	2.80	2.75
13	4.67	3.81	3.41	3.18	3.03	2.92	2.83	2.77	2.71	2.67
14	4.60	3.74	3.34	3.11	2.96	2.85	2.76	2.70	2.65	2.60
15	4.54	3.68	3.29	3.06	2.90	2.79	2.71	2.64	2.59	2.54
16	4.49	3.63	3.24	3.01	2.85	2.74	2.66	2.59	2.54	2.49
17	4.45	3.59	3.20	2.96	2.81	2.70	2.61	2.55	2.49	2.45
18	4.41	3.55	3.16	2.93	2.77	2.66	2.58	2.51	2.46	2.41
19	4.38	3.52	3.13	2.90	2.74	2.63	2.54	2.48	2.42	2.38
20	4.35	3.49	3.10	2.87	2.71	2.60	2.51	2.45	2.39	2.35
21	4.32	3.47	3.07	2.84	2.68	2.57	2.49	2.42	2.37	2.32
22	4.30	3.44	3.05	2.82	2.66	2.55	2.46	2.40	2.34	2.30
23	4.28	3.42	3.03	2.80	2.64	2.53	2.44	2.37	2.32	2.27
24	4.26	3.40	3.01	2.78	2.62	2.51	2.42	2.36	2.30	2.25
25	4.24	3.39	2.99	2.76	2.60	2.49	2.40	2.34	2.28	2.24
	1	2	3	4	5	6	7	8	9	10
26	4.23	3.37	2.98	2.74	2.59	2.47	2.39	2.32	2.27	2.22
27	4.21	3.35	2.96	2.73	2.57	2.46	2.37	2.31	2.25	2.20
28	4.20	3.34	2.95	2.71	2.56	2.45	2.36	2.29	2.24	2.19
29	4.18	3.33	2.93	2.70	2.55	2.43	2.35	2.28	2.22	2.18
30	4.17	3.32	2.92	2.69	2.53	2.42	2.33	2.27	2.21	2.16
32	4.15	3.29	2.90	2.67	2.51	2.40	2.31	2.24	2.19	2.14
34	4.13	3.28	2.88	2.65	2.49	2.38	2.29	2.23	2.17	2.12
36	4.11	3.26	2.87	2.63	2.48	2.36	2.28	2.21	2.15	2.11
38	4.10	3.24	2.85	2.62	2.46	2.35	2.26	2.19	2.14	2.09
40	4.08	3.23	2.84	2.61	2.45	2.34	2.25	2.18	2.12	2.08
42	4.07	3.22	2.83	2.59	2.44	2.32	2.24	2.17	2.11	2.06
44	4.06	3.21	2.82	2.58	2.43	2.31	2.23	2.16	2.10	2.05
46	4.05	3.20	2.81	2.57	2.42	2.30	2.22	2.15	2.09	2.04
48	4.04	3.19	2.80	2.57	2.41	2.29	2.21	2.14	2.08	2.03
50	4.03	3.18	2.79	2.56	2.40	2.29	2.20	2.13	2.07	2.03
55	4.02	3.16	2.78	2.54	2.38	2.27	2.18	2.11	2.06	2.01
60	4.00	3.15	2.76	2.53	2.37	2.25	2.17	2.10	2.04	1.99
65	3.99	3.14	2.75	2.51	2.36	2.24	2.15	2.08	2.03	1.98
70	3.98	3.13	2.74	2.50	2.35	2.23	2.14	2.07	2.02	1.97
80	3.96	3.11	2.72	2.49	2.33	2.21	2.13	2.06	2.00	1.95
100	3.94	3.09	2.70	2.46	2.31	2.19	2.10	2.03	1.97	1.93
125	3.92	3.07	2.68	2.44	2.29	2.17	2.08	2.01	1.96	1.91
150	3.90	3.06	2.66	2.43	2.27	2.16	2.07	2.00	1.94	1.89
200	3.89	3.04	2.65	2.42	2.26	2.14	2.06	1.98	1.93	1.88
400	3.86	3.02	2.62	2.39	2.23	2.12	2.03	1.96	1.90	1.85
1000	3.85	3.00	2.61	2.38	2.22	2.11	2.02	1.95	1.89	1.84
∞	3.84	3.00	2.60	2.37	2.21	2.10	2.01	1.94	1.88	1.83

Table 4a Quantiles $F_{m_1,m_2;q}$ of the F–distribution for $q = 0.95$

m_2 \ m_1	12	14	16	20	30	50	75	100	500	∞
1	244	245	246	248	250	252	253	253	254	254
2	19.4	19.4	19.4	19.4	19.5	19.5	19.5	19.5	19.5	19.5
3	8.74	8.71	8.69	8.66	8.62	8.58	8.56	8.55	8.53	8.53
4	5.91	5.87	5.84	5.80	5.75	5.70	5.68	5.66	5.64	5.63
5	4.68	4.64	4.60	4.56	4.50	4.44	4.42	4.41	4.37	4.36
6	4.00	3.96	3.92	3.87	3.81	3.75	3.72	3.71	3.68	3.67
7	3.57	3.53	3.49	3.44	3.38	3.32	3.29	3.27	3.24	3.23
8	3.28	3.24	3.20	3.15	3.08	3.02	3.00	2.97	2.94	2.93
9	3.07	3.03	2.99	2.93	2.86	2.80	2.77	2.76	2.72	2.71
10	2.91	2.86	2.83	2.77	2.70	2.64	2.61	2.59	2.55	2.54
11	2.79	2.74	2.70	2.65	2.57	2.51	2.47	2.46	2.42	2.40
12	2.69	2.64	2.60	2.54	2.47	2.40	2.36	2.35	2.31	2.30
13	2.60	2.55	2.51	2.46	2.38	2.31	2.28	2.26	2.22	2.21
14	2.53	2.48	2.44	2.39	2.31	2.24	2.21	2.19	2.14	2.13
15	2.48	2.42	2.38	2.33	2.25	2.18	2.14	2.12	2.08	2.07
16	2.42	2.37	2.33	2.28	2.19	2.12	2.09	2.07	2.02	2.01
17	2.38	2.33	2.29	2.23	2.15	2.08	2.04	2.02	1.97	1.96
18	2.34	2.29	2.25	2.19	2.11	2.04	2.00	1.98	1.93	1.92
19	2.31	2.26	2.21	2.15	2.07	2.00	1.96	1.94	1.89	1.88
20	2.28	2.22	2.18	2.12	2.04	1.97	1.93	1.91	1.86	1.84
21	2.25	2.20	2.16	2.10	2.01	1.94	1.90	1.88	1.82	1.81
22	2.23	2.17	2.13	2.07	1.98	1.91	1.87	1.85	1.80	1.78
23	2.20	2.15	2.11	2.05	1.96	1.88	1.84	1.82	1.77	1.76
24	2.18	2.13	2.09	2.03	1.94	1.86	1.82	1.80	1.75	1.73
25	2.16	2.11	2.07	2.01	1.92	1.84	1.80	1.78	1.73	1.71
	12	14	16	20	30	50	75	100	500	∞
26	2.15	2.09	2.05	1.99	1.90	1.82	1.78	1.76	1.71	1.69
27	2.13	2.08	2.04	1.97	1.88	1.81	1.76	1.74	1.68	1.67
28	2.12	2.06	2.02	1.96	1.87	1.79	1.75	1.73	1.67	1.65
29	2.10	2.05	2.01	1.94	1.85	1.77	1.73	1.71	1.65	1.64
30	2.09	2.04	1.99	1.93	1.84	1.76	1.72	1.70	1.64	1.62
32	2.07	2.01	1.97	1.91	1.82	1.74	1.69	1.67	1.61	1.59
34	2.05	1.99	1.95	1.89	1.80	1.71	1.67	1.65	1.59	1.57
36	2.03	1.98	1.93	1.87	1.78	1.69	1.65	1.62	1.56	1.55
38	2.02	1.96	1.92	1.85	1.76	1.68	1.63	1.61	1.54	1.53
40	2.00	1.95	1.90	1.84	1.74	1.66	1.61	1.59	1.53	1.51
42	1.99	1.94	1.89	1.83	1.73	1.65	1.60	1.57	1.51	1.49
44	1.98	1.92	1.88	1.81	1.72	1.63	1.58	1.56	1.49	1.48
46	1.97	1.91	1.87	1.80	1.71	1.62	1.57	1.55	1.48	1.46
48	1.96	1.90	1.86	1.79	1.70	1.61	1.56	1.54	1.47	1.45
50	1.95	1.89	1.85	1.78	1.69	1.60	1.55	1.52	1.46	1.44
55	1.93	1.88	1.83	1.76	1.67	1.58	1.53	1.50	1.43	1.41
60	1.92	1.86	1.82	1.75	1.65	1.56	1.51	1.48	1.41	1.39
65	1.90	1.85	1.80	1.73	1.63	1.54	1.49	1.46	1.39	1.37
70	1.89	1.84	1.79	1.72	1.62	1.53	1.48	1.45	1.37	1.35
80	1.88	1.82	1.77	1.70	1.60	1.51	1.45	1.43	1.35	1.32
100	1.85	1.79	1.75	1.68	1.57	1.48	1.42	1.39	1.31	1.28
125	1.83	1.77	1.73	1.66	1.55	1.45	1.40	1.36	1.27	1.25
150	1.82	1.76	1.71	1.64	1.53	1.44	1.38	1.34	1.25	1.22
200	1.80	1.74	1.69	1.62	1.52	1.41	1.35	1.32	1.22	1.19
400	1.78	1.72	1.67	1.60	1.49	1.38	1.32	1.28	1.17	1.13
1000	1.76	1.70	1.65	1.58	1.47	1.36	1.30	1.26	1.13	1.08
∞	1.75	1.69	1.64	1.57	1.46	1.35	1.28	1.24	1.11	1.00

Table 4b Quantiles $F_{m_1,m_2;\,q}$ of the F-distribution for $q = 0.99$

m_2 \ m_1	1	2	3	4	5	6	7	8	9	10
1	4052	4999	5403	5625	5764	5859	5928	5981	6022	6056
2	98.5	99.0	99.2	99.2	99.3	99.3	99.4	99.4	99.4	99.4
3	34.1	30.8	29.5	28.7	28.2	27.9	27.7	27.5	27.3	27.2
4	21.2	18.0	16.7	16.0	15.5	15.2	15.0	14.8	14.7	14.6
5	16.3	13.3	12.1	11.4	11.0	10.7	10.5	10.3	10.2	10.1
6	13.7	10.9	9.78	9.15	8.75	8.47	8.26	8.10	7.98	7.87
7	12.2	9.55	8.45	7.85	7.46	7.19	6.99	6.84	6.72	6.62
8	11.3	8.65	7.59	7.01	6.63	6.37	6.18	6.03	5.91	5.81
9	10.6	8.02	6.99	6.42	6.06	5.80	5.61	5.47	5.35	5.26
10	10.0	7.56	6.55	5.99	5.64	5.39	5.20	5.06	4.94	4.85
11	9.65	7.21	6.22	5.67	5.32	5.07	4.89	4.74	4.63	4.54
12	9.33	6.93	5.95	5.41	5.06	4.82	4.64	4.50	4.39	4.30
13	9.07	6.70	5.74	5.21	4.86	4.62	4.44	4.30	4.19	4.10
14	8.86	6.51	5.56	5.04	4.70	4.46	4.28	4.14	4.03	3.94
15	8.68	6.36	5.42	4.89	4.56	4.32	4.14	4.00	3.89	3.80
16	8.53	6.23	5.29	4.77	4.44	4.20	4.03	3.89	3.78	3.69
17	8.40	6.11	5.18	4.67	4.34	4.10	3.93	3.79	3.68	3.59
18	8.29	6.01	5.09	4.58	4.25	4.01	3.84	3.71	3.60	3.51
19	8.18	5.93	5.01	4.50	4.17	3.94	3.77	3.63	3.52	3.43
20	8.10	5.85	4.94	4.43	4.10	3.87	3.70	3.56	3.46	3.37
21	8.02	5.78	4.87	4.37	4.04	3.81	3.64	3.51	3.40	3.31
22	7.95	5.72	4.82	4.31	3.99	3.76	3.59	3.45	3.35	3.26
23	7.88	5.66	4.76	4.26	3.94	3.71	3.54	3.41	3.30	3.21
24	7.82	5.61	4.72	4.22	3.90	3.67	3.50	3.36	3.26	3.17
25	7.77	5.57	4.68	4.18	3.86	3.63	3.46	3.32	3.22	3.13
	1	2	3	4	5	6	7	8	9	10
26	7.72	5.53	4.64	4.14	3.82	3.59	3.42	3.29	3.18	3.09
27	7.68	5.49	4.60	4.11	3.78	3.56	3.39	3.26	3.15	3.06
28	7.64	5.45	4.57	4.07	3.76	3.53	3.36	3.23	3.12	3.03
29	7.60	5.42	4.54	4.04	3.73	3.50	3.33	3.20	3.09	3.00
30	7.56	5.39	4.51	4.02	3.70	3.47	3.30	3.17	3.07	2.98
32	7.50	5.34	4.46	3.97	3.65	3.43	3.25	3.13	3.02	2.93
34	7.44	5.29	4.42	3.93	3.61	3.39	3.22	3.09	2.98	2.89
36	7.40	5.25	4.38	3.89	3.57	3.35	3.18	3.05	2.95	2.86
38	7.35	5.21	4.34	3.86	3.54	3.32	3.15	3.02	2.92	2.83
40	7.31	5.18	4.31	3.83	3.51	3.29	3.12	2.99	2.89	2.80
42	7.28	5.15	4.29	3.80	3.49	3.27	3.10	2.97	2.86	2.78
44	7.25	5.12	4.26	3.78	3.47	3.24	3.08	2.95	2.84	2.75
46	7.22	5.10	4.24	3.76	3.44	3.22	3.06	2.93	2.82	2.73
48	7.20	5.08	4.22	3.74	3.43	3.20	3.04	2.91	2.80	2.71
50	7.17	5.06	4.20	3.72	3.41	3.19	3.02	2.89	2.78	2.70
55	7.12	5.01	4.16	3.68	3.37	3.15	2.98	2.85	2.75	2.66
60	7.08	4.98	4.13	3.65	3.34	3.12	2.95	2.82	2.72	2.63
65	7.04	4.95	4.10	3.62	3.31	3.09	2.93	2.80	2.69	2.61
70	7.01	4.92	4.08	3.60	3.29	3.07	2.91	2.78	2.67	2.59
80	6.96	4.88	4.04	3.56	3.26	3.04	2.87	2.74	2.64	2.55
100	6.90	4.82	3.98	3.51	3.21	2.99	2.82	2.69	2.59	2.50
125	6.84	4.78	3.94	3.47	3.17	2.95	2.79	2.66	2.55	2.47
150	6.81	4.75	3.92	3.45	3.14	2.92	2.76	2.63	2.53	2.44
200	6.76	4.71	3.88	3.41	3.11	2.89	2.73	2.60	2.50	2.41
400	6.70	4.66	3.83	3.37	3.06	2.85	2.69	2.56	2.45	2.37
1000	6.66	4.63	3.80	3.34	3.04	2.82	2.66	2.53	2.43	2.34
∞	6.63	4.61	3.78	3.32	3.02	2.80	2.64	2.51	2.41	2.32

Table 4b Quantiles $F_{m_1,m_2;q}$ of the F–distribution for $q = 0.99$

m_2 \ m_1	12	14	16	20	30	50	75	100	500	∞
1	6106	6143	6170	6209	6261	6302	6324	6334	6360	6366
2	99.4	99.4	99.4	99.4	99.5	99.5	99.5	99.5	99.5	99.5
3	27.1	26.9	26.8	26.7	26.5	26.4	26.3	26.2	26.1	26.1
4	14.4	14.3	14.2	14.0	13.8	13.7	13.6	13.6	13.5	13.5
5	9.89	9.77	9.68	9.55	9.38	9.24	9.17	9.13	9.04	9.02
6	7.72	7.60	7.52	7.40	7.23	7.09	7.02	6.99	6.90	6.88
7	6.47	6.36	6.27	6.16	5.99	5.86	5.79	5.75	5.67	5.65
8	5.67	5.56	5.48	5.36	5.20	5.07	5.00	4.96	4.88	4.86
9	5.11	5.00	4.92	4.81	4.65	4.52	4.45	4.42	4.33	4.31
10	4.71	4.60	4.52	4.41	4.25	4.12	4.05	4.01	3.93	3.91
11	4.40	4.29	4.21	4.10	3.94	3.81	3.74	3.71	3.62	3.60
12	4.16	4.05	3.97	3.86	3.70	3.57	3.49	3.47	3.38	3.36
13	3.96	3.86	3.78	3.66	3.51	3.38	3.31	3.27	3.19	3.17
14	3.80	3.70	3.62	3.51	3.35	3.22	3.15	3.11	3.03	3.00
15	3.67	3.56	3.49	3.37	3.21	3.08	3.01	2.98	2.89	2.87
16	3.55	3.45	3.37	3.26	3.10	2.97	2.90	2.86	2.78	2.75
17	3.46	3.35	3.27	3.16	3.00	2.87	2.80	2.76	2.68	2.65
18	3.37	3.27	3.19	3.08	2.92	2.78	2.71	2.68	2.59	2.57
19	3.30	3.19	3.12	3.00	2.84	2.71	2.64	2.60	2.51	2.49
20	3.23	3.13	3.05	2.94	2.78	2.64	2.57	2.54	2.44	2.42
21	3.17	3.07	2.99	2.88	2.72	2.58	2.51	2.48	2.38	2.36
22	3.12	3.02	2.94	2.83	2.67	2.53	2.46	2.42	2.33	2.31
23	3.07	2.97	2.89	2.78	2.62	2.48	2.41	2.37	2.28	2.26
24	3.03	2.93	2.85	2.74	2.58	2.44	2.37	2.33	2.24	2.21
25	2.99	2.89	2.81	2.70	2.54	2.40	2.33	2.29	2.19	2.17

	12	14	16	20	30	50	75	100	500	∞
26	2.96	2.86	2.78	2.66	2.50	2.36	2.29	2.25	2.16	2.13
27	2.93	2.82	2.75	2.63	2.47	2.33	2.25	2.22	2.12	2.10
28	2.90	2.80	2.72	2.60	2.44	2.30	2.23	2.19	2.09	2.06
29	2.87	2.77	2.69	2.57	2.41	2.27	2.20	2.16	2.06	2.03
30	2.84	2.74	2.66	2.55	2.39	2.25	2.17	2.13	2.03	2.01
32	2.80	2.70	2.62	2.50	2.34	2.20	2.12	2.08	1.98	1.96
34	2.76	2.66	2.58	2.46	2.30	2.16	2.08	2.04	1.94	1.91
36	2.72	2.62	2.54	2.43	2.26	2.12	2.04	2.00	1.90	1.87
38	2.69	2.59	2.51	2.40	2.23	2.09	2.01	1.97	1.86	1.84
40	2.66	2.56	2.48	2.37	2.20	2.06	1.98	1.94	1.83	1.80
42	2.64	2.54	2.46	2.34	2.18	2.03	1.98	1.91	1.80	1.78
44	2.62	2.52	2.44	2.32	2.15	2.01	1.93	1.89	1.78	1.75
46	2.60	2.50	2.42	2.30	2.13	1.99	1.91	1.86	1.76	1.73
48	2.58	2.48	2.40	2.28	2.12	1.97	1.89	1.84	1.73	1.70
50	2.56	2.46	2.38	2.26	2.10	1.95	1.87	1.82	1.71	1.68
55	2.53	2.42	2.34	2.23	2.06	1.91	1.83	1.78	1.67	1.64
60	2.50	2.39	2.31	2.20	2.03	1.88	1.79	1.75	1.63	1.60
65	2.47	2.37	2.29	2.18	2.00	1.85	1.76	1.72	1.60	1.57
70	2.45	2.35	2.27	2.15	1.98	1.83	1.74	1.70	1.57	1.54
80	2.42	2.31	2.23	2.12	1.94	1.79	1.70	1.65	1.53	1.49
100	2.37	2.27	2.19	2.07	1.89	1.74	1.65	1.60	1.47	1.43
125	2.33	2.23	2.15	2.03	1.85	1.69	1.60	1.55	1.41	1.37
150	2.31	2.20	2.12	2.00	1.83	1.67	1.57	1.52	1.38	1.33
200	2.27	2.17	2.09	1.97	1.79	1.63	1.53	1.48	1.33	1.28
400	2.23	2.13	2.04	1.92	1.74	1.58	1.48	1.42	1.25	1.19
1000	2.20	2.10	2.02	1.90	1.72	1.54	1.44	1.38	1.19	1.11
∞	2.18	2.08	2.00	1.88	1.70	1.52	1.42	1.36	1.15	1.00

Table 5 Probabilities $p_k = \frac{\lambda^k}{k!} e^{-\lambda}$ of the Poisson distribution

$k \backslash \lambda$	0,1	0,2	0,3	0,4	0,5	0,6	0,7
0	0,904837	0,818731	0,740818	0,670320	0,606531	0,548812	0,496585
1	0,090484	0,163746	0,222245	0,268128	0,303265	0,329287	0,347610
2	0,004524	0,016375	0,033337	0,053626	0,075816	0,098786	0,121663
3	0,000151	0,001091	0,003334	0,007150	0,012636	0,019757	0,028388
4	0,000004	0,000055	0,000250	0,000715	0,001580	0,002964	0,004968
5		0,000002	0,000015	0,000057	0,000158	0,000356	0,000696
6			0,000001	0,000004	0,000013	0,000036	0,000081
7					0,000001	0,000003	0,000008

$k \backslash \lambda$	0,8	0,9	1,0	1,5	2,0	2,5	3,0
0	0,449329	0, 406570	0,367879	0,223130	0,135335	0,082085	0,049787
1	0,359463	0,365913	0,367879	0,334695	0,270671	0,205212	0,149361
2	0,143785	0,164661	0,183940	0,251021	0,270671	0,256516	0,224042
3	0,038343	0,049398	0,061313	0,125510	0,180447	0,213763	0,224042
4	0,007669	0,011115	0,015328	0,047067	0,090224	0,133602	0,168031
5	0,001227	0,002001	0,003066	0,014120	0,036089	0,066801	0,100819
6	0,000164	0,000300	0,000511	0,003530	0,012030	0,027834	0,050409
7	0,000019	0,000039	0,000073	0,000756	0,003437	0,009941	0,021604
8	0,000002	0,000004	0,000009	0,000142	0,000859	0,003106	0,008101
9			0,000001	0,000024	0,000191	0,000863	0,002701
10				0,000004	0,000038	0,000216	0,000810
11					0,000007	0,000049	0,000221
12					0,000001	0,000010	0,000055
13						0,000002	0,000013
14							0,000003
15							0,000001

Table 5 Probabilities $p_k = \frac{\lambda^k}{k!} e^{-\lambda}$ of the Poisson distribution

$k \backslash \lambda$	4,0	5,0	6,0	7,0	8,0	9,0	10,0
0	0,018316	0,006738	0,002479	0,000912	0,000335	0,000123	0,000045
1	0,073263	0,033690	0,014873	0,006383	0,002684	0,001111	0,000454
2	0,146525	0,084224	0,044618	0,022341	0,010735	0,004998	0,002270
3	0,195367	0,140374	0,089235	0,052129	0,028626	0,014994	0,007567
4	0,195367	0,175467	0,133853	0,091226	0,057252	0,033737	0,018917
5	0,156293	0,175467	0,016623	0,127717	0,091604	0,060727	0,037833
6	0,104196	0,146223	0,160623	0,149003	0,122138	0,091090	0,063055
7	0,059540	0,104445	0,137677	0,149003	0,139587	0,117116	0,090079
8	0,029770	0,065278	0,103258	0,130377	0,139587	0,131756	0,112599
9	0,013231	0,036266	0,068838	0,101405	0,124077	0,131756	0,125110
10	0,005292	0,018133	0,041303	0,070983	0,099262	0,118580	0,125110
11	0,001925	0,008242	0,022529	0,045171	0,072190	0,097020	0,113736
12	0,000642	0,003434	0,011264	0,026350	0,048127	0,072765	0,094780
13	0,000197	0,001321	0,005199	0,014188	0,029616	0,050376	0,072908
14	0,000056	0,000472	0,002228	0,007094	0,016924	0,032384	0,052077
15	0,000015	0,000157	0,000891	0,003311	0,009026	0,019431	0,034718
16	0,000004	0,000049	0,000334	0,001448	0,004513	0,010930	0,021699
17	0,000001	0,000014	0,000118	0,000596	0,002124	0,005786	0,012764
18		0,000004	0,000039	0,000232	0,000944	0,002893	0,007091
19		0,000001	0,000012	0,000085	0,000397	0,001370	0,003732
20			0,000004	0,000030	0,000159	0,000617	0,001866
21			0,000001	0,000010	0,000061	0,000264	0,000889
22				0,000003	0,000022	0,000108	0,000404
23				0,000001	0,000008	0,000042	0,000176
24					0,000003	0,000016	0,000073
25					0,000001	0,000006	0,000029
26						0,000002	0,000011
27						0,000001	0,000004
28							0,000001
29							0,000001

Table 6 Quantiles $\chi^2_{m;q}$ of the χ^2–distribution

m \ q	0.005	0.01	0.025	0.05	0.1	0.9	0.95	0.975	0.99	0.995
1	(1)	(2)	(3)	(4)	(5)	2.71	3.84	5.02	6.63	7.88
2	0.0100	0.020	0.051	0.103	0.21	4.61	5.99	7.38	9.21	10.60
3	0.0717	0.115	0.216	0.352	0.58	6.25	7.81	9.35	11.34	12.84
4	0.207	0.297	0.484	0.711	1.06	7.78	9.49	11.14	13.28	14.86
5	0.412	0.554	0.831	1.15	1.61	9.24	11.07	12.83	15.09	16.75
6	0.676	0.872	1.24	1.64	2.20	10.64	12.59	14.45	16.81	18.55
7	0.989	1.24	1.69	2.17	2.83	12.02	14.07	16.01	18.48	20.28
8	1.34	1.65	2.18	2.73	3.49	13.36	15.51	17.53	20.09	22.96
9	1.73	2.09	2.70	3.33	4.17	14.68	16.92	19.02	21.67	23.59
10	2.16	2.56	3.25	3.94	4.87	15.99	18.31	20.48	23.21	25.19
11	2.60	3.05	3.82	4.57	5.58	17.28	19.68	21.92	24.73	26.76
12	3.07	3.57	4.40	5.23	6.30	18.55	21.03	23.34	26.22	28.30
13	3.57	4.11	5.01	5.89	7.04	19.81	22.36	24.74	27.69	29.82
14	4.07	4.66	5.63	6.57	7.79	21.06	23.68	26.12	29.14	31.32
15	4.60	5.23	6.26	7.26	8.55	22.31	25.00	27.49	30.58	32.80
16	5.14	5.81	6.91	7.96	9.31	23.54	26.30	28.85	32.00	34.27
17	5.70	6.41	7.56	8.67	10.09	24.77	27.59	30.19	33.41	35.72
18	6.26	7.01	8.23	9.39	10.86	25.99	28.87	31.53	34.81	37.16
19	6.84	7.63	8.91	10.12	11.65	27.20	30.14	32.85	36.19	38.58
20	7.43	8.26	9.59	10.85	12.44	28.41	31.41	34.17	37.57	40.00
21	8.03	8.90	10.28	11.59	13.24	29.62	32.67	35.48	38.93	41.40
22	8.64	9.54	10.98	12.34	14.04	30.81	33.92	36.78	40.29	42.80
23	9.26	10.20	11.69	13.09	14.85	32.01	35.17	38.08	41.64	44.18
24	9.89	10.86	12.40	13.85	15.66	33.20	36.42	39.36	42.98	45.56
25	10.52	11.52	13.12	14.61	16.47	34.38	37.65	40.65	44.31	46.93
26	11.16	12.20	13.84	15.38	17.29	35.56	38.89	41.92	45.64	48.29
27	11.81	12.88	14.57	16.15	18.11	36.74	40.11	43.19	46.96	49.64
28	12.46	13.56	15.31	16.93	18.94	37.92	41.34	44.46	48.28	50.99
29	13.12	14.26	16.05	17.71	19.77	39.09	42.56	45.72	49.59	52.34
30	13.79	14.95	16.79	18.49	20.60	40.26	43.77	46.98	50.89	53.67
40	20.71	22.16	24.43	26.51	29.05	51.81	55.76	59.34	63.69	66.77
50	27.99	29.71	32.36	34.76	37.69	63.17	67.51	71.42	76.16	79.49
60	35.53	37.48	40.48	43.19	46.46	74.40	79.08	83.30	88.38	91.96
70	43.28	45.44	48.76	51.74	55.33	85.53	90.53	95.02	100.43	104.23
80	51.17	53.54	57.15	60.39	64.28	96.58	101.88	106.63	112.33	116.33
90	59.20	61.75	65.65	69.13	73.29	107.57	113.15	118.14	124.12	128.31
100	67.33	70.06	74.22	77.93	82.36	118.50	124.34	129.56	135.81	140.18

(1)=0.00004; (2)=0.00016; (3)=0.00098; (4)=0.0039; (5)=0.0158

References

1. Amman, H. M. (ed.) (1996): Handbook of Computational Economics. Elsevier: Amsterdam
2. Anthony, M., Biggs, N. L. (1996): Mathematics for Economics and Finance. Methods and Modelling. Cambridge University Press: Cambridge
3. Baltagi, B. H. (1999): Econometrics, 2nd edition. Springer: Berlin, Heidelberg
4. Baltagi, B. H. (1998): Solutions Manual for Econometrics. Springer: Berlin, Heidelberg
5. Baxter, M., Rennie, A. (1997): Financial Calculus. An Introduction to Derivative Pricing. Cambridge University Press: Cambridge
6. Chiang, A. C. (1984): Fundamental Methods of Mathematical Economics, 3rd edition. McGraw-Hill: New York
7. Cissell, R., Cissell, H., Flaspohler, D. C. (1990): Mathematics of Finance. Houghton Mifflin: Boston
8. Elliott, R. J., Kopp, P. E. (1999): Mathematics of Financial Markets. Springer: New York, Berlin, Heidelberg
9. Elton, F., Gruber, M. (1992): Futures and Options, 4th edition. Wiley: New York
10. Glenberg, A. M. (1998): Learning from Data: An Introduction to Statistical Reasoning. Erlbaum: Mahwah (NJ)
11. Jacques, I. (1999): Mathematics for Economics and Business. Addison-Wesley: Harlow
12. Jeffrey, A. (1995): Handbook of Mathematical Formulas and Integrals. Academic Press: San Diego (Calif.)
13. Levy, A. (1992): Economic Dynamics. Applications of Difference Equations, Differential Equations and Optimal Control. Avebury: Aldershot
14. Mansfield, E. (1994): Statistics for Business and Economics: Methods and Applications, Norton: New York
15. Moore, J. C. (1999): Mathematical Methods for Economic Theory. Springer: Berlin
16. Pestman, W. R. (1998): Mathematical Statistics – an Introduction. de Gruyter: Berlin, New York
17. Simon, C. P., Blume L. (1994): Mathematics for Economists. Norton: New York
18. Sirjaev, A. N. (1996): Probability, 2nd edition (Transl. from the Russian). Springer: New York, Heidelberg
19. Sydsaeter, K., Strom A., Berck, P. (1993): Economists' Mathematical Manual, 3rd edition. Springer: Berlin, Heidelberg
20. Watson C., Billingsley, P., Croft, D., Huntsberger, D. (1993): Statistics for Management and Economics, 5th edition. Houghton Mifflin: Boston
21. Wilmott, P., Howison, S., Dewynne, J. (1998): The Mathematics of Financial derivatives. A Student Introduction. Cambridge University Press: Cambridge

Index